JULY	AUGUST	SEPTEMBER	OCTOBER	NOVEMBER	DECEMBER

asparagus
aubergines
beetroot
bell peppers
broad beans
broccoli
brussels sprouts
carrots
cauliflower
celeriac
celery
chicory
coriander
courgettes
cucumbers
fennel
garlic
globe artichokes
jerusalem artichokes
kale
kohlrabi
leeks
lettuce
lovage
marsh samphire
nettles
onions
parsnips
peas
potatoes
pumpkins
rocket
savoy cabbage
sorrel
spinach
squash
swede
sweet potatoes
sweetcorn
swiss chard
tomatoes
turnips
watercress
wild mushrooms

THE SOUP BOOK

Soil Association

THE SOUP BOOK

EDITOR-IN-CHIEF **SOPHIE GRIGSON**

London, New York, Melbourne,
Munich, and Delhi

Photography William Reavell

Editor Michael Fullalove
Designer John Round

Project Editor Robert Sharman
Designer Kathryn Wilding
Senior Jacket Creative Nicola Powling
Managing Editor Dawn Henderson
Managing Art Editor Christine Keilty
Production Editor Kelly Salih
Production Controller Alice Holloway
Creative Technical Support Sonia Charbonnier

First published in Great Britain in 2009
by Dorling Kindersley Limited
80 Strand, London WC2R 0RL

A Penguin Company
Copyright © 2009 Dorling Kindersley
Text copyright © 2009 Dorling Kindersley

2 4 6 8 10 9 7 5 3 1

ISBN 978-1-4053-4785-3

Colour reproduction by Colourscan, Singapore
Printed and bound in Singapore by Star Standard

**Discover more at
www.dk.com**

www.soilassociation.org

contents

foreword by sophie grigson

I have no hesitation in insisting that of all types of food, soup is the most universally relevant. Soup can be whatever you want it to be. It has the potential to make itself at home on any dining table or lap or rug laid out on the grass, no matter whether as part of a multi-coursed banquet for kings and queens, or the main nourishment for humble cash-strapped commoners. There are no eating occasions when a well-judged slurp of soup would not be welcome. Or at least none that I can think of.

This really is the joy of soup. It can be thick or thin, elegant or rustic, subtle or brassy, light or filling, vegetarian, meaty, fishy, vegan, dairy free, wheat free, hot or cold, health-giving, revitalizing, comforting and many, many more fine, upstanding adjectives. The one blot on this cavalcade of praise is the poorly made soup, or worse still, the instant hot-water-'n'-mix sort of a soup that is sprinkled out of a packet with no regard for taste. For that, I have no time, and I hope, too, that with this book in hand, you will jettison such abominations.

Anyone can make a good soup. Yes, anyone. The simplest of soups, those that are an elementary assembly job of ingredients whizzed up in a liquidizer or processor, could be made by a six year old with minimal assistance, and still merit bags of praise. From there it is only a small step to that wonderful crowd of cooked and puréed vegetable soups. Once this technique is mastered, a vast world of possibilities opens up before you. As long as you make sure you start with good fresh ingredients (soup should never be just a dustbin job for the wrinkled remnants at the back of the vegetable rack), preferably organic or locally sourced, and you pay a gentle degree of attention to what you are doing, you can hardly go wrong. And in the unlikely event that you do, there may well be remedies (see pages 34–35) to speedily restore your reputation as a fine soup-maker.

In this book you will find soups of every hue and texture, and complexity. Many of the most famous soups of the world have found their way here – starlets such as the hearty chowders of the Newfoundland fishermen, or warming Hungarian Goulash. There's Vichyssoise, the posh version of leek and potato soup, Minestrone, the Italian mama's favourite, Russian Borscht, and cool, Spanish Gazpacho, so invigorating on a searingly hot day. Scattered amongst these are swathes of lesser known, though equally satisfying, soups of many types, from a simple pumpkin and apple soup to Indian-inspired broths or more surprising fruit soups.

As well as the soups themselves, you will find a neat guide to garnishes great and small, and suggestions for bread accompaniments – from a straightforward crusty white loaf to golden American cornbread. In short, everything you'll ever need to know about soup is gathered here in *The Soup Book*.

introduction by the soil association

What has a book about soup got to do with the global food crisis and building a more sustainable and organic food and farming future?

Actually everything! In preparing a simple bowl of soup for your family and loved ones sourced from fresh, organic, in season and ideally local ingredients you are taking powerful direct action to prepare the earth for a more resilient and sustainable future, both for yourself and for future generations. Whether your ingredients are coming freshly grown from your garden or allotment, or you've bought directly from a real person at the farm gate or farmers' market, making the connection between the food you eat and the place it comes from is crucial to a healthy sense of cultural identity.

In a world where the problems we face seem so enormous and intractable, making the food connection is coined perfectly by poet and philosopher Wendell Berry when he wrote "Eating is an agricultural act". By eating food – in this case soup – with a good story you are contributing to the solution at a local level, which, scaled up, has global implications.

This book has been planned with real food enthusiasts in mind. It is organized by produce, so you can look up whatever seasonal produce you've come across and find a range of different, wholesome recipes for it. The Soil Association has been working for over sixty years to promote a healthier food culture that puts the health and welfare of our environment, our farm animals and people at centre stage. We believe in the power of individual citizens to "be the change" and this soup book is a part of that revolution in our food culture.

Patrick Holden

Director of the Soil Association

We would like to thank the following for kindly donating recipes:
Darina Allen • Dan Barber • Raymond Blanc • Sally Clarke • Jeff Cox • Monty Don
Josephine Fairley • Livia Firth • Skye Gyngell • Shaun Hill • Juliet Kindersley
Daphne Lambert • Allegra McEvedy • Clodagh McKenna • Jeannette Orrey
Arthur Potts Dawson • Thane Prince • Sarah Raven • Rosemary Shrager
Geetie Singh • Rebecca Sullivan • Eric Treuille • Alice Waters

techniques

The cornerstone of many soups is a well-made stock and, though the ingredients for it may seem humble and the preparation simple, the contribution it makes is vital.

making stock

The four stocks most commonly called for in soup-making are chicken stock, brown stock, fish stock, and vegetable stock. Made from bones and/or common vegetables and flavourings, they are easy to prepare and freeze well for up to three months. If produced from meat bones, stock is clear and relatively fat-free, though it will be gelatinous enough to set when cold. Vegetable stock is lighter and requires a careful balance of ingredients to make it flavoursome. Stocks should not be seasoned with salt – they are one of the building blocks for a soup, not a dish in their own right.

selection of stocks

brown stock is so called because it is produced from meat bones that have been "browned" by cooking in fat. It jellies when cold.

vegetable stock can be given extra depth by the addition of mushrooms, potato, and tomatoes that will offset the sweetness of the other veg.

fish stock is quick to make, ideally from the bones and heads of salmon or mild-flavoured white fish, especially flat fish like sole and plaice.

chicken stock serves as the base for many a fine soup. Some raw or cooked chicken bones and a few standard aromatics are all that's required to produce a rich, gelatinous stock.

This recipe gives an ideal list of ingredients, but as long as you have the chicken carcase, onion, carrot, and one or two of the herbs, you can turn out a fine stock.

chicken stock

⊘ **MAKES** 1.5 L (2¾ PINTS)   ⏱ **PREP** 5 MINS **COOK** 3 HRS   ❄ **FREEZE** 3 MONTHS

1 raw or cooked chicken carcase,
   roughly broken into pieces
1 onion, quartered
1 carrot, quartered
1 leek, quartered
1 celery stalk, quartered

1 bay leaf
2 parsley stalks
a sprig of thyme
8 black peppercorns
1.7 litres (3 pints) cold water

1 Put the chicken, vegetables, and all the flavourings into a large pan, cover with the water, and bring to the boil. Cover with a lid, lower the heat, and simmer for 2–3 hours, skimming off any foam from time to time.

2 Ladle the stock through a sieve into a clean bowl, pressing the ingredients firmly against the sides of the sieve with the back of the ladle to squeeze out as much liquid as possible.

3 If you're using the stock straightaway, remove any globules of fat from the surface by skimming the top of the stock with a piece of kitchen paper folded in two.

4 Otherwise, leave the stock to cool before chilling it in a covered container for up to 3 days. A layer of congealed fat will form on the surface. Scoop this off before use.

microwave chicken stock
If you are short of time, you can also make chicken stock in a microwave. Put the broken-up chicken carcase into a large microwaveable bowl along with the onion, carrot, leek, and celery. Add the bay leaf, parsley, thyme and peppercorns, then cover with boiling water. Cover the bowl with cling film (roll it back at one edge to allow the steam to escape) and microwave on full power for 25 minutes. Leave to stand for a further 25 minutes, then strain.

For a rich meat-based stock, use either beef or lamb bones, but never a mixture of the two. If you have any bacon rinds or vegetable trimmings to hand, pop them in the pot too.

brown stock

⊘ MAKES 2.5 L (4¼ PINTS)   **◑ PREP** 10 MINS **COOK** 3½–4½ HRS   **✳ FREEZE** 3 MONTHS

1.35kg (3lb) raw or cooked beef or lamb bones
2–3 onions, halved
2–3 carrots, halved

a bouquet garni (see p24)
2.5–3 litres (4½–5¼ pints) cold water
1 tsp black peppercorns

1 If you're using raw bones, roast them with the onions and carrots in an oven preheated to 200°C (400°F/Gas 6), turning them frequently, for 30 minutes or until browned. If you're using cooked bones, start the stock from step 2.

2 Put all the ingredients into a large pan, bring to the boil, then skim off any foam that rises to the surface with a slotted spoon. Lower the heat, cover with a lid, and simmer for 3–4 hours. Strain the stock through a sieve, pressing the ingredients against the sides of the sieve to extract all the liquid. Leave to cool, then chill in a covered container for up to 3 days. Before use, remove any solidified fat from the surface with a slotted spoon, then bring the stock to the boil.

hale and hearty
A meaty stock based on beef or lamb makes a world of difference to hearty broth-based soups like French onion soup.

This is an excellent stock, with a good balance of flavours. The potato means it will not be clear, but since it is being used in a soup, that doesn't matter.

vegetable stock

⊘ MAKES 1 L (1¾ PINTS)   **● PREP** 5 MINS **COOK** 35 MINS   **❋ FREEZE** 3 MONTHS

1 leek, thickly sliced
1 large carrot, thickly sliced
2 celery stalks, thickly sliced
1 onion, roughly chopped
75g (2½oz) button, chestnut, or open-cup
   mushrooms, quartered

1 medium potato, thickly sliced
1 tomato, quartered
3 parsley stalks
2 bay leaves
4 sprigs thyme
1.5 litres (2¾ pints) cold water

1 Put all the ingredients into a large pan. Bring to the boil, then lower the heat, cover with a lid, and simmer very gently for 30 minutes.

2 Strain the stock through a fine sieve, pressing the ingredients well against the sides of the sieve to extract all the liquid. Leave to cool completely, then chill in a covered container for up to 3 days before use.

light and fragrant
A flavoursome vegetable stock makes a good alternative to chicken stock, whether you are vegetarian or not.

Ask the fishmonger for the bones when getting fish filleted, and check if they have any extra that they can give you. Fish bones will freeze, well-wrapped, for up to two months.

fish stock

◉ **MAKES** 1.5 L (2¾ PINTS)   🕐 **PREP** 5 MINS **COOK** 30 MINS   ❄ **FREEZE** 2 MONTHS

675g–1kg (1½–2¼lb) salmon or white fish bones, heads, and skin (don't use those from dark, oily fish such as mackerel, herring, and sardines – they will give the stock an unpleasant flavour)
6 black peppercorns
1 sprig of thyme

1 bay leaf
2 parsley stalks
2 small carrots
1 onion
2 celery stalks
1 generous glass of dry white wine
1.7 litres (3 pints) cold water

1 Put the fish heads and bones into a large pan, breaking or cutting them up with a knife to fit. Add the black peppercorns, thyme, bay leaf, and parsley.

2 Roughly chop the vegetables and add to the pot with the wine. Place the pan over a moderate heat and let the wine bubble for 3 minutes. Add the water and bring to the boil.

3 Lower the heat and simmer, uncovered, for 20–25 minutes – no longer or the stock may begin to develop a bitter taste. Skim off any scum from time to time with a slotted spoon.

4 Strain the stock through a fine sieve into a bowl, pressing the solids against the side of the sieve to extract all the liquid. Leave to cool completely, then chill in a covered container for up to 3 days.

5 The finished stock should be thin in texture, with a delicate flavour. It will make an excellent base for all kinds of fish soup.

Careful preparation of vegetables is essential – not only do properly cut vegetables contribute to the finished appearance of a soup, they cook more evenly too.

preparing vegetables

Vegetables are best prepared just before cooking: washed, peeled, and cut ahead of time, they are left exposed to air and moisture, which can lead them to deteriorate and lose their vitamins. Most often vegetables can be cut by hand, so a good sharp knife is vital. Use a large or small knife depending on the vegetable you're cutting. Here's how to prepare those most commonly used in soups.

chopping or crushing garlic

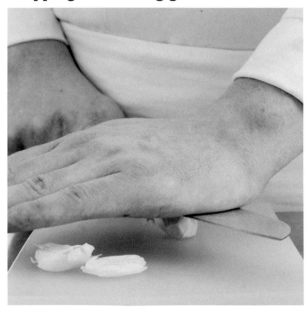

1 Lay the clove of garlic on a chopping board with the blade of a large knife on top of it. Strike the blade with the heel of your hand to break the skin of the clove, but don't press down so hard that you smash the garlic.

2 Peel off the skin, then chop off the ends of the garlic. Chop the garlic roughly, then sprinkle it with a little salt to stop it sticking to the blade. You can then chop it finely or crush smooth with the flat blade.

chopping onions

1 Cut the onion in half lengthways with a chef's knife. Peel away the skin, but leave the root intact – it will help keep the halves together as you chop.

2 With the onion flat side down on the chopping board, make two or three horizontal slices, cutting up to – but not through – the root.

3 Now, slice the onion finely vertically, taking care once again to cut up to but not through the root.

4 Turn the onion through 90 degrees and slice across to make even-sized dice. Discard the root when you get to it.

skinning and deseeding tomatoes

1 With a sharp knife, cut an "X" in the base of the tomato.

2 Immerse it in boiling water for around 20 seconds or until the skin begins to split.

3 Remove the tomato with a slotted spoon and plunge it into iced water to cool it.

4 When it's cool enough to handle, use a paring knife to peel off the skin.

5 Slice the tomato in half, then squeeze the seeds into a bowl and discard.

6 Slice the tomato half first into strips and then into dice.

cleaning and chopping leeks

1 With a large knife, trim off the root and some of the dark green leaf at the top, then slice the leek in two lengthways and fan it open.

2 Rinse the leek under cold running water to remove the soil that tends to collect between the layers, then pat it dry with kitchen paper.

3 Sit the halved leek on the chopping board and slice it into thick or thin strips, according to the recipe.

chopping carrots

sweating vegetables

Peel the carrot, then slice it lengthways. Cut the lengths crossways, then stack them and cut into batonnets. Slice across the batonnets to make even-sized dice.

Sweating chopped vegetables in oil or butter gives a soup a more pronounced flavour. Heat a little fat over a low heat, stir in the vegetables, then add a pinch of salt, cover, and cook for 5–10 minutes or until soft but not brown.

Chopped herbs release more of their flavour than whole, but before the leaves of some herbs like rosemary can be chopped, they need to be stripped from their woody stalks.

preparing herbs

chopping herbs with tender stalks

1 To chop the leaves of herbs with tender stalks like basil, roll them together into a tight bunch.

2 Holding the bunch of leaves steady with one hand, slice across them with a chef's knife.

3 Using the knife in a rocking motion, chop the leaves finely, turning them 90 degrees halfway through.

using a mezzaluna

removing woody stalks

making a bouquet garni

A mezzaluna makes light work of chopping herbs. Rock it from side to side across them until they're chopped to your liking.

To strip the leaves of herbs with woody stalks, run the thumb and forefinger of one hand along the stalk.

For a classic soup flavouring, tie a sprig of thyme and parsley with a bay leaf. You could also include sage or rosemary.

Spices lend an extra dimension to many soups and, whether you're using them fresh or dried, they usually require a little straightforward preparation.

preparing spices

bruising whole spices

Before use, whole fresh spices like lemongrass are usually bruised with the blade of a heavy knife and your hand.

grating roots

Roots like ginger can be finely chopped by hand, but it's often easiest to grate them. Peel off the skin beforehand.

deseeding chillies

Scraping out the seeds from chillies lessens their heat. Wear a pair of rubber or plastic gloves to do it.

frying in oil

When spices are fried till lightly coloured, their flavour gets trapped in the oil. The oil is used along with the spices.

dry-roasting

To dry-roast spices, place them in an oven preheated to 160°C (325°F/Gas 3), or fry them in a dry pan, till lightly browned.

crushing

Dried or dry-roasted spices can be crushed by hand in a pestle and mortar or by machine in a spice mill.

Dried beans, peas, and lentils are perfect for soup-making. Little effort is required to prepare them – all you need to do is think ahead.

preparing pulses

The basic preparation of pulses is simple: first, you need to sort and rinse them; then (in nearly all cases) you need to soak them; finally, the pulses have to be cooked until tender. This can take anything from around half an hour to 3 hours. Once cooked, pulses are well-suited to puréeing, but they also work well left whole in soups.

sorting and rinsing

soaking

Whatever kind of pulse you're using, start by sorting and rinsing them. Place the pulses in a colander and carefully pick out any husks or pieces of grit, then rinse the pulses well under cold running water.

Apart from lentils and split peas, all pulses need to be soaked for at least 8 hours, and preferably overnight. Place them in a bowl, add three times their volume of cold water, then cover and place in the fridge.

adding flavour

The flavour of pulses can be rather bland, so it's usually a good idea to add some aromatics. A bouquet garni (see p24) or a sprig of herbs will do the trick: bay leaf, parsley, rosemary, or thyme all work well. A pinch of cumin, coriander, chilli, or caraway is another option, but you could also pop a carrot into the pan or an onion studded with cloves. Alternatively, you can cook pulses in a well-flavoured stock, but never season it with salt – it will prevent them from softening.

cooking pulses

Drain the soaked pulses, then place them in a large pan along with any flavourings. Pour in four times their volume of cold water and add 1 tbsp vegetable oil to stop them sticking. Bring rapidly to the boil, and boil hard for 10 minutes, skimming away any foam with a slotted spoon. Lower the heat, part-cover with a lid, and simmer until tender. The cooking time will depend on the variety of pulse (see right).

COOKING TIMES

Here are approximate cooking times for the pulses most commonly used in soups.

black beans	1 hour
black-eyed beans	1–1½ hours
borlotti beans	1–1½ hours
butter beans	1–1½ hours
cannellini beans	1–1½ hours
chickpeas	2–3 hours
flageolet beans	1½ hours
haricot beans	1–1½ hours
lentils (split)	25 minutes
lentils (whole)	45 minutes
pinto beans	1–1½ hours
red kidney beans	1–1½ hours
split peas	45 minutes

Among the easiest soups to prepare are those you whiz to a purée in a blender. The alternative is to use a food mill – this requires a little more effort, but the results are smoother.

puréeing

The secret to success with puréed soups is thorough cooking, so that the starchy ingredients that give the soup its body can be blended to a smooth purée. For that reason, always cook root vegetables and dried beans till they are extremely tender, but never overcook potatoes, or they will become glutinous and gluey. There is also a range of semi-puréed soups, in which some of the ingredients are blended to thicken the broth, while the rest are left whole for interest.

in a blender

1 Before blending, test the ingredients are really tender with a knife – they are only ready to purée when completely soft.

2 Blend the soup until you have a smooth consistency with no lumps. Do it in batches so you don't overload the machine.

3 The consistency of a puréed soup will vary according to the ingredients used and the way in which they're processed. But, in general, it should be totally smooth and lump-free. To remove all traces of skins, seeds, and fibres, you may need to push the purée through a fine sieve.

using a food mill

Working the ingredients through a food mill is particularly successful for soups that contain ingredients with skins and seeds, which blenders sometimes can't cope with.

semi-puréed soups

To thicken a soup but keep some texture for interest, purée around half of it and then return it to the pan. Gently reheat the soup before serving.

A little butter or cream stirred into a soup just before serving will enrich it (see pp32–3), but there will be times when you want to thicken a soup rather more. Here's how to do it.

thickening

There are several quick and easy ways you can give body to a soup at the end of cooking. You could whisk egg yolk or a mixture of egg yolk and cream into the hot liquid. Another option is to use starch, in the form of cornflour, plain flour, or rice flour. Or you could make a paste from flour and butter and stir this into the soup before serving. But perhaps the oldest method of thickening a soup is with bread, either stirred into the broth at the last minute or incorporated into it earlier in the cooking process.

with starch

with flour and butter

Mix a little cornflour, rice flour, or plain flour to a thin paste with some cold water. Stir the mixture into the pan of hot soup, bring back to the boil, and simmer, stirring all the time, for 1–2 minutes or until the soup thickens.

Combine two parts softened butter to one part flour. Gradually whisk small pieces of the paste into the hot soup at the end of cooking. Allow the flour to cook for 1–2 minutes, stirring all the time.

with egg

Added towards the end of cooking, egg yolk or a mixture of egg yolk and cream will thicken a hot soup and make it velvety. Remove the pan from the heat to incorporate the mixture, then reheat the soup gently, whisking until thick. Do not allow it to boil or it will curdle.

with bread

Bread has long been used to thicken country soups. For gazpacho (left), breadcrumbs are blended into the soup at an early stage. But bread can also be added to a broth at the last minute, and stirred until it breaks up and thickens the soup.

Butter or cream stirred into a soup at the last minute will greatly improve its character, adding body and shine. For interest, you can flavour the butter and serve it at the table.

enriching

Both cream and butter make a quick and simple garnish for individual servings of soup (see p36–39), but if you have another garnish in mind, you can add them to the soup to enrich it while it's still in the pan. Butters flavoured with herbs, nuts, or smoked fish are another way of enriching a soup, although these are best served separately, to be added to the soup by your guests.

with cream

with butter

Add the cream at the end of cooking and, in the case of a puréed soup, after blending. Stir it in well, then check the seasoning. If you've added a substantial amount, you may want to reheat the soup gently before serving.

Cut a knob of chilled unsalted butter into cubes. Remove the pan from the heat and whisk it in a cube at a time – the soup should become glossy and smooth. Do not reheat the soup or the butter will separate.

with a flavoured butter

Flavoured butters are an ideal accompaniment to puréed soups and bisques. They are also easy to prepare and work well with a variety of ingredients. Blend the flavourings of your choice into the butter, then place the butter on a sheet of greaseproof paper and roll it tightly into a cylindrical shape. Chill it in the fridge or freezer until you're ready to dish up the soup, then simply slice it into rounds. You could also serve the butter at the table and allow your guests to help themselves. Here are recipes for two flavoured butters that are great with a whole range of soups.

herb butter Mix 60g (2oz) softened butter with 6 blanched and finely chopped spinach leaves, 1 chopped shallot, 1 tsp each chopped parsley, chervil, and tarragon, and some salt and pepper. Roll in greaseproof paper and chill till needed.

lemon and chilli butter Combine 60g (2oz) softened butter with 1 tsp finely grated lemon zest and ¼ tsp crushed dried chilli flakes (or more if you like your food quite spicy). Season to taste with salt.

There's no need to worry if your soup hasn't turned out quite as you had intended – even the most accomplished cook occasionally produces a dish that's less than perfect.

rescuing

Whether you are unhappy with the finished consistency or think the soup is too highly seasoned, here are some quick fixes to put things right.

too thin

There are a number of ways you can thicken a soup that's too thin. You could whisk in a paste of butter and flour or a mixture of eggs and cream (as here). Or you could add some rice flour, cornflour, or plain flour blended with water (for more details, turn to pp30–1). Another option is to stir in a few instant potato flakes or a little instant oat cereal.

too thick

Depending on the liquid you've used to produce the soup, thin it with a little stock, milk, or water. Once the soup has reached the desired consistency, taste it, season, and reheat gently.

stringy or lumpy

Even a soup you've whizzed in a blender can turn out lumpy or stringy. Ladle it into a fine sieve, then use the back of the ladle, a wooden spoon, or a pestle to push the ingredients through. Reheat gently before serving.

too salty

If you only ever add salt towards the end of cooking and use home-made stock that's unseasoned, the chances of your soup being too salty are slim. But if it is, there are a couple of things you can do. Add a couple of raw potatoes cut in half and simmer the soup gently until they're cooked, then remove and discard. Alternatively, add a little sugar and, if the soup is also too thick, some cream, milk, or water.

From a single piece of seafood to a simple swirl of cream, a well-chosen garnish transforms a soup, adding extra colour, as well as texture and flavour.

garnishing

For some soups, a garnish is an essential component – the soured cream stirred into Borscht, for instance, or the cheese-topped croûtes served with French onion soup. For others, a garnish is a way of introducing contrasting textures and flavours. Many ingredients can act as a garnish if they also complement the flavours of the soup, but here is a selection to suit almost every occasion.

with cream

Dolloped, swirled, or drizzled, cream makes an excellent garnish for thick puréed soups. Use single cream, double cream, whipped cream, soured cream, or crème fraîche. Yogurt is an alternative if you're counting the calories.

with herbs

Fresh sage leaves or parsley fried in olive oil until crisp make a flavoursome garnish for gutsy soups, but a sprinkling of chopped parsley, chervil, or coriander instantly adds fragrance and colour to almost any soup.

with shellfish

A whole prawn, crab claw, grilled scallop, or (as here) an oyster poached and served in its shell makes a spectacular garnish for a seafood soup. A wild garlic flower provides the finishing touch for this dish.

with olive oil

As much a condiment as a garnish, a drizzle of fragrant, full-bodied extra virgin olive oil brings a Mediterranean flavour to soups, while looking appetizing and glossy on the surface.

with vegetables

Raw or cooked, vegetables make eye-catching and healthy garnishes. If small, like peas, they can be served whole. Otherwise, slice them into decorative strips, dice, or rings.

with bacon

Grilled until crisp and then crumbled, bacon makes a tasty garnish that looks attractive floating on the surface of a pale puréed soup. Here it is accompanied by pieces of pan-fried scallop.

with seeds or nuts

Toasted seeds or nuts not only look pretty, they also lend a satisfying crunch. Served with a vegetable soup, they are a good source of protein too.

with croûtons

Small dice of fried bread are a classic garnish. For about 40 croûtons, cut 4 slices of day-old white bread (crusts removed) into 1cm (½in) dice. Heat 2 tbsp sunflower oil and 30g (1oz) unsalted butter in a large frying pan until hot, then fry the dice, stirring constantly, for 10 minutes or until golden. Drain on kitchen paper before serving. For extra flavour, stir in a finely chopped garlic clove a couple of minutes before the croûtons are due to be done.

with croûtes

Large croûtons are known as croûtes. To make them, cut a day-old baguette into 1cm (½in) slices, and toast until golden. Alternatively, place on a baking sheet and bake in an oven preheated to 180°C (350°F/Gas 4) for 15 minutes.

ways of serving croûtes

Croûtes are a versatile garnish. Rubbed with garlic, then topped with cheese and flashed under the grill, they are perfect for French onion soup (above). For fish soups, spread them thickly with a garlicky rouille sauce.

A well-stocked storecupboard will save you time and help you rustle up soups even at short notice. With the right ingredients, it will also be a source of inspiration.

storecupboard essentials

Putting together soups from the contents of your kitchen cupboards is a satisfying experience. What's more, you don't need a larder the size you can walk in. With a few well-chosen basics to hand, you'll always have the wherewithal for turning out a tasty soup. These are the required items.

onions

basic vegetables

Onions, garlic, carrots, and leeks are the basis for countless soups, so it makes sense to have them available at all times. Obviously, they are perishable – store them in a cool, dark place.

frozen stock, stock cubes, and bouillons

A supply of home-made stock is a must. Make it in advance and keep it in the freezer. For those occasions when you're in a real hurry, have some good-quality stock cubes and a vegetable bouillon to hand, too.

a selection of oils

From the best-quality olive oil for garnishing to the more work-a-day varieties, such as sunflower oil, used for sweating and frying, a good selection of oils is invaluable. The more unusual, like sesame oil, are available in small bottles – a blessing when space is at a premium.

garlic

flavourings

Salt and whole black peppercorns are indispensable in the kitchen, but there are other flavourings it's worth having in your storecupboard, too. Wine vinegars, sherry vinegar, Worcestershire sauce, soy sauce, and fish sauce are made frequent use of in soups.

dried or canned pulses

Canned or dried, pulses are one of the staples of soup-making.
Dried pulses do not keep indefinitely, so buy them from shops
with a healthy turnover, and ensure you use them within a year
– no amount of cooking will soften them after that. Canned pulses
need almost nothing in the way of preparation – simply drain,
rinse, then drain them again.

dried pulses

dried spices

You don't need a taste for particularly spicy food to make use
of a wide range of spices – a pinch of chilli flakes or a tablespoon
of crushed coriander seeds may be all that's required to give a
soup that extra dimension. Among the dried spices most often
called for are cumin, coriander, caraway, nutmeg, fenugreek,
star anise, cinnamon, and ginger.

herbs – fresh and dried

For the rounded flavour and complexity they give to soups,
herbs are invaluable. The more popular, such as parsley and
chives, are available fresh all year round, but it's handy to keep
dried and frozen herbs in your larder as well. They are generally
more pungent than fresh, so use them sparingly. And keep an
eye on expiry dates: frozen herbs will keep well for up to six
months; dried for up to four. If you grow your own herbs, why
not dry or freeze them for use during the winter.

fresh herbs

canned ingredients

Canned tomatoes are excellent in soups, and in winter are likely
to be more flavoursome than fresh tomatoes. They even come ready
chopped. Make some shelf space for a can of tomato purée, too, and
a tin of sweetcorn. Some coconut milk might also be handy.

dried pasta and noodles

Dried pasta and noodles are at the heart of many comforting soups,
so it's worth making them a permanent feature of your storecupboard.
If space is an issue, a small supply of vermicelli, rice noodles, and
udon noodles will serve you well.

dried pasta

However well we plan, we all have food left over at times. Cooked chicken and ham are obvious candidates for soup, but you can make good use of many other leftovers, too.

making use of leftovers

The ideal home for leftovers is in comforting rustic-style soups. Add the ingredient sparingly to begin with, then use your discrimination to decide on balance, texture, and seasoning. Recycling food calls for ingenuity and skill, so never give in to temptation and use your soup pan as a bin, or your soup-making skills will acquire a poor reputation. Here are some thrifty ideas for using leftover food.

stale bread

stale bread

Stale white bread is the perfect starting point for making croûtons and croûtes (see p39), which are a welcome addition to a wide range of soups. Whizzed in a blender or food processor to form breadcrumbs, stale bread is also an essential ingredient in the chilled Spanish soup Gazpacho (see p107).

cooked meat

Cooked chicken, turkey, or game are all excellent in soups, as is cooked ham. Cured meats such as chorizo and salami work equally well. In general, leftovers of red meats are not suitable for making soup, although the bones from cooked beef or lamb can go straight into the cooking pot for stock.

egg yolks and whites

eggs yolks and egg whites

Making use of leftover egg yolks is never a problem. Whisk them into a hot soup towards the end of cooking – they will thicken it and give a velvety texture. Although less versatile, leftover egg whites are useful for clarifying consommé.

cooked vegetables

Cut into dice, shredded, or left whole if small like sweetcorn and peas, cooked vegetables can be added to a soup just before serving and heated through. Alternatively, they can be popped in the blender along with the other ingredients and puréed.

leftover cabbage

home-made gravy

Capitalize on gravy's richness and depth of flavour by stirring it into meaty soups just before serving. If the sauce has acquired a skin since you first prepared it, carefully remove this beforehand with a slotted spoon.

boiled pasta

Small pasta shapes that have been cooked but not dressed with sauce can turn a simple soup into a square meal. Add them at the last minute and then heat them gently through.

chunks of cheese

scraps of cheese

Small chunks of Cheddar, Parmesan, and Gruyère need never go to waste when you make your own soups. Grate the cheese finely and use it to top croûtes. Grilled until golden brown and bubbling, these make a hearty topping for soups.

red or white wine

A small glass of white wine splashed into a fish soup will help bring out the flavour of the seafood, while a little red wine added to a rich meaty soup will lend body and depth.

cold potatoes

Cooked potato is a positive boon when making soups, since it gives extra substance. Whiz it in the blender with the other ingredients or dice it and add it to the pan just before serving and heat gently through.

leftover potatoes

recipe choosers

vegetarian

mango and curry leaf soup
🕒 35 mins **page 325**

creamy pistachio soup
🕒 1 hr **page 229**

beetroot and apple soup
🕒 1 hr 20 mins **page 78**

jerusalem artichoke soup
🕒 50–60 mins **page 164**

creamy kidney bean soup
🕐 3 hrs 35 mins **page 209**

tuscan bean soup
1 hr 35 mins page 204

sweetcorn chowder
40 mins page 96

chilled

tomato borscht
🕐 50 mins **page 104**

white gazpacho
🕐 20 mins **page 230**

watercress soup
🕐 25 mins **page 130**

porcini mushroom soup
🕐 35–45 mins (plus standing) **page 195**

mexican chilli bean soup
🕐 50 mins **page 207**

creamy kidney bean soup
🕐 3 hrs 35 mins **page 209**

cannellini bean and carrot soup
🕐 1 hr 10 mins **page 211**

rosemary's bean soup with italian cheese crisps
🕐 25–30 mins (plus soaking) **page 214**

lentil soup
🕐 55 mins **page 217**

harissa and chickpea soup
🕐 1 hr 10 mins **page 221**

split pea and bacon soup
🕐 1 hr 40 mins **page 225**

soupe de poissons
🕐 1 hr 20 mins **page 239**

creamy smoked trout soup
🕐 25 mins **page 251**

italian wedding soup
🕐 1 hr 50 mins **page 314**

pichelsteiner
🕐 1 hr 30 mins **page 315**

white bean soup
🕐 2 hrs 30 mins **page 212**

minted pea and ham soup
🕐 35–40 mins **page 93**

tuscan bean soup
🕐 1 hr 35 mins **page 204**

healthy

carrot and orange soup
🕐 50 mins **page 71**

roasted red pepper soup
🕐 2 hrs 25 mins **page 112**

baby broad bean soup
🕐 1 hr 20 mins **page 91**

vegetable and chervil soup
🕐 30 mins **page 66**

widow's soup
🕐 45 mins **page 67**

beetroot and apple soup
🕐 1 hr 20 mins **page 78**

asparagus and morel soup
🕐 35 mins **page 83**

fennel and apple soup
🕐 40 mins **page 84**

edamame noodle soup
🕐 20 mins **page 88**

broad bean and mint soup
🕐 55 mins **page 89**

aubergine and red pepper soup
🕐 1 hr 5 mins **page 100**

classic tomato soup
🕐 1 hr 15 mins **page 101**

tomato borscht
🕐 50 mins **page 104**

roast tomato soup
🕐 45 mins **page 106**

gazpacho
🕐 30 mins **page 107**

spinach and rosemary soup
🕐 40 mins **page 122**

spicy

pork vindaloo broth
🕐 3 hrs 35 mins (plus chilling) **page 312**

mango and snapper broth
🕐 30 mins (plus marinating) **page 249**

maple carrot ginger soup
🕐 1 hr 15 mins–1 hr 25 mins **page 69**

edamame noodle soup
🕐 20 mins **page 88**

aubergine and red pepper soup
🕐 1 hr 5 mins **page 100**

smoked tomato soup
🕐 45 mins **page 110**

curried broth with peppers
🕐 40 mins **page 111**

spicy spinach soup
🕐 50 mins (plus marinating) **page 125**

spicy watercress soup
🕐 50 mins **page 132**

zuppa di verdure
🕐 2–3 hrs 30 mins (plus soaking) **page 146**

ribollita
🕐 50 mins **page 147**

garbure
🕐 40 mins **page 148**

turnip soup with pimento, chilli, and noodles
🕐 40 mins **page 167**

keralan prawn soup
🕐 1 hr **page 277**

sopa de tortilla
🕐 1hr 5 mins **page 109**

mussels in ginger and chilli broth
🕐 50–55 mins **page 265**

curried parsnip soup
🕐 55 mins **page 169**

bigos
🕐 2 hrs 40 mins **page 184**

cuban black bean soup
🕐 2 hrs 5 mins (plus soaking) **page 202**

mexican chilli bean soup
🕐 50 mins **page 207**

butterbean soup with rocket pesto
🕐 40 mins **page 210**

cannellini bean and carrot soup
🕐 1 hr 10 mins **page 211**

kichidi
🕐 1 hr 5 mins **page 219**

hot and sour chicken broth
🕐 30 mins **page 295**

beef chilli soup
🕐 45 mins **page 307**

spiced lamb broth
🕐 3 hrs **page 316**

thai chicken soup
🕐 55 mins **page 292**

main meals

sausage and bean soup
🕐 50–55 mins **page 296**

bouillabaisse
🕐 1 hr 5 mins **page 234**

hungarian goulash soup
🕐 2 hrs 15 mins **page 308**

quick

chilled melon and ginger soup
🕐 15 mins page 320

pumpkin soup

watercress soup

white gazpacho

summer vegetables

Thane Prince's recipe books and teaching promote simple cooking with the best local ingredients. "This French country-style soup is delicious topped with a little pesto."

allotment soup

⊘ SERVES 6   **🕐 PREP** 20 MINS, PLUS OVERNIGHT SOAKING   **❄ FREEZE** UP TO 3 MONTHS
COOK 1 HR 20 MINS   WITHOUT THE GREEN BEANS

85g (3oz) dried haricot beans, soaked
   overnight in water, then drained
2 tbsp olive oil
1 medium leek, finely sliced
1 small turnip, cut into 1cm (½in) dice
2 medium carrots, cut into 1cm (½in) dice
1 large courgette, cut into 1cm (½in) dice
1 celery stalk, cut into 1cm (½in) dice

1 large potato, cut into 1cm (½in) dice
2 tomatoes, skinned and cut into
   1cm (½in) dice
2 garlic cloves, finely chopped
2 litres (3½ pints) cold water
salt and freshly ground black pepper
175g (6oz) fine green beans, cut into
   2cm (¾in) lengths

1 Put the soaked haricot beans in a saucepan with plenty of cold unsalted water. Bring to the boil, cover with a lid, and boil for 15 minutes. Lower the heat, then simmer for 1 hour or until tender and drain.

2 Meanwhile, heat the oil in a large saucepan, add the leek, turnip, carrots, courgette, celery, potato, tomatoes, and garlic, and cook, stirring often, for 10–15 minutes or until they are soft but not brown. Add the water, season with salt and freshly ground black pepper, then bring to the boil, cover with a lid, and simmer for 45 minutes or until all the vegetables are tender.

3 Add the cooked haricot beans to the pan, along with the green beans, and cook for 5 minutes or until tender. Divide the soup among six bowls and serve with some crusty bread.

Raymond Blanc OBE, Chef Patron of Le Manoir aux Quat' Saisons, Oxfordshire, writes, "This soup offers a multitude of flavours which can vary according to the seasons."

vegetable and chervil soup

SERVES 4–6   **PREP** 20 MINS **COOK** 10–12 MINS   ❄ **FREEZE** UP TO 3 MONTHS
AT END OF STEP 2

15g (½oz) unsalted butter
1 onion, finely chopped
1 garlic clove, finely chopped
2 large carrots, finely sliced
3 celery sticks, sliced into ½cm (¼in) pieces
2 medium leeks, sliced into 1cm
  (¾in) chunks
salt and freshly ground white pepper

1 large courgette large, halved lengthways
  and cut into ½cm (¼in) slices
2 ripe tomatoes, quartered and
  roughly chopped
15g (½oz) unsalted butter or soured cream
25g (scant 1oz) chervil, finely chopped
crème fraîche, to serve (optional)

1 Melt the butter in a pan and sweat the onion, garlic, carrots, celery, and leeks for 5 minutes (do not allow them to colour). Season with salt and freshly ground white pepper.

2 Add 1 litre (1¾ pints) boiling water, the courgette and tomatoes (using boiling water will reduce the cooking time and also keep the lively colours). Fast boil for a further 5 minutes only – it is vital that you do not spoil the fresh, clean flavours of your vegetables by overcooking.

3 Whisk in the butter or sour cream (or both!) and add the chervil. Taste and correct the seasoning if required, and blend the soup if you would like a finer texture. Pour into a large tureen and serve to your guests. A spoon of crème fraîche would always be welcome.

A Maltese tale tells of a poor widow who had only home-grown vegetables, eggs from her chickens, and a little soft cheese. She made this simple, delicious soup. **Sophie Grigson**

widow's soup

SERVES 4–6 **PREP** 7 MINS **COOK** 40 MINS   **FREEZE** NOT SUITABLE

1 tbsp olive oil
1 large onion, chopped
1 large potato, chopped
175g (6oz) cauliflower florets, quartered
175g (6oz) carrots, sliced
1 small lettuce, shredded
175g (6oz) shelled fresh peas or thawed
    frozen peas
250g (9oz) tomatoes, skinned and roughly
    chopped, or half a 400g (14oz)
    tin chopped tomatoes

1½ tbsp tomato purée
1 tsp sugar
1 tsp red wine vinegar
salt and freshly ground black pepper
6 eggs
250g (9oz) ricotta cheese or firm young
    goat's cheese

1 Heat the oil in a large pan, and fry the onion until soft, but not coloured. Add the potato, cauliflower, carrots, lettuce, and fresh peas, if using. Stir, then add the tomatoes, tomato purée, sugar, vinegar, salt and pepper, and enough water (or stock) to cover generously. Bring to the boil and simmer until the vegetables are almost tender. If using thawed frozen peas, add them now. Taste and adjust the seasoning.

2 Reduce the heat so that the surface of the soup is barely trembling. Break the eggs one at a time onto a saucer, and slip them into the soup. Poach the eggs until the white has just set, about 8–10 minutes.

3 Cut the cheese into 4–6 pieces, according to the number of serving bowls, and place one in each bowl. Carefully place one egg in each bowl, and ladle the soup around the eggs and cheese before serving.

This spicy, exotically flavoured carrot soup makes an elegant starter. Serve it with lime wedges so that guests can adjust the flavour to their liking. **Angela Nilsen**

carrot soup with coconut and lemongrass

⊚ SERVES 4　　🕐 **PREP** 15 MINS **COOK** 35 MINS　　❄ **FREEZE** UP TO 3 MONTHS

2 tbsp vegetable oil or sunflower oil
1 onion, chopped
1 lemongrass stalk, trimmed and tough
　outer layer discarded
2 garlic cloves, chopped
2 tsp finely grated root ginger
1 tbsp red Thai curry paste

450g (1lb) carrots, sliced
900ml (1½ pints) hot vegetable stock
3 kaffir lime leaves
165ml (6fl oz) can coconut milk
salt and freshly ground black pepper
lime wedges, to serve

1 Heat the oil in a large saucepan, add the onion, and fry for 3–4 minutes or until starting to soften. Meanwhile, finely chop the lemongrass, then add to the pan, along with the garlic and ginger, and fry for 2 minutes. Add the curry paste and fry for 1 minute, stirring all the time, then add the carrots and fry for 2 minutes. Pour in the stock, add the lime leaves, and simmer for 20–25 minutes or until the carrots are tender.

2 Remove from the heat and take out and discard the lime leaves. Pour in the coconut milk, then whiz in a blender or food processor until smooth. The soup shouldn't be too thick – dilute with more stock if it is. Season to taste, then serve with a grating of black pepper and lime wedges.

The maple syrup helps the carrot to caramelize in the oven, giving this soup its deep, rich flavour. If you cannot find lovage, use chopped chives to finish. **Sophie Grigson**

maple-roasted carrot and ginger soup

SERVES 8   **PREP** 20 MINS **COOK** 55–65 MINS   **FREEZE** UP TO 3 MONTHS

2kg (4½lb) carrots, cut into roughly little-finger-sized pieces
2 onions, cut into eighths
4cm (1¾in) piece of stem ginger, cut into matchsticks
4 garlic cloves, peeled
3 tbsp sunflower oil

4 tbsp maple syrup
1½ litres (2¾ pints) chicken or vegetable stock
a couple of squeezes of lemon juice (optional)
salt and freshly ground black pepper
chopped lovage, to serve

1 Preheat the oven to 220°C/425°F/Gas Mark 7. Place the carrots in a roasting tin with all the rest of the ingredients except the stock, lemon juice, salt and pepper, and the lovage. Mix thoroughly with your hands, then smooth down lightly. Roast for some 45–60 minutes, turning occasionally, until the vegetables are very tender and patched here and there with brown.

2 Cool slightly, then scrape into a liquidizer, including as much as you can scrape off of the brown sticky residues at the bottom of the tin. Add half the stock and liquidize until smooth, adding more stock if necessary. You may need to do this in batches.

3 Pour into a saucepan, stir in the last of the stock, adding extra if necessary to thin the soup, and then taste and correct the seasoning, adding a couple of squeezes of lemon juice if you find the sweetness too intense. Adequate seasoning will also balance this. Heat up well just before serving, and sprinkle each bowlful with chopped lovage.

A light, refreshing soup with a hint of spice, this is the perfect start to a summer meal. Try adding a swirl of cream or a spoonful of low-fat plain yogurt before serving.

carrot and orange soup

⊘ SERVES 4   **⏱ PREP** 10 MINS **COOK** 40 MINS   **❄ FREEZE** UP TO 3 MONTHS

2 tsp light olive oil or sunflower oil
1 leek, sliced
500g (1lb 2oz) carrots, sliced
1 potato, about 115g (4oz), chopped
½ tsp ground coriander
pinch of ground cumin

300ml (10fl oz) orange juice
500ml (16fl oz) vegetable or chicken stock
1 bay leaf
salt and freshly ground black pepper
2 tbsp chopped coriander, to garnish

1 Place the oil, leek, and carrots in a large saucepan and cook over a low heat for 5 minutes, stirring frequently, or until the leek has softened. Add the potato, coriander, and cumin, then pour in the orange juice and stock. Add the bay leaf and stir occasionally.

2 Increase the heat, bring the soup to the boil, then lower the heat, cover, and simmer for 40 minutes, or until the vegetables are very tender.

3 Allow the soup to cool slightly, then transfer to a blender or food processor and process until smooth, working in batches if necessary.

4 Return to the saucepan and add a little extra stock or water if the soup is too thick. Bring back to a simmer, then transfer to heated serving bowls and sprinkle with chopped coriander.

Pushing this colourful, zingy soup through a sieve may seem fiddly, but it does wonders for the texture and is worth the effort. **Marie-Pierre Moine**

carrot cream with onion and cumin

SERVES 4   **PREP** 20 MINS **COOK** 30 MINS   **FREEZE** UP TO 3 MONTHS
BEFORE CREAM IS ADDED

2 tbsp sunflower, groundnut or mild olive oil
2 large Spanish onions, peeled
　and coarsely chopped
1 tsp cumin seeds
1 tsp ground cumin
1kg (2¼lb) carrots, peeled and
　coarsely chopped

sea salt and freshly ground black pepper
juice and grated zest of 1 small
　unwaxed orange
120ml (4fl oz) single cream
1 tbsp finely chopped flat-leaf parsley

1 Place a large sauté pan over a medium-high heat. Add the oil and tip in the onion and cumin. Cook for 3–5 minutes, or until softened, stirring frequently. Add the carrots and 1.5 litres (2¾ pints) water, then season lightly. Bring to a simmer, reduce the heat, cover and cook for 20 minutes, or until the carrots are very tender. Turn off the heat and allow to cool a little.

2 Pour into a blender or food processor and whiz until smooth. Place a sieve over a saucepan (or the sauté pan if possible). Pour the soup into the sieve and push it through with the back of a wooden spoon.

3 Taste and adjust the seasoning. Stir in the orange juice and zest. Reheat until piping hot and stir in the cream, then the parsley. Season with a little extra pepper. Serve hot.

Sally Clarke was one of the first British chefs to champion seasonal, organic food at her London restaurant, Clarkes. "This chilled, fresh-tasting soup is perfect in summer."

beetroot and tomato soup

⊘ SERVES 6   **🕐 PREP** 20 MINS, PLUS 3 HRS CHILLING   **❄ FREEZE** UP TO 3 MONTHS
COOK 55 MINS   AT THE END OF STEP 2

90ml (3fl oz) olive oil, plus extra to garnish
½ head new-season garlic, roughly chopped
1 large onion, roughly chopped
4 celery stalks, roughly chopped
1 bulb fennel, roughly chopped
500g (1lb 2oz) very ripe plum tomatoes, roughly chopped
500g (1lb 2oz) very ripe beefsteak tomatoes, roughly chopped
250g (9oz) cooked beetroot, roughly chopped

2 tbsp freshly chopped basil (stalks reserved), plus 6 sprigs, to garnish
salt and freshly ground black pepper
50g (1¾oz) red, yellow, or pink baby beetroot, to garnish
1 tbsp chives, with blossoms if available, to garnish
115g (4oz) red, yellow, or orange cherry tomatoes, to garnish
crème fraîche, to garnish (optional)

1 Preheat the oven to 200°C (400°F/Gas 6). In a casserole pan over a low heat, cook the garlic, onion, celery, and fennel in the oil, stirring, for 6–8 minutes. Add the tomatoes, beetroot, and basil stalks. Season. Barely cover with water, bring to the boil, then place, uncovered, in the oven for 40 minutes.

2 Transfer to a blender and whiz until smooth, adding a little water if necessary. Pass through a sieve, pushing as much as you can through with the back of the ladle. Season, then chill in the fridge for at least 3 hours.

3 Cook the baby beetroot in boiling salted water for 20–25 minutes or until tender, then drain, cool, and peel. Top, tail, and halve or quarter, depending on size. Season and stir in half the chopped basil, half the chives, and a drizzle of oil. Halve and season the cherry tomatoes.

4 Stir the soup well, check the seasoning, and half-fill six chilled bowls. Spoon the baby beetroots and cherry tomatoes into the centre of each bowl, then garnish with a drizzle of olive oil or a generous scoop of crème fraîche, the basil sprigs, and the rest of the chives, snipped.

This thickly textured, satisfying soup is a Russian classic to enjoy at any time of year and on any occasion. Try it with grated carrot piled on top and hunks of dark rye bread.

borscht

SERVES 4   **PREP** 15 MINS **COOK** 1½ HRS   **FREEZE** UP TO 3 MONTHS

45g (1½ oz) butter or goose fat
2 large beetroot, roughly grated
1 onion, roughly grated
1 carrot, roughly grated
1 celery stalk, roughly grated
400g can chopped tomatoes
1 garlic clove, crushed (optional)

1.7 litres (3 pints) hot vegetable stock
2 bay leaves
4 cloves
2 tbsp lemon juice
salt and freshly ground black pepper
200ml (7fl oz) soured cream

1 Melt the butter in a large saucepan over a medium heat. Add the beetroot, onion, carrot, and celery, and cook, stirring, for 5 minutes or until just softened. Add the tomatoes and garlic, if using, and cook for 2–3 minutes, stirring frequently, then stir in the stock.

2 Tie the bay leaves and cloves in a small piece of muslin and add to the pan. Bring the soup to the boil, then lower the heat, cover, and simmer for 1 hour 20 minutes. Discard the muslin bag, stir in the lemon juice, and season to taste with salt and pepper. Ladle the soup into warm bowls and add a swirl of soured cream to each one.

BEETROOT
You can find a variety of types of beetroot at your local farmers' market – red has the richest flavour. Be gentle when washing as heavy scrubbing may damage the skin and cause "bleeding".

For adults only, with a finishing kick of gin, this dramatic-looking dark pink dish carries distinct eastern European flavours of dill, caraway, and soured cream. **Sophie Grigson**

beetroot and gin soup

SERVES 4–6   **PREP** 10 MINS **COOK** 50 MINS   **FREEZE** UP TO 3 MONTHS
BEFORE GIN IS ADDED

2 stems of fresh parsley
1 bay leaf
2 large sprigs of fresh dill or fennel
2 tbsp sunflower oil
1 onion, chopped
½ tbsp caraway seeds
3 tbsp risotto rice (eg arborio)
650g (1½lb) beetroot, peeled and grated

1 tbsp lemon juice
1 litre (1¾ pints) beef stock, chicken stock, or vegetable stock
salt and freshly ground black pepper
2 tbsp gin or vodka
soured cream or crème fraîche, to serve
chopped fresh dill or chives, to serve

1 Make a bouquet garni (see p24) using the parsley, bay leaf, and sprigs of dill or fennel. Heat the oil in a saucepan and sweat the onion, caraway seeds, and bouquet garni over a low heat, covered, for 10 minutes.

2 Add the rice to the pan, and stir for about 1 minute to coat it in the juices. Add the beetroot and lemon juice (to set the colour), and continue cooking, stirring constantly, for a further 2–3 minutes.

3 Pour in the stock, season with salt and pepper, and bring to the boil. Simmer for 25–30 minutes, until both the beetroot and rice are tender. Remove and discard the bouquet garni. Add a splash of water – about 120ml (4fl oz) – to the pan.

4 Whiz the soup in a blender until smooth, in batches if needed. Return to the pan, adjust the seasoning, and stir in the gin. Reheat thoroughly, without letting the soup boil. Serve steaming hot, with a generous swirl of soured cream in each bowl and a sprinkling of dill or chives.

in praise of...
beetroot
The underrated and under-used, yet vastly versatile beetroot is good to eat all year round, as one of its many virtues is that it stores so well. A sweet-sour, ruby-coloured soup is guaranteed to convert even the most beetroot-averse of diners.
Juliet Kindersley

Juliet Kindersley and her husband Peter rear and produce organic meat from Sheepdrove Organic Farm in Berkshire. "We like this with plenty of lemon, sugar, salt, and pepper."

beetroot and apple soup

SERVES 6–8   **PREP** 20 MINS **COOK** 1 HR   ❄ **FREEZE** UP TO 3 MONTHS
WITHOUT THE HERB CREAM

1 onion, halved
2 garlic cloves
3 tbsp olive oil
salt and freshly ground black pepper
350g (12oz) raw beetroot, peeled and halved
1 potato, halved
4 eating apples, peeled and cored
1.5 litres (2¾ pints) hot vegetable stock
  or chicken stock

1–2 tbsp dark brown sugar
juice of 1 lemon
2 tbsp finely chopped parsley, chives,
  dill, or coriander, or a mixture
200g (7oz) crème fraîche, soured cream,
  or thick creamy yogurt

1 Grate the onion and garlic in a food processor. Heat the oil in a large pan over a low heat, add the onion, garlic, and a pinch of salt, and cook gently, stirring once or twice, for 5 minutes or until soft. Meanwhile, grate the beetroot, potato, and apples in the food processor.

2 Add the beetroot, potato, and apples to the pan and stew gently for 10 minutes, stirring occasionally. Pour in the stock, bring to the boil, then cover with a lid and simmer gently for 45 minutes or until the beetroot is cooked through.

3 Transfer the mixture to a blender and whiz till smooth. You may need to do this in batches. Season with the sugar, lemon juice, and some salt and freshly ground black pepper.

4 Stir the chopped herbs into the cream or yoghurt, then ladle the soup into warm bowls and drop a big spoonful of green-speckled cream into the middle of the deep pink soup.

Rebecca Sullivan founded Dirty Girl Kitchen and Reap and Sow. "This is a fantastic way to cook beetroot. The cheese complements the round sweetness of the beets."

beetroot soup with goat's cheese

SERVES 4   **PREP TIME** 15 MINS **COOK** 45 MINS   **FREEZE** UP TO 3 MONTHS
WITHOUT THE GOAT'S CHEESE

HOT OR COLD

500-600g (1lb 2oz-1lb5oz) beetroot
500g (1lb 2oz) ripe tomatoes, halved
250g (9oz) apples, diced
2 tbsp olive or sunflower oil

1 medium onion, peeled and finely chopped
500ml (16fl oz) good strong beef stock
salt and freshly ground black pepper
125g (4½oz) Childwickbury goat's cheese

1 Preheat the oven to 190°C (375°F/Gas 5). Wearing gloves to prevent staining your hands, peel and coarsely grate the beetroot and set aside, then place the tomatoes and apples in an ovenproof dish and drizzle with half the oil. Roast for 25–30 minutes, or until soft and pulpy, then rub them through a sieve to remove the skin and pips.

2 Heat the remaining oil in a pan and sweat the onion for a few minutes until soft. Add the beetroot and stock and bring to the boil, then season to taste and simmer gently for 10 minutes, or until the beetroot is tender. Stir in the tomato and apple purée, transfer to a blender and process until completely smooth. Taste and adjust the seasoning.

3 To serve cold, chill in the fridge then divide between four bowls. To serve hot, reheat until piping hot but not boiling. In either case, crumble the cheese over each bowl. Serve with crusty bread and butter.

Sarah Raven, presenter on BBC Gardeners' World, says, "This is a wonderful sweet, earthy soup, which I eat all year round. It is best served warm rather than piping hot."

swiss chard and coconut soup

🍵 **SERVES** 6   🕐 **PREP** 10 MINS **COOK** 20 MINS   ❄️ **FREEZE** UP TO 3 MONTHS

250g (9oz) Swiss chard (or spinach)
125g (4½oz) Red Giant mustard, kale
  or more chard
2 medium onions, finely chopped
1 garlic clove, finely chopped

2 tbsp olive oil
750ml (1¼ pints) vegetable stock
2 x 400ml cans coconut milk
salt and black pepper

1 Prepare the chard and Red Giant mustard or kale, stripping the green leaves from the stems and shredding it into ribbons.

2 Sweat the onion and garlic gently in the oil for about 10 minutes, or until soft. Add the shredded greens, stock and coconut milk and bring to the boil. Simmer for 10 minutes then whiz everything up together with a wand or food processor. Season to taste and serve.

SWISS CHARD
Now a familiar sight at the farmers' market or greengrocer. The leaves should be firm and green, not limp or yellowing. Do not wash it before storing in the fridge as it can wilt, and use it quickly for maximum nutritional value.

If you are a fan of puréed soups, you can whiz the mixture in a blender at the end of cooking, then pass it though a fine sieve and reheat gently before serving.

cream of asparagus soup

⊘ SERVES 4   **◷ PREP** 10 MINS **COOK** 40 MINS   **❄ FREEZE** UP TO 3 MONTHS
BEFORE EGG AND CREAM ADDED

1 litre (1¾ pints) water
salt and freshly ground black pepper
60g (2oz) butter
500g (1lb 2oz) white or green asparagus,
    trimmed, peeled (reserve the trimmings),
    and cut into 2.5cm (1in) lengths
300ml (10fl oz) milk

30g (1oz) plain flour
pinch of caster sugar
pinch of freshly grated nutmeg
2 medium egg yolks
2 tbsp whipping cream
1½ tbsp chopped flat-leaf parsley

1 Put the water into a saucepan with 1 level tsp salt and 20g (¾oz) of the butter. Add the asparagus trimmings, bring to the boil, then cover and simmer for 15 minutes over a medium heat. Strain through a sieve (reserving the cooking liquid) and discard the trimmings.

2 Bring the cooking liquid to the boil and add the trimmed asparagus. Return to the boil, cover, and cook for 10–12 minutes or until al dente, then drain, reserving the cooking liquid. Add enough of the milk to the cooking liquid to make 1 litre (1¾ pints) in all.

3 Melt the remaining butter in a pan, add the flour, and cook over a low heat, stirring, for 2–3 minutes or until smooth. Gradually add the milk mixture, stirring vigorously with a whisk to make sure there are no lumps. Bring to the boil and cook, uncovered, over a low heat for 5 minutes, stirring occasionally. Add the sugar and nutmeg and season with salt and freshly ground black pepper.

4 Stir the egg yolks into the cream and slowly add the mixture to the soup, stirring carefully to get a smooth texture. Add the asparagus and reheat gently. Do not let the soup boil. Serve garnished with the parsley.

This soup is for early summer when asparagus first appears and when fresh morel mushrooms are in season. It should taste fresh and light, so cooking times are brief. **Shaun Hill**

asparagus and morel soup

⊘ SERVES 4   **🕐 PREP** 15 MINS **COOK** 20 MINS   **❄ FREEZE** NOT SUITABLE

1.5 litres (2¾ pints) chicken stock
1 small potato, cut into 2cm (¾in) dice
1 small leek, trimmed and cut into
   2cm (¾in) lengths
400g (14oz) asparagus, trimmed and
   cut into 5cm (2in) lengths

1 tbsp olive oil
1 tbsp crème fraîche
25g (scant 1oz) unsalted butter
salt and freshly ground black pepper
4 large fresh morels (or 4 dried morels soaked
   in lukewarm water for 30 minutes)

1 Heat the stock in a large saucepan, add the potato, and bring to the boil. Lower the heat and simmer for 5 minutes. Add the leek and asparagus and cook, uncovered, for 7–8 minutes. Pick out four attractive asparagus tips and reserve for garnishing. Transfer the contents of the pan to a blender and whiz until smooth. Add the olive oil, crème fraîche, and 20g (¾oz) of the butter, then season with salt and freshly ground black pepper.

2 Halve the morels lengthways and brush clean inside and out. Stew gently in a pan with the remaining butter for a few minutes until cooked. Meanwhile, reheat the soup. Serve garnished with the morels and reserved asparagus tips.

ASPARAGUS
Buy spears with plump, firm stems and tight buds. Organic asparagus is expensive to produce (keeping the beds weeded is a labour of love) but, for its subtle flavour of freshly cut grass, it is well worth the indulgence.

Fennel will store better in the fridge if you remove the feathery fronds, but be sure to save a good handful of those for this soup as a garnish. **Celia Brooks Brown**

fennel and apple soup

⊘ **SERVES** 4   🕐 **PREP** 10 MINS **COOK** 30 MINS   ❄ **FREEZE** UP TO 3 MONTHS

2 tbsp virgin rapeseed oil or olive oil
4 spring onions, sliced
2 cloves garlic, chopped
600g (1lb 5oz) fennel (trimmed weight), roughly chopped
1 celery heart with leaves, or 3 celery stalks, chopped

1 cooking apple, peeled, cored and roughly chopped
sea salt
750ml (1¼ pints) vegetable stock
fennel fronds, to serve

1 Heat the oil in a large pan over a medium heat and add the spring onions. Soften for 3 minutes, then add the garlic. Cook for 1–2 minutes until fragrant, then add the fennel, celery and apple with a little salt. Stir, cover and sweat for 10 minutes, stirring frequently.

2 Pour in the stock and bring to the boil. Simmer for 15 minutes, until the fennel is tender. Cool briefly, then purée with a hand blender. Taste and adjust the seasoning. Serve hot, or allow to cool, chill for several hours and serve cold. Serve each bowl scattered with torn fennel fronds.

FENNEL
In the market, look for firm, unblemished bulbs that are heavy for their size, with bright green fronds. If you are considering growing your own, bear in mind that fennel thrives in warm conditions.

The last-minute addition of paprika-flavoured chorizo gives spice to this hearty soup. Keep the texture chunky by processing only briefly. **Marie-Pierre Moine**

fennel soup with beans, thyme, and chorizo

SERVES 4 | **PREP** 15 MINS PLUS SOAKING OVERNIGHT **COOK** 1 HOUR | **FREEZE** UP TO 3 MONTHS WITHOUT CHORIZO

250g (9oz) dried haricot beans
1 tbsp sunflower, groundnut or mild olive oil
1 Spanish onion, finely chopped
2 cloves garlic, crushed
1 head fennel, cored and finely chopped

2 tsp dried fennel seeds
1 tbsp finely chopped fresh parsley
2 tsp thyme leaves
salt and pepper
100g (3½oz) diced cubed chorizo

1 Soak the beans overnight in plenty of cold water then drain and rinse. Put a heavy pan over a medium heat. Add the oil, spread in the onion and stir for 2 minutes. Add the garlic, fennel and fennel seeds, parsley and half the thyme and cook for 3–5 minutes until slightly softened. Tip in the beans. Stir, pour in 2 litres (3½ pints) water and season lightly.

2 Bring to a simmer and cook for 40 minutes, or until the beans are tender, skimming from time to time. Remove from the heat and leave to cool a little. Transfer to a food processor or blender and whiz briefly until partly puréed. Return to the pan, taste and adjust the seasoning.

3 Gently reheat the soup. Meanwhile, place a small non-stick pan over a moderately high heat and fry the chorizo for 2–3 minutes until crisp and coloured, stirring frequently. Drain on a plate lined with kitchen paper.

4 Ladle the soup into bowls, add a little chorizo to each and finish with a scattering of thyme. Serve immediately.

This rustic soup owes its substance to haricot beans.
Buy fresh beans when they are available in early summer
– they are quicker to cook and easier to digest. **Marie-Pierre Moine**

pistou soup

⊙ **SERVES** 6–8　　🕐 **PREP** 30 MINS **COOK** 1½ HOURS　　❄ **FREEZE** UP TO 3 MONTHS
WITHOUT THE PISTOU

for the pistou
3 garlic cloves, smashed and peeled
coarse sea salt to taste
leaves from a large handful of fresh basil
2 small tomatoes, skinned, seeds removed
　and chopped (see p22)
freshly ground black pepper
25g (scant 1oz) mimolette cheese, grated
3 tbsp olive oil

1 ham hock, or a thick piece of smoked
　bacon, about 150g (5½oz)

200g (7oz) fresh white haricot beans,
　such as cannellini, shelled
100g (3½oz) fresh red haricot beans,
　such as borlotti, shelled
250g (9oz) flat green beans, sliced
2 medium floury potatoes, diced
3 tomatoes, skinned, seeds removed
　and chopped (see p22)
4 medium courgettes, chopped
salt and freshly ground black pepper
100g (3½oz) small macaroni

1 To make the pistou, pound the garlic in a mortar with a pestle, then add a little salt and the basil and pound to a paste. Add the tomatoes and continue pounding and mixing until you have a thick sauce. Add pepper, the cheese, and the oil, mix well, and adjust the seasoning.

2 For the soup, put 2 litres (3½ pints) cold water in a large stewing pot. Add the ham hock. Bring to a simmer, then partly cover and leave to bubble gently for 30 minutes, skimming occasionally.

3 Meanwhile, put the haricot beans in a saucepan, cover with plenty of cold water, and bring to the boil. Simmer for 10 minutes, drain and refresh. Add all the vegetables to the stewing pot. Season lightly. Return to a simmer, then part-cover and bubble gently for 1 hour, skimming occasionally.

4 Remove the ham hock and shred the meat. Lift half of the ingredients out of the pan, mash with a fork, then return to the soup with the ham. Add the macaroni and cook until just tender. Stir in the pistou, and serve.

Edamame, or fresh soya beans, are widely available as frozen whole pods from Asian supermarkets – thaw them slightly before using. **Celia Brooks Brown**

edamame noodle soup

SERVES 4   **PREP** 10 MINS **COOK** 10 MINS   **FREEZE** NOT SUITABLE

500g (1lb 2oz) edamame in the pod or 225g
  (8oz) podded weight
4 tbsp white miso paste
400g (14oz) cooked udon noodles
1 tbsp brown sugar, or to taste
juice of 1 lemon

for the hot garlic oil
1 small red chilli, snipped
1 clove garlic
½ tsp coarse sea salt
2 tbsp sesame oil

1 Remove the edamame from the pod, if necessary, and set aside. Bring 1 litre (1¾ pints) of water to the boil in a large pan. Meanwhile, make the hot garlic oil. With a mortar and pestle, pound the chilli, garlic and salt together until smooth then stir in the sesame oil.

2 Place the miso in a small bowl and mix with a slosh of boiling water from the pan, stirring until you have a pourable paste. Add the edamame, noodles and sugar to the water in the pan and cook for 3 minutes, or until the edamame are tender but still bright green.

3 Turn off the heat and stir in the diluted miso paste, then add lemon juice to taste. Ladle into warm bowls and drizzle with the hot garlic oil before serving.

This soup is a beautiful cool, pale green, flecked with mint and bright, skinned beans. Do not reheat once you have mixed in the yogurt, as it may curdle. **Sophie Grigson**

broad bean and mint soup

⊘ **SERVES** 4   🕐 **PREP** 30 MINS **COOK** 25 MINS   ❄ **FREEZE** UP TO 3 MONTHS
BEFORE YOGURT IS ADDED

450g (1lb) broad beans (podded weight),
    thawed if frozen
1 onion, chopped
1 stem celery, thinly sliced
30g (1oz) butter
2 tbsp pudding rice
1 generous sprig summer savory, or thyme

1 litre (1¾ pints) chicken or vegetable stock
salt and pepper
110g (4oz) Greek yogurt
handful of fresh mint leaves, chopped
4 small sprigs of mint
paprika or cayenne pepper, to serve

1 If the beans are fresh, drop them into a pan of boiling water and simmer for 1 minute. Drain and run under the cold tap. Then, whether using fresh or frozen, skin each bean by slitting the tough outer skin with a fingernail or a small sharp knife and squeezing out the bright green beanlet inside. Take about one eighth, chop roughly and set aside.

2 Over a low heat in a covered pan, sweat the onion and celery gently in the butter for 10 minutes, or until very tender. Add the rice and savory or thyme and cook for another minute, uncovered. Now add the unchopped beans, 900ml (1½ pints) of stock, salt and pepper, bring to the boil and simmer for 10 minutes, or until the rice is tender. Remove the herbs then blend in batches, adding more stock if you want a looser consistency.

3 Shortly before serving, reheat thoroughly, then remove from the heat. Stir in a tablespoonful of the yogurt, together with the reserved chopped beans and the mint. Mix in the remaining yogurt, a tablespoon at a time, until it is all added. Taste and adjust seasoning and serve while still warm, floating a sprig of mint and a light dusting of paprika or cayenne on the surface of each bowl.

This soup is a perfect spring starter. Try serving it topped with a splash of extra virgin olive oil and cubes of bread fried in olive oil. **Marie-Pierre Moine**

baby broad bean soup

SERVES 4–6   **PREP** 20 MINS **COOK** 1 HOUR   **FREEZE** UP TO 3 MONTHS
WITHOUT THE CROÛTONS

3 slices toasting bread, for croûtons
6 tbsp olive oil
3 large mild onions, sliced
1 leek, sliced
1.5kg (3lb 3oz) broad beans, shelled

4 garlic cloves, crushed
a small handful of fresh chives, chopped
4 new potatoes, peeled and chopped
salt and freshly ground black pepper
leaves from a bunch of fresh radishes

1 To make the croûtons, cut the bread into 1.5cm (½in) cubes. Heat 3 tbsp oil in a large frying pan over a fairly hot heat. Add the bread cubes and spread them out. Fry for a minute, then stir and turn them over. Fry for another minute. Spread the croûtons over a plate lined with kitchen paper. Pat with more kitchen paper to drain off excess oil. Set aside.

2 In a big stewing pot or flameproof casserole, heat the remaining oil over a moderate heat. Add the onions and leek. Soften for 10 minutes, stirring frequently.

3 Add the broad beans to the pot with the garlic, chives, and potatoes. Stir, then pour in about 3 litres (5¼ pints) water. Season lightly and stir in the radish leaves. Turn up the heat a little and bring to the boil, then leave to bubble gently for 15–20 minutes.

4 Allow to cool a little, then work through a food mill. Alternatively, whiz briefly in a blender, then press through a sieve. (If you prefer, you can omit the sieving, in which case the soup will serve 6–8 people.) Reheat until piping hot before serving, topped with the croûtons.

Quick to make, this soup transforms everyday ingredients into a splendid light lunch. Frozen peas, with their natural sweetness, make a good match for the fresh mint. **Roopa Gulati**

minted pea and ham soup

⊙ SERVES 4–6   **🕑 PREP** 15 MINS **COOK** 20–25 MINS   **❄ FREEZE** UP TO 2 MONTHS
BEFORE CRÈME FRAÎCHE IS ADDED

2 shallots, finely chopped
40g (1¼oz) butter
1 potato, peeled and chopped
300ml (10fl oz) vegetable stock, hot
500g (1lb) frozen peas, defrosted

2 handfuls of fresh mint leaves, plus 2 tbsp
  extra for garnishing
150g (5oz) cooked ham, diced
salt and freshly ground black pepper
150ml (5fl oz) crème fraîche

1 Soften the shallots in the butter in a pan over a low heat for 2–3 minutes. Add the potato and continue cooking, covered, for another 7–10 minutes or until the potato is tender. Pour over the stock and simmer for 10–15 minutes.

2 In a separate pan, boil 400ml (14fl oz) water and cook the peas for 2–3 minutes. Add the mint leaves for the last 20 seconds of cooking. Tip the peas and mint into a sieve placed over a bowl, reserving the cooking liquid in the bowl. Add the peas and mint to the stock and whiz the soup using a blender until smooth, pouring in enough cooking liquid from the peas to loosen the consistency. Stir in the diced ham.

3 For the garnish, stretch a sheet of cling film tightly over a dinner plate. Brush with olive oil and press the extra mint leaves onto the surface. Cover with another layer of cling film and cook in the microwave for 2 minutes, until crisp. Reheat the soup, seasoning with salt and pepper to taste. Serve with a dollop of crème fraîche in the centre, garnished with the dried mint leaves.

Try this hearty soup with slices of dark German rye bread and a glass of white wine or wheat beer. Warming and perfect for a wintry day.

pea and sausage soup

⊘ SERVES 6   **⏱ PREP** 20 MINS **COOK** 20 MINS   **❄ FREEZE** UP TO 3 MONTHS
WITHOUT THE SAUSAGES

30g (1oz) butter
1 large carrot, peeled and diced
1 small leek, diced
2 stalks celery, diced
1 medium potato, peeled and diced
½ bunch fresh parsley, chopped

125ml (4fl oz) dry white wine
1.2 litres (2 pints) hot chicken stock
3 Toulouse sausages
750g (1lb 10oz) peas (frozen or fresh)
salt and pepper

1 Preheat the oven to 180°C (350°F/Gas 4). In a large saucepan, melt the butter and add the carrot, leek, celery and potato and cook, stirring, until softened. Add the parsley, wine and stock and simmer for 15 minutes.

2 Place the sausages on a baking tray and cook, turning occasionally, for 15–20 minutes, or until cooked through and golden brown on all sides, then slice and set aside.

3 Add the peas to the pot and cook for 3–4 minutes, or until just al dente. Season and process to a puree in a blender. Return to the pot and heat through. Serve in 6 bowls, garnished with the sliced cooked sausage.

If you don't have chilli-flavoured olive oil, stir a very little piquante pimenton, harissa or smoked paprika into fruity olive oil and drizzle over the servings. **Marie-Pierre Moine**

mexican sweetcorn soup

SERVES 4   **PREP** 15 MINS **COOK** 20 MINS   **FREEZE** UP TO 3 MONTHS

3 tbsp olive oil
1 Spanish onion, finely chopped
1 red pepper, halved, cored, deseeded
  and finely chopped
1 clove garlic, crushed
1 tsp fennel seeds

1 tsp fresh thyme leaves
400g (14oz) sweetcorn kernels
  (drained and rinsed, if canned)
salt and pepper
100ml (3½fl oz) single cream
1½ tbsp chilli-flavoured olive oil, to serve

1 Heat the oil in a large sauté pan over a moderate heat, add the onion, pepper (reserving a scant tablespoon to finish), garlic, fennel seeds and thyme, and stir-fry for 3 minutes. Add the sweetcorn and season lightly. Continue stirring and cooking for 2 minutes, then pour in 500ml (16fl oz) hot water, stir, and bring to a simmer. Lower the heat, cover, and simmer for 15 minutes or until the vegetables are tender and cooked through. Stir in the cream and leave to cool for a few minutes.

2 Process the soup until smooth in a blender (you may need to do this in batches). Return to the pan and reheat gently, stirring occasionally. Taste and adjust the seasoning. Ladle into bowls and add the reserved red pepper. Drizzle over a little chilli-flavoured olive oil and serve immediately.

SWEETCORN
A seasonal delight. Look for locally grown cobs with the squeaky, stiff leaves that are a sign of freshness. The grains should be firm and bright yellow, not wrinkled. Use as soon as possible, as the corn will quickly lose its sweetness.

If you have grown your own sweetcorn, wait until the very last minute to harvest it – the quicker you get it from the plot to the pan, the sweeter it will be. **Celia Brooks Brown**

sweetcorn chowder

SERVES 4–6   **PREP** 10 MINS **COOK** 30 MINS   ❄ **FREEZE** UP TO 1 MONTH
WITHOUT MILK OR CREAM CHEESE

4 fresh corn on the cob
500ml (16fl oz) water
salt
2 bay leaves
2 tbsp olive oil
1 large onion, chopped
4 fresh sage leaves, chopped, or ½ tsp
    dried sage, crushed
1 tsp fresh thyme leaves, or ½ tsp
    dried thyme

1 medium carrot, chopped
2 celery sticks, chopped
1 large potato, chopped
200g (7oz) cream cheese
120ml (4fl oz) milk
salt and freshly ground black pepper
single cream, to serve
dusting of paprika, to serve

1 Stand each corn cob upright in a large bowl and strip the kernels by cutting downward with a sharp knife. Set the kernels aside. Place the cobs in a large saucepan and add water, a generous dose of salt, and bay leaves. Bring to the boil and simmer, covered, for 15 minutes. Remove and discard the cobs and bay leaves.

2 Heat the oil in a saucepan and cook the onions until translucent. Add the herbs and remaining vegetables except the corn kernels. Cook for about 5 minutes, until softened. Add the corn cob stock and simmer until the potato is collapsing. Meanwhile, place the sweetcorn kernels in a saucepan and barely cover with cold water. Bring to the boil and cook for 2 minutes. Set aside.

3 Add the cream cheese and milk to the soup mixture, then purée until smooth. Stir in the corn kernels with their cooking liquid. Give the chowder one more whiz if desired, to break up the corn kernels slightly. Reheat and adjust the seasoning. Ladle into warm bowls. Drizzle with streaks of single cream and dust with paprika.

Nutmeg and saffron bring out the delicate, nutty taste of the artichoke. Fresh is best, but canned and drained, or frozen and defrosted, artichoke hearts also work well. **Marie-Pierre Moine**

globe artichoke soup

SERVES 4   **PREP** 20 MINS **COOK** 20 MINS   ❄ **FREEZE** UP TO 3 MONTHS
BEFORE CREAM IS ADDED

1 tbsp olive oil
20g butter
½ Spanish onion, finely chopped
1 shallot, finely chopped
1 clove garlic, crushed
¼ tsp ground nutmeg
a few saffron strands

800g (1¾lb) artichoke hearts, chopped
salt and pepper
100ml (3½fl oz) single cream
4 thin rashers smoky streaky bacon
  or pancetta
a large handful of baby spinach
  leaves, chopped

1 Bring a full kettle to the boil. Put a sauté pan over a moderate heat and add the oil and butter. Tip in the onion, shallot, garlic, nutmeg and saffron, and stir for 3 minutes. Add the artichoke hearts and season lightly. Continue stirring and cooking for 3 minutes. Pour 1 litre (1¾ pints) of hot water from the kettle into the sauté pan and stir to mix. Bring to a simmer. Reduce the heat, cover and simmer for 10 minutes, or until the vegetables are tender and cooked through. Leave to cool for several minutes.

2 Pour the soup into a blender and process until smooth, then pour back into the pan. Reheat gently, stirring occasionally. Meanwhile, heat the cream until simmering in a separate small saucepan over a moderate heat.

3 Place a non-stick frying pan over a moderately high heat. Once the pan is hot, add the bacon or pancetta. Sizzle for 2 minutes, until crisp and coloured. Turn over with tongs and cook the other side until crisp. Drain on a plate lined with kitchen paper. Spread the spinach in the same pan and stir until wilted. Turn off the heat.

4 Stir the simmering cream into the soup. Taste and adjust the seasoning. Ladle the soup into bowls and add the spinach, stir lightly, then float a rasher of bacon or pancetta in the middle of each bowl. Serve immediately.

Jeff Cox was an editor on one of America's first organic gardening magazines, and now writes on cooking and gardening from his home in Sonoma, California.

broccoli soup

⊘ SERVES 4-6   **🕐 PREP TIME** 10 MINS **COOK** 40 MINS   **❄ FREEZE** UP TO 3 MONTHS
WITHOUT THE CREAM

1 tbsp lemon juice
675g (1½ lb) broccoli florets
45g (1½oz) butter
60g (2oz) celery, finely chopped
125g (4½oz) white part of leeks, chopped

4 tbsp plain flour
1.5 litres (2¾ pints) hot chicken stock
salt and pepper
125ml (4fl oz) double cream
2 tbsp snipped chives, to serve

1 Bring a large pot of salted water to the boil and add ½ tbsp of the lemon juice. Add half the florets and cook for 3 minutes, or until just tender. Remove to a colander and run cold water over them to stop the cooking. Let them drain and set aside.

2 In a large saucepan, melt the butter over a medium-low heat. Add the celery and leeks and cook, stirring, for 5–7 minutes or until the vegetables are tender. Add the flour and stir it in thoroughly, then whisk in the stock until the flour is entirely absorbed. Turn the heat to high and bring to a vigorous boil, then reduce the heat to low and simmer for 5 minutes.

3 Chop the uncooked broccoli into small pieces and add to the soup. Simmer for 15 minutes, or until very tender. Process in a blender until almost smooth – you want to retain a slightly grainy texture. Return the puree to the saucepan, season to taste with salt and pepper and the rest of the lemon juice, then add the cream and the reserved broccoli. Reheat and serve, sprinkled with chives.

This is a two-in-one soup, a mild and gentle aubergine cream yanked into high gear with a swirl of the sweeter, hotter red pepper. **Sophie Grigson**

aubergine and red pepper soup

SERVES 6   **PREP** 25 MINS **COOK** 40 MINS   ❄ **FREEZE** UP TO 3 MONTHS SEPARATELY

for the aubergine soup
2 tbsp extra virgin olive oil
1 onion, chopped
1 carrot, roughly sliced
2 tbsp chopped parsley
1 tbsp crushed coriander seeds
2 large aubergines, diced
1 tbsp risotto or pudding rice
750ml (1¼ pints) chicken or vegetable stock
salt and pepper

for the pepper soup
2 tbsp extra virgin olive oil
2 cloves garlic, chopped
1–2 fresh red chillies, deseeded and chopped
2 red peppers, deseeded and cut into strips
250g (9oz) tomatoes
1 tbsp tomato purée
1 tbsp caster sugar
salt and pepper
600ml (1 pint) chicken or vegetable stock
handful of fresh basil leaves

1 To make the aubergine soup, put the first seven ingredients in a saucepan, cover and sweat over a low heat for 15 minutes. Add the stock and season. Bring to the boil and simmer for 15 minutes until the carrots and rice are tender. Cool slightly and whiz to a purée in a blender.

2 To make the red pepper soup, place the olive oil, garlic, chilli and red pepper in a pan, and sauté until the peppers are very tender. Blanch and skin the tomatoes (see p22), then quarter, deseed and roughly chop, before adding to the pan along with the tomato purée, sugar, salt and pepper. Cook for a further 5–10 minutes until very thick. Stir in the stock and bring to the boil, then cool slightly and whiz to a purée in a blender.

3 Reheat both soups in separate pans, then taste and adjust seasonings. Divide the aubergine soup between 6 soup bowls and add a ladle of the pepper soup, swirling it in lightly. Sprinkle with basil and serve at once.

Easy to make from kitchen cupboard ingredients, using canned tomatoes, this delicious soup can be enjoyed all year round to brighten the dullest day.

classic tomato soup

⊘ SERVES 4   **🕐 PREP** 20 MINS **COOK** 55 MINS   **❄ FREEZE** UP TO 3 MONTHS

1 tbsp olive oil
1 onion, chopped
1 garlic clove, sliced
2 celery sticks, sliced
1 carrot, sliced
1 potato, chopped

2 x 400g cans tomatoes
750ml (1¼ pints) vegetable or chicken stock
1 bay leaf
1 tsp sugar
salt and pepper

1 Heat the oil in a large saucepan over a medium-low heat, add the onion, garlic and celery and fry, stirring frequently, until softened but not coloured.

2 Add the carrot and potato and stir for 1 minute, then add the tomatoes with their juices, the stock, bay leaf, and sugar. Season to taste, bring to the boil, then reduce the heat, cover, and simmer for 45 minutes, or until the vegetables are very soft.

3 Remove from the heat and allow to cool slightly, then process in a blender or food processor until smooth, working in batches if necessary. Taste and adjust the seasoning, then reheat and serve.

This extra-special version of the old standard – using fresh, sun-dried, and roasted tomatoes, takes the humble tomato to new heights. **Sofia Larrinua-Craxton**

cream of tomato soup

SERVES 4–6   **PREP** 30 MINS **COOK** 40 MINS   **FREEZE** UP TO 3 MONTHS
BEFORE CREAM IS ADDED

50g (1¾oz) butter
1 tbsp olive oil
2 onions, finely chopped
2 celery sticks, finely chopped
2 carrots, finely diced
2 garlic cloves, minced
12 plum tomatoes, about 1kg (2¼lb), quartered, roasted, and roughly chopped

8 plum tomatoes, about 600–720g (1¼–1½lb), skinned and finely chopped
6 sun-dried tomatoes, finely chopped
1 litre (1¾ pints) hot vegetable stock
2–3 tbsp double cream
salt and freshly ground black pepper

1 Heat the butter and olive oil in a heavy saucepan over a medium heat. Add the onions, and sauté for 8–10 minutes, stirring frequently, until very soft but not coloured. Next, add the celery and carrots, and continue cooking gently without burning for another 10 minutes, stirring from time to time. Add the garlic and sauté for another 2 minutes, stirring.

2 Mix together the roasted plum tomatoes, fresh tomatoes, and sun-dried tomatoes. Tip into the pan with any juices, and cook, stirring, for 5 minutes to allow the flavours to combine; if the sauce looks too thick or starts catching on the bottom of the pan, add a little of the hot vegetable stock. Pour in the remaining vegetable stock, and simmer the soup for 15–20 minutes.

3 Blend the soup to a smooth purée using a food processor or hand-held blender. Pass through a sieve or mouli into a clean pan, unless you prefer to make a peasant-style soup. Add the double cream a teaspoon at a time until you are happy with the taste and texture. Season with salt and pepper, reheat very gently if needed, and serve.

In Russia and the Ukraine, borscht often includes tomatoes as well as beetroot. This version may seem unusual, but you will love its rich colour and fantastic taste. **Sofia Larinua-Craxton**

tomato borscht

⊘ SERVES 4   **🕐 PREP** 25 MINS **COOK** 25 MINS   **❄ FREEZE** UP TO 3 MONTHS

2 tbsp olive oil
1 small onion, finely chopped
1 garlic clove, chopped
225g (8oz) raw beetroot, peeled
 and finely grated
1 tsp freshly ground toasted cumin seeds
¼ tsp ground cinnamon
225g (8oz) ripe fresh tomatoes, skinned
 and roughly chopped

250ml (8fl oz) tomato juice
1 tbsp sun-dried tomatoes,
 very finely chopped
600ml (1 pint) vegetable stock
1 tbsp light soy sauce
salt and freshly ground black pepper
toasted cumin seeds, to serve
soured cream or crème fraîche, to serve

1 Heat the oil in a heavy pan over a low heat. Gently cook the onion and garlic for about 5 minutes, then add the beetroot. Sweat gently for a further 10 minutes, stirring from time to time, until softened but not browned.

2 Add the ground spices, tomatoes, tomato juice, and sun-dried tomatoes, then pour in the stock. Bring to the boil. Reduce the heat slightly, cover, and simmer very gently for 15 minutes or until all the vegetables are soft. Remove from the heat. Blend or process until velvety smooth. Check the seasoning, adding the soy sauce, salt, and pepper to taste.

3 Serve chilled, at room temperature, or slightly warm. If you do reheat the soup, do so gently over a low heat. To serve, spoon into serving bowls, and garnish with toasted cumin seeds and a spoonful of soured cream or crème fraîche.

For home-made food in a jiffy, roast the vegetables up to three days in advance and keep them in the fridge. This soup then takes just minutes to prepare. **Sofia Larrinua-Craxton**

roast tomato soup

SERVES 4   **PREP** 10 MINS **COOK** 30 MINS   **FREEZE** UP TO 3 MONTHS

8 plum tomatoes, about 675g (1½lb) in total, quartered
1 red onion, cut into 8 wedges
2 garlic cloves, unpeeled

3 tbsp olive oil
sea salt and freshly ground black pepper
1 litre (1¾ pints) hot vegetable stock
3 tbsp sun-dried tomato paste

1 Preheat the oven to 180°C (350°F/Gas 4). Put the tomatoes, onion, and garlic on baking trays covered with greaseproof paper. Drizzle with the oil, and season well with salt and freshly ground black pepper. Roast until they are soft, caramelized, and slightly browned – allow 10–15 minutes for the garlic, 15–20 minutes for the onion, and 25 minutes for the tomatoes. Squeeze the garlic from their skins once they have cooled slightly.

2 Transfer to a blender, add the stock and tomato paste, then whiz until smooth but still slightly chunky. Season with salt and freshly ground black pepper, reheat gently, and serve hot.

TOMATOES
Pick out firm tomatoes that smell of the vine. Go organic for the best flavour, but also because organic tomatoes contain more health-promoting antioxidants than those cultivated by conventional means.

Geetie Singh, who is behind Britain's first organic pub, The Duke of Cambridge, writes, "A wonderfully refreshing summer lunch, this soup is fantastically quick to make."

gazpacho

🍥 **SERVES** 6–8 🕐 **PREP** 30 MINS ❄ **FREEZE** UP TO 3 MONTHS

1 red pepper, deseeded and chopped
10 spring onions, trimmed and chopped, or 1 red onion, finely chopped
5 garlic cloves, chopped
1 cucumber, finely chopped
1kg (2¼lb) ripe tomatoes, finely chopped
1 tbsp fresh thyme, marjoram, parsley, mint, or basil, chopped

100g (3½oz) stale bread
1 fresh chilli, deseeded and finely chopped, or ½ tsp cayenne pepper (optional)
2 tbsp red wine vinegar
3 tbsp olive oil, plus extra to serve
100ml (16fl oz) chilled water
salt and freshly ground black pepper

1 Place a serving bowl in the fridge. Put the pepper, spring onions or onion, garlic, cucumber, and tomatoes in a mixing bowl, then add the herbs.

2 Whiz the bread in a blender to make breadcrumbs, then add to the mixing bowl along with the chilli, if using, the vinegar and oil. Gradually add the water – 100ml will give a nice thick consistency, but you can use more if you prefer.

3 Transfer to the blender and whiz briefly – I like there to be still the odd chunk of cucumber, but you can blend the soup until smooth, if you prefer. Season generously with salt and freshly ground black pepper. Transfer to the serving bowl, add a few ice cubes, and drizzle with olive oil.

Fresh lime juice, coriander, and dried poblano chillies – not to mention the corn tortillas – give a Mexican flavour to this spicy tomato soup.

sopa de tortilla

◉ **SERVES** 4   🕐 **PREP** 15 MINS **COOK** 50 MINS   ❄ **FREEZE** UP TO 3 MONTHS
AT THE END OF STEP 3

5 tbsp sunflower oil
½ onion, finely chopped
2 large garlic cloves, finely chopped
450g (1lb) tomatoes, skinned
1.5 litres (2¾ pints) chicken stock
  or vegetable stock
1 or 2 dried poblano chillies, deseeded

2 soft corn tortillas, cut into strips
3 tbsp chopped fresh coriander
2 tbsp fresh lime juice
salt and freshly ground black pepper
85g (3oz) Gruyère cheese, grated
2 limes, cut into wedges, to serve

1 Heat 1 tbsp of the oil in a large saucepan over a medium heat. Add the onion and fry, stirring, for 5 minutes, or until softened. Add the garlic and stir for 30 seconds. Using a blender, whiz with the tomatoes until smooth.

2 Tip the tomato-onion purée into the pan and simmer for 8–10 minutes, stirring constantly. Stir in the stock and bring to the boil. Reduce the heat, partially cover the pan, and simmer for 15 minutes, or until thickened.

3 Place a non-stick frying pan over a medium heat. Add the chillies and press them against the pan with a spatula until they blister. Turn them over and repeat. Remove from the pan, cut into small pieces, and set aside.

4 Heat the remaining oil in the frying pan until sizzling hot. Add the tortilla strips in batches and fry until just crisp. Remove with a slotted spoon and drain on kitchen paper.

5 When ready to serve, add the chillies to the soup, bring to the boil and simmer for 3 minutes, or until the chillies are soft. Stir in the coriander and lime juice, and season with salt and pepper to taste. Divide the toasted tortilla strips between 4 soup bowls. Ladle in the soup and top with a sprinkling of cheese. Serve with wedges of lime.

Dan Barber, the top US chef with a Blue Hill restaurant in Manhattan and another on a farm outside New York, teaches all his staff the principles of good farming.

smoked tomato soup

⏺ **SERVES** 4   ⏱ **PREP** 15 MINS **COOK** 30 MINS   ❄ **FREEZE** UP TO 3 MONTHS

10 large plum tomatoes, about 1.1kg (2½lb)
   total in weight, 2 halved and deseeded,
   8 coarsely chopped
60ml (2fl oz) extra virgin olive oil
1 large onion, finely chopped
1 large leek, cut in half lengthways and
   then thinly sliced crossways
1½ tsp coriander seeds
2 garlic cloves, crushed

2 bay leaves
1 tsp finely grated fresh horseradish or
   drained bottled horseradish
250ml (8fl oz) hot chicken stock
pinch of sugar
60g (2oz) unsalted butter, softened
salt and freshly ground black pepper
basil leaves, to garnish

1 Scatter a handful of apple, pecan, or hickory wood barbecue chips in a medium-sized, cast-iron frying pan or wok, cover tightly with a lid, and place over a medium heat. When the chips start to smoke, put the 4 tomato halves on a rack, and set the rack in the pan. Replace the lid and smoke the tomatoes for 2–3 minutes or until barely softened. Transfer to a plate and allow to cool slightly, then skin.

2 Heat the oil in a large pan, add the onion and leek, and cook over a medium heat, stirring frequently, for 10 minutes or until softened but not browned. Add the coriander, garlic, bay leaves, and horseradish and cook for 2 minutes or until fragrant. Add the chopped tomatoes, stock, and sugar, cover with a lid, and cook over a medium heat for 10 minutes or until the tomatoes are soft. Pick out and discard the bay leaves.

3 Transfer to a blender, add the butter and smoked tomatoes, and whiz until smooth. You may need to do this in batches. Strain through a sieve into a clean pan and season with salt and freshly ground black pepper. Serve garnished with basil leaves.

This fragrant soup is seasoned with a blend of spices often used to give Indian pickles and preserves their distinctive tang. It is best enjoyed with hot naan bread. **Roopa Gulati**

curried broth with peppers

◉ SERVES 4 **🕐 PREP** 15 MINS **COOK** 25 MINS **❄ FREEZE** UP TO 3 MONTHS

2 tbsp vegetable oil
1 star anise
½ tsp chilli flakes
½ tsp nigella seeds
1½ tsp fennel seeds
¼ tsp fenugreek seeds
2 onions, diced
4cm (1½in) piece of root ginger, peeled and grated
1 orange pepper, diced

1 yellow pepper, diced
2 tbsp basmati rice
¾ tsp turmeric
½ tsp garam masala
1 litre (1¾ pints) hot vegetable stock
1 tbsp date palm sugar
grated zest and juice of 1 large lemon
salt and freshly ground black pepper
2 tbsp coriander leaves, roughly chopped

1 Heat the oil in a large saucepan over a medium heat, add the star anise, chilli, nigella, fennel, and fenugreek, and stir-fry for 30 seconds. Lower the heat, add the onions and ginger, then cover and cook for 5 minutes or until the onions have softened. Stir in the peppers and fry for 2–3 minutes.

2 Add the rice, turmeric, and garam masala, stir well, and cook for 1 minute. Pour in the stock, then add the sugar and lemon zest. Season with salt and freshly ground black pepper and simmer for 15 minutes or until the soup has thickened slightly and the peppers and rice are tender. Sharpen with the lemon juice and serve garnished with coriander.

CHOOSING PEPPERS
Look for bright, shiny peppers that feel firm, and avoid any that have soft spots or are pale or shrivelled. Yellow peppers and orange peppers are ripe versions of green peppers. As a consequence, they are sweeter.

Make this soup near the end of the summer when tomatoes and peppers are plentiful. It freezes well and is also a cheering stalwart for winter meals. **Roopa Gulati**

roasted red pepper, fennel and tomato soup

SERVES 4–6   **PREP** 25 MINS **COOK** 2 HRS   **FREEZE** UP TO 3 MONTHS

1 large fennel bulb, peeled
1 red onion
2 red peppers, halved and deseeded
500g (1lb) tomatoes
4 garlic cloves, in their skins
1.5 tsp sugar
2 tbsp olive oil
1 large sprig of fresh rosemary, leaves only

1–2 tbsp vegetable oil
1.5 tsp fennel seeds
½ tsp nigella seeds
400ml (14fl oz) passata
1 litre (2 pints) vegetable stock
1 red chilli, split and deseeded
salt and freshly ground black pepper
handful of fennel leaves

1 Preheat the oven to 200°C (400°F/Gas 6). Cut the fennel and onion into wedges. Slice a cross into the base of each tomato and squeeze the juice and seeds into a bowl. Strain the juice and set aside.

2 Line a roasting tin with baking parchment and add the fennel, onion, peppers, tomatoes, and garlic cloves. Sprinkle over the sugar, drizzle with the olive oil, and scatter the rosemary on top. Roast the vegetables for about 1 hour, until the tomatoes are soft. Cool the vegetables before peeling the blackened skin from the peppers. Peel the garlic and discard the skins.

3 Heat the vegetable oil in a large pan and toss in the fennel and nigella seeds, swirling them around for a few seconds. Pour over the passata, the stock and the reserved tomato juice, and bring to the boil. Add the roasted vegetables, pop the chilli into the pan and season with salt and pepper to taste. Half cover with a lid and simmer for about 45 minutes.

4 Using a blender, whiz the soup until smooth and press through a sieve. Reheat, re-season, and finish with a sprinkling of fennel leaves.

Rich, slightly nutty avocado works well with peppery wild rocket. Hass avocados are particularly good, but always buy extra in case one turns out to be blemished. **Marie-Pierre Moine**

avocado and rocket soup

⊘ SERVES 4   **◷ PREP** 15 MINS PLUS 1 HR CHILLING   **❄ FREEZE** NOT SUITABLE
COOK NONE

CHILLED

3 large (or 4 medium) ripe avocados
juice of 1 lemon
150g (5½oz) wild rocket
750ml (1¼ pints) cold light chicken
   or vegetable stock

¼ tsp harissa
salt and pepper

1 Skin the avocados and remove their stones, then chop the flesh and put it in a blender or food processor with the lemon juice. Coarsely chop the rocket (save a few sprigs to decorate) and add to the avocados. Pour over the stock. Add the harissa and season, then blend until smooth. Transfer to a bowl, cover and refrigerate for 1 hour.

2 Before serving, taste and adjust the seasoning. Pour into bowls or glasses, add an ice cube or two to each and decorate with sprigs of rocket. Serve chilled.

This lovely, cool summer soup is just perfect when it's too hot to cook. Track sorrel down at your local farmer's market; its lemon-spinach flavour is unique. **Sophie Grigson**

avocado, cucumber, and sorrel soup

⊘ **SERVES** 4–6   ⏱ **PREP** 5–10 MINS   ❄ **FREEZE** NOT SUITABLE

1 ripe, buttery avocado, stoned and peeled
a generous handful of sorrel leaves (discard any tough stalks)
¼ large cucumber, roughly diced but not skinned

75g (2½oz) Greek yogurt
1–2 cloves of garlic, peeled and chopped
salt and pepper
avocado oil, to serve

1 Put the avocado in a blender with the sorrel, cucumber, yogurt, and garlic, add a good slurp of water, and then flick the switch. As soon as it is smoothly blended, taste and adjust the seasoning, adding more sorrel, or salt or pepper, or thinning down with a little more water.

2 Once you are happy, divide between 6 serving bowls or cups and drizzle a thin thread of avocado oil on the surface. Serve at once, or at least within the next hour while it is fresh and vivid.

STONING AND PEELING AN AVOCADO

Slice the avocado in two, cutting all the way round, then separate the two halves by twisting gently.

Strike the stone with the blade of a large knife, then lift the knife to remove the stone.

Cut the avocado in half again and carefully remove the skin with a paring knife.

This refreshing soup can be prepared ahead and makes an elegant starter for a summer meal. For a lunch or dinner party, try serving it with smoked salmon. **Marie-Pierre Moine**

cucumber and dill soup

⊘ SERVES 4   **⏱ PREP** 30 MINS PLUS 3 HRS CHILLING   **✳ FREEZE** NOT SUITABLE

2 medium cucumbers
salt and pepper
1 litre (1¾ pints) whole or semi-skimmed milk

small bunch of fresh dill
150ml (5fl oz) bio natural yogurt

1 Peel the cucumbers, leaving one or two strips of skin on for colour. Slice, put into a colander and sprinkle with a teaspoon of salt. Toss and stand it over a bowl for one hour. Meanwhile, put the milk in another bowl, add a few whole dill fronds, stir and refrigerate for an hour to allow the flavours to infuse slightly.

2 Rinse the cucumber under the cold water tap, pressing down to extract as much moisture as possible. Remove the dill fronds from the milk. Put the milk and cucumber in a blender or food processor. Add a few more fronds of dill and some pepper and blend well. Pour into a bowl and refrigerate for 3 hours.

3 Place a sieve over a second bowl, pour in the chilled soup and push through with the back of a wooden spoon, adding 100–150ml (3½–5fl oz) of chilled water, and return to the refrigerator until ready to serve.

4 Stir in the yogurt, taste, and adjust the seasoning if necessary. Whisk until frothy with a handheld or balloon whisk then pour into cups, bowls or glasses. Decorate with a little more dill and serve immediately.

This is delicious in the autumn, when it will use up any particularly mature cucumbers, though you may need to remove any hard seeds and bitter skin. **Celia Brooks Brown**

cucumber and walnut soup

○ SERVES 4–6   **● PREP** 10–15 MINS PLUS 30 MINS CHILLING   **❄ FREEZE** NOT SUITABLE

2 medium cucumbers, about 700g (1lb 9oz) in total
500g (1lb 2oz) Greek or thick and creamy yogurt
1 clove garlic
coarse sea salt

50g (1¾oz) walnuts, plus more chopped walnuts for garnish
handful of fresh mint leaves, finely chopped
2 tbsp fresh lemon juice
freshly ground black pepper
extra virgin olive oil, to serve

1 Peel, seed and finely dice the cucumbers. Be punctilious about this to ensure your soup is delicately flavoured without any bitterness.

2 In a medium bowl, or large measuring jug, mix together the yogurt and 250ml (8fl oz) cold water until combined. Pound the garlic with a large pinch of coarse sea salt in a mortar until smooth. Scrape it into the yogurt. Pound the walnuts in the garlicky mortar to a coarse paste; do not crush them too fine. Add to the yogurt mixture with the cucumber, mint, lemon juice and a good grinding of pepper and stir well. Taste for seasoning.

3 Cover and chill for 30 minutes or more. Pour into bowls and garnish with a drizzle of olive oil and a few chopped walnuts.

CUCUMBERS
Go for locally grown cucumbers that feel firm and avoid any with soggy, limp ends. Ensure that you store them in the refrigerator for no longer than a week, as they contain mostly water and will quickly lose their vibrancy.

Cooked cucumber has a subtle flavour which combines particularly well with the more assertive but still delicate tarragon. **Marie-Pierre Moine**

hot cucumber and tarragon soup

⊘ SERVES 4   **◷ PREP** 15 MINS **COOK** 20 MINS   **❄ FREEZE** NOT SUITABLE

2 medium-large or 3 small cucumbers
1 tbsp sunflower or rapeseed oil
50g (1¾oz) chilled butter, diced
2 tbsp chopped fresh tarragon
800ml (1¾ pints) light vegetable
  or chicken stock

salt and pepper
2 tbsp cornflour
4 heaped tsp cream cheese (optional)

1 Peel the cucumbers, cut crossways in half, then cut each half lengthways. With a pointed teaspoon, scoop out and discard all the seeds and chop the flesh coarsely.

2 Place a sauté pan over a moderate heat. Add the oil and 15g (½oz) of the butter. Once the butter has melted, add the cucumber and half the tarragon. Stir for 2 minutes, then pour in the stock and season lightly.

3 Bring to a simmer, reduce the heat a little, then cover and simmer gently for 10–15 minutes. Stir in the cornflour. Cook for 2 minutes. Take off the heat and leave to cool a little.

4 Transfer to a blender or food processor and blend until smooth. Return to the pan and whisk in the remaining butter. Taste and adjust the seasoning, stir in the rest of the tarragon and serve hot. If you like, add a dollop of cream cheese (if using) to each serving at the last minute.

For absolute decadence, omit the poached eggs and top each bowl with a little chopped hard-boiled egg and a shucked oyster in its half shell. **Carolyn Humphries**

samphire soup with poached eggs

⊙ **SERVES** 4   🕐 **PREP** 10 MINS **COOK** 30 MINS   ❅ **FREEZE** UP TO 3 MONTHS

200g (7oz) fresh or frozen samphire
good knob of unsalted butter
1 large leek, washed thoroughly and sliced
1 large potato, diced
1 thick slice of lemon
small handful of fresh parsley

900ml (1½ pints) light vegetable
 or chicken stock
pepper
a little milk
1 tbsp white wine vinegar
4 eggs

1 Wash the samphire, then boil in a little water for 3–5 minutes or until tender. Drain, rinse with cold water, and drain again. Put on a board and scrape the green flesh off any thick stalks with a stringy central core (you won't need to with young, fresh samphire).

2 Melt the butter in a large saucepan. Add the leek and potato and fry gently, stirring, for 2 minutes or until soft but not browned. Add the lemon, parsley, stock, and pepper – it's unlikely to need salt as samphire is very salty. Bring to the boil, reduce the heat, cover, and simmer gently for 20 minutes, or until the vegetables are really soft. Discard the lemon and whiz in a blender with the samphire flesh. Return to the pan, taste and add more pepper if necessary. If freezing, cool and freeze at this point, then defrost and continue. Thin with a little milk, if desired, then reheat gently.

3 Meanwhile, bring a large pan of water to the boil and add the vinegar. Swirl round to make an eddy and break in the eggs one at a time. Poach until cooked to your liking, then remove with a slotted spoon. Ladle into wide, shallow soup plates then rest a poached egg in the centre of each.

This spin on a popular Indian curry makes an innovative first course. The crackling curry leaves, toasted spices, and tangy tamarind work well with the yogurt base. **Roopa Gulati**

whipped yogurt soup with sautéed courgette

⊘ **SERVES** 4   ⏱ **PREP** 30 MINS, PLUS 20 MINS STANDING   ❄ **FREEZE** NOT SUITABLE
COOK 25 MINS

3 tbsp vegetable oil
2 dried red chillies
1 tsp mustard seeds
¼ tsp fenugreek seeds
1 tsp cumin seeds
12 curry leaves
3 tbsp gram flour
½ tsp turmeric
400ml (14fl oz) Greek yogurt
400ml (14fl oz) cold water

2 tbsp tamarind pulp
2 tbsp chopped coriander leaves, to garnish

for the sautéed courgette topping
2 tbsp vegetable oil
1 small red onion, diced
1 courgette, finely diced
1 green chilli, deseeded and finely chopped
salt flakes, to season

1 Heat the oil in a wok over a medium heat. Toss in the chillies and mustard seeds and swirl around for a few seconds before adding the fenugreek, cumin, and curry leaves. Lower the heat and stir-fry for a few seconds. Sprinkle in half the flour and stir-fry for 2–3 minutes or until lightly toasted. Remove from the heat, add the turmeric, and leave to cool slightly.

2 Whisk the remaining flour with the yogurt and water and add to the wok. Return to the heat and, whisking all the time, bring to a simmer and cook for 3–4 minutes. Add more water, if needed, to loosen the consistency. I like to leave the whole spices in, but you can sieve the soup at this stage. Season with salt and enough tamarind to sharpen.

3 For the sautéed courgette topping, heat the oil in a frying pan and soften the onion for 3–4 minutes over a low heat. Turn the heat up, add the courgette and green chilli and continue cooking for a further minute. Season with salt and add to the hot soup. Finish with the chopped coriander.

A very simple soup, easy to make and with very few ingredients, this is lifted out of the ordinary by the gentle aniseed tang of dill.

courgette and potato soup

SERVES 4   **PREP** 10 MINS **COOK** 15 MINS   **FREEZE** UP TO 3 MONTHS

2 large potatoes, peeled and diced
500ml (16fl oz) hot chicken stock
1 tsp salt
1 tbsp olive oil
3 medium courgettes, peeled, finely diced
   or grated

1 onion, peeled, finely diced or grated
white pepper
100ml (3½fl oz) double cream
300ml (10fl oz) milk
small bunch of fresh dill, chopped

1 Place the potatoes into a large pan with the hot stock and salt, bring to the boil and simmer for about 5 minutes, or until tender. Blend with a stick blender until smooth and return to the saucepan.

2 In another saucepan, heat the olive oil, add the courgettes and onion and fry over a gentle heat for 2–3 minutes or until slightly softened but not coloured. Stir in a dash of the pepper, the cream, milk and puréed potato broth and simmer gently for 5 minutes, or until the courgettes have softened. Add dill and season to taste. Serve hot.

COURGETTES
A welcome addition to vegetable boxes, courgettes should be firm, unblemished, feel heavy, and have glossy skin. Avoid those that are shrivelling. Smaller courgettes have the best flavour.

Darina Allen of the world-class Ballymaloe Cookery School in Ireland says "Add the greens at the last minute, otherwise they will overcook and the soup will lose its fresh taste."

spinach and rosemary soup

🌑 **SERVES** 6   🕐 **PREP** 15 MINS **COOK** 25 MINS   ❄ **FREEZE** UP TO 3 MONTHS

50g (2oz) butter
110g (4oz) finely chopped onion
150g (5½oz) diced potato
salt and freshly ground black pepper
450ml (15fl oz) hot vegetable stock, chicken stock, or water
450ml (15fl oz) creamy milk (¼ cream and ¾ milk)

350g (12oz) spinach, destalked and chopped
1 tbsp chopped fresh rosemary
2 tbsp single cream, to garnish
sprig of rosemary or rosemary flowers, to garnish

1 Melt the butter in a heavy-bottomed pan. When it is starting to foam, add the diced onion and potato, and stir to coat well. Season well with salt and freshly ground black pepper, then cover the pan with a lid and sweat the vegetables on a gentle heat for 10 minutes.

2 Add the stock and milk, bring to the boil, then simmer for 5 minutes or until the potato and onion are completely cooked. Add the spinach and boil the soup with the lid off for 2–3 minutes or until tender. Do not overcook. Add the chopped rosemary, then whiz the soup in a blender until smooth. You may need to do this in batches. Return to the pan and reheat gently.

3 Serve in warm bowls garnished with a swirl of cream and a sprig of rosemary. If you have a rosemary bush in bloom, sprinkle a few flowers over the top for extra pzazz. This is good with crusty bread or cheese scones.

Skye Gyngell is head chef at Petersham Nurseries Café in Richmond, Surrey, where she champions seasonal and local produce. "This soup is easy to make and sings of the garden."

spinach and parmesan soup with crème fraîche

◉ SERVES 4   **● PREP** 10 MINS **COOK** 15–20 MINS   **❄ FREEZE** UP TO 3 MONTHS
BEFORE PARMESAN IS ADDED

300g (10oz) young spinach leaves
25g (scant 1oz) unsalted butter
2 banana shallots, finely sliced
1 garlic clove, finely chopped
sea salt and freshly ground black pepper

1 litre (1¾ pints) chicken stock
100ml (3½fl oz) crème fraîche
100g (3½oz) Parmesan cheese, grated
grated lemon zest, to garnish

1 Wash the spinach thoroughly, drain and shake until almost dry. Place a large pan over a medium heat. Add the spinach, cover and cook until it just wilts. Drain in a colander and set aside.

2 Rinse and dry the saucepan. Add the butter to the pan and melt over a low heat, then add the shallots and sweat for five minutes, or until softened and translucent. Add the garlic and cook for 1–2 minutes, then season with a little salt and some pepper.

3 Add the cooked spinach and stir once or twice. Pour in the stock and turn up the heat. Bring to a simmer then immediately remove from the heat. Purée the soup in a blender until smooth. Return it to the saucepan and stir in the crème fraîche. Add the grated Parmesan cheese and check the seasoning. Then either reheat gently and serve warm, or allow to cool and enjoy at room temperature. Add a sprinkling of grated lemon zest before serving.

Here, the astringent bite of green chillies and root ginger is tempered by the subtlety of herbs and delicate spinach leaves. Add a dollop of cream just before serving. **Roopa Gulati**

spicy spinach soup

SERVES 4   **PREP** 12 MINS PLUS 90 MINS MARINATING   **FREEZE** UP TO 2 MONTHS
COOK 40 MINS   BEFORE CUMIN SEEDS ARE ADDED

for the chicken
2 garlic cloves, finely chopped
3cm (1¼in) piece of root ginger, finely chopped
¾ tsp garam masala
juice of 2 limes
3 tbsp Greek-style yoghurt
salt to season
2 boneless chicken thighs, without skin
drizzle of vegetable oil

for the soup
3 tbsp vegetable oil
1 onion, finely chopped

2 green chillies, deseeded and finely chopped
1 garlic clove, finely chopped
2 tbsp ground almonds
1 litre (1¾ pints) hot chicken stock
3cm (1¼in) piece of root ginger, peeled
500g (1lb 2oz) baby spinach leaves
large handful coriander leaves,
handful mint leaves
1 tsp sugar
salt and freshly ground black pepper
1 tsp roasted and ground cumin seeds, to garnish

1 Mix the garlic, ginger and garam masala with the lime juice, yoghurt and salt. Add the chicken and coat. After 1–2 hours heat some vegetable oil in a griddle pan. Drain any excess yoghurt off the chicken, drizzle with vegetable oil and cook for 5–7 minutes on each side. Cool, then cut into small pieces. Pour any cooking juices over the chicken and set aside.

2 Heat the oil in a large saucepan over a low heat. Add the onions, chilli and garlic and cover. Cook for about 10 minutes, stirring occasionally. Add the ground almonds and cook for a further minute, stirring. Add the chicken stock and root ginger. Season well and simmer for 10 minutes.

3 Bring to a boil and add the spinach. When it wilts, add the herbs and sugar. Turn the heat off and remove the root ginger. Blend until smooth. Pour the soup into a clean pan. Add the chicken and reheat gently. Check the seasoning and serve sprinkled with roasted ground cumin seeds.

in praise of...
lettuce
If you grow your own
vegetables, it is easy
to end up with an
abundance of lettuces,
and soup is a great
way to use them for
something delicious
and different.
Celia Brooks Brown

Don't used lettuces that have bolted for this – they will have bitter cores. Some of the leaves may still be good to use, though. Have a taste first. **Celia Brookes Brown**

lettuce soup with peas

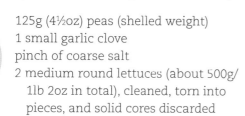

◉ SERVES 4   **🕑 PREP** 30 MINS, PLUS 30 MINS CHILLING   **❄ FREEZE** NOT SUITABLE

125g (4½oz) peas (shelled weight)
1 small garlic clove
pinch of coarse salt
2 medium round lettuces (about 500g/
    1lb 2oz in total), cleaned, torn into
    pieces, and solid cores discarded

250ml (8fl oz) plain yogurt
2cm (¾in) piece fresh ginger, peeled
    and finely grated
handful of mint leaves
juice of ½ lemon
salt and freshly ground black pepper

1 Bring a small amount of water to the boil in a pan, add the peas, and cook for 1 minute. Drain (reserving the cooking water), cool under cold running water, and refrigerate. Cut the garlic in half, remove any green at the centre, and discard. Crush the halves with a pinch of coarse salt.

2 Combine the garlic with all the other ingredients (except the peas) in a food processor or blender, adding just enough of the reserved cooking water to get the blades moving or until the desired consistency is achieved – this will vary according to the type of lettuce and the kind of machine you are using, but it is nice if you can get it fairly smooth, with a bit of texture.

3 Transfer the soup to a large bowl and chill for 30 minutes. When ready to serve, stir through the cooked peas, leaving a few to garnish.

LETTUCE
Search your farmers' market for lettuces with fresh-looking leaves and a silky, slightly firm heart. Avoid any that are wilted or bruised. To clean, pat the leaves with damp kitchen paper, then tear them – rather than cut – to size.

Serve this velvety smooth soup hot, topped with shavings of Parmesan cheese, or chilled with an extra swirl of cream or crème fraîche.

watercress soup

⊘ SERVES 4　　　**⊙ PREP** 10 MINS **COOK** 15 MINS　　　**❄ FREEZE** 3 MONTHS

HOT OR COLD

25g (scant 1oz) butter
1 onion, finely chopped
175g (6oz) watercress
3 ripe pears, cored and roughly chopped
1 litre (1¾ pints) vegetable stock

salt and freshly ground black pepper
200ml (7fl oz) double cream
juice of ½ lemon
Parmesan cheese, shaved, to serve
olive oil, to drizzle

1 Melt the butter in a saucepan and cook the onion for 10 minutes, or until soft, stirring occasionally to prevent burning. Meanwhile, trim the watercress and pick off the leaves. Add the watercress stalks to the onion with the pears and stock, and season with salt and pepper.

2 Bring to the boil, cover, and simmer gently for 15 minutes. Remove from the heat and pour into a blender along with the watercress leaves. Process until the soup has a very smooth texture.

3 Stir in the cream and lemon juice, adjust the seasoning, and serve sprinkled with Parmesan shavings and drizzled with a little oil. The soup can be made up to 4 hours in advance and refrigerated until ready to use. To serve chilled, pour the soup into chilled bowls, top with crushed ice, and drizzle with a little olive oil.

WATERCRESS
Locally produced watercress with fresh, round leaves and thick stalks are best. Unwashed leaves will keep in the fridge for several days, but ready-washed ones must be eaten quickly.

Peppery watercress, curry leaf oil and caramelized pear make a marvellous melange of flavours. The oil can be made a few days before and kept refrigerated. **Roopa Gulati**

spicy watercress soup

⊙ SERVES 4–6   **◔ PREP** 20 MINS **COOK** 30 MINS   **❄ FREEZE** UP TO 1 MONTH
AT THE END OF STEP 2

3 tbsp fresh curry leaves
150ml (5fl oz) olive oil
2 tbsp olive oil
1 onion, chopped
2 medium potatoes, chopped
1 litre (1¾ pints) hot vegetable stock
250g (9oz) watercress
2 tbsp crème fraîche
salt and freshly ground black pepper

for the garnish
1 conference pear, peeled and finely diced
2 tbsp icing sugar
pinch of coarsely ground black peppercorns
1 tbsp crème fraîche

1 First make the curry leaf oil. Drop the leaves into a pan of boiling water and cook for about 30 seconds. Remove and refresh with cold water. Pat dry with kitchen paper and transfer to a blender. Warm the oil and gradually pour into the blender as the leaves are being processed. Blend to a smooth paste. Line a sieve with kitchen paper and pour the curry leaf mixture into it – the oil will slowly drip through.

2 For the soup, heat the olive oil in a large pan and add the onion and potato. Cover and fry over a gentle heat, stirring frequently, until softened but not coloured. Pour in the stock and simmer for another 10 minutes, until the potatoes are cooked. Add the watercress and cook for a further minute. Season, and stir in 2–3 tsp of the curry leaf oil off the heat. Blend with a stick blender until smooth and sieve to remove any tough fibres.

3 For the garnish, toss the pear in icing sugar seasoned with pepper. Heat a frying pan over a moderate heat and fry the pear until caramelized.

4 Reheat and re-season the soup and whisk in 2 tbsp of crème fraîche. Ladle into bowls, and top with an extra dollop of crème fraîche. Scatter over the pears and finish with an extra drizzle of curry leaf oil.

This makes good use of peppery late-season rocket that may have become a bit leathery. If your rocket is in bloom, the flowers have a distinctive savoury flavour. **Celia Brooks Brown**

rocket and parmesan soup

⊘ **SERVES** 4   🕐 **PREP** 10 MINS **COOK** 30 MINS   ❄ **FREEZE** UP TO 3 MONTHS

2 tbsp olive oil
2 medium onions, chopped
650g (1lb 7oz) potatoes, washed but not
   peeled, cut in 2cm (¾in) cubes
sea salt
4 small or 2 large garlic cloves, crushed

1 litre (1¾ pints) vegetable stock
1 Parmesan rind, about 3 x 9cm (1¼ x 3½in),
   cut into tiny dice
125g (4½oz) rocket leaves, roughly chopped
fresh Parmesan, to serve
rocket flowers, to serve (optional)

1 Heat the oil in a soup pan over a medium heat. Add the onions and cook, stirring frequently, until soft and translucent. Add the potatoes with a little salt, stir, cover, and cook for 5 minutes, stirring frequently.

2 Add the garlic and stir for a few seconds until fragrant, then pour in the stock. Bring to the boil, add the Parmesan rind, then simmer for about 10 minutes, stirring occasionally, until the potato is soft.

3 Add the rocket, stir and cook for 3–5 minutes, until tender but still bright green. Cool briefly, then purée the soup with a hand blender until smooth. Taste for seasoning. Serve each bowl with grated or shaved fresh parmesan, and a few rocket flowers if you have them.

ROCKET
A versatile ingredient with a pronounced peppery flavour. Go for locally grown rocket, choosing fresh leaves and firm stalks. You can store unwashed rocket in the fridge for several days. Pre-washed leaves will only last a day.

A real tonic on a chilly spring day, this soup with its bright sorrel sharpness is always welcome. Later in the summer, when the temperature rises, serve it chilled. **Sophie Grigson**

sorrel soup

SERVES 6   **PREP** 15 MINS **COOK** 30–35 MINS   ❄ **FREEZE** UP TO 3 MONTHS
WITHOUT CREAM OR YOGURT

HOT OR COLD

3 big handfuls of large-leaved sorrel
2 tbsp extra virgin olive oil
1 onion, chopped
400g (14oz) potatoes, peeled and diced
1 bay leaf
2 sprigs of parsley

2 sprigs of thyme
1.5 litres (2¾ pints) light chicken
   or vegetable stock
salt and pepper
6 tbsp double cream (optional) or 3 tbsp
   Greek yogurt

1 Cut out and discard the larger tougher stems of the sorrel, then shred the leaves roughly. Warm the oil in a large saucepan and add the onion, potatoes, bay leaf, parsley, and thyme, tied together with string to form a bouquet garni. Stir to coat in oil, then cover and sweat over a low heat for 10 minutes or so.

2 Uncover and pour in the stock, then season with salt and pepper. Bring up to the boil and simmer for 15 minutes or so until the potato is very tender. Take off the heat, remove the bouquet garni, then stir in the sorrel. Liquidize in batches and return to the pan. Reheat when required, stir in the cream if using, then taste and adjust the seasoning. Serve straight away. Alternatively, when the weather is warm, chill the soup down for a few hours in the refrigerator, then serve with a teaspoonful of Greek yogurt floating in each bowlful.

SORREL
Look for sorrel at farmers' markets. If you're lucky, you might even be able to forage for it. Look for firm stalks and fresh, green, spear-shaped leaves. Mature leaves are best in soups and sauces, but take care not to overcook.

If you don't grow this old-fashioned herb yourself, ask around among your gardening friends or head down to the nearest garden centre to see if they sell it. **Sophie Grigson**

lovage soup

🍲 **SERVES** 4–6   🕐 **PREP** 10 MINS **COOK** 30 MINS   ❄ **FREEZE** UP TO 3 MONTHS
BEFORE CREAM IS ADDED

60g (2 oz) butter
1 onion, chopped
250–300g (9–10oz) floury potatoes,
   peeled and diced
1 large carrot, diced
a large handful of fresh lovage leaves

1–1.2 litres (1¾–2 pints) chicken, light game
   or vegetable stock
salt and pepper
6 tbsp double cream
cayenne pepper

1 Melt the butter in a large pan and add the onion, potato, carrot and lovage. Stir, then cover and sweat over a low heat for 10 minutes.

2 Add the stock and a little salt and pepper. Bring up to the boil and simmer for 15 minutes until all the vegetables are very tender. Cool slightly, liquidize and, if you would like a smoother soup, pass through a sieve. Taste and adjust the seasoning if necessary. Reheat when needed and stir in the cream. Serve with a dusting of cayenne pepper.

LOVAGE
When buying cut leaves, choose strong stems and yellow-green leaves, but remember that they don't keep for long. If you choose to grow your own, you will find that lovage can grow to a considerable height.

This is a favourite soup in Portugal, where fresh coriander is used enthusiastically. It is essentially a potato and onion soup, liquidized with lots of fresh coriander. **Sophie Grigson**

potato and coriander soup

⊘ **SERVES** 4–6   🕐 **PREP** 10–15 MINS **COOK** 30 MINS   ❄ **FREEZE** UP TO 3 MONTHS

1 small bunch of fresh coriander
2 onions, chopped
2 cloves garlic, chopped
3 tbsp olive oil

2lb (900g) potatoes, peeled and cubed
2 pints (1.2 litres) chicken stock, vegetable
    stock or water
salt and pepper

1 Cut the stalks from the coriander and tie them in a bundle with string. Chop the leaves finely and reserve.

2 Fry the onion and garlic gently in the oil until tender without browning. Add the potatoes and coriander stalks, stir, then cover and sweat over a low heat for 5 minutes.

3 Now add the stock, salt and pepper and bring to the boil. Simmer until the potatoes are very tender. Remove the bundle of coriander stalks. Liquidize, adding a little more stock or water if the soup is too thick. Stir in the coriander leaves and reheat gently without boiling. Taste and adjust the seasoning. Serve immediately.

CORIANDER
You can easily grow hardy coriander in a pot on your windowsill. Cook it, eat it raw, or use it as a garnish. Cut bunches should be kept in water or in a sealed pack in the fridge, but make sure you use them within a week.

A fantastic way to use this much maligned, fragrant weed – choose young and tender specimens and wear a double layer of latex gloves to pick them. **Celia Brooks Brown**

nettle soup

🌀 **SERVES** 4   🕐 **PREP** 10 MINS **COOK** 20 MINS   ❄ **FREEZE** UP TO 3 MONTHS

2 tbsp virgin rapeseed oil or olive oil
4 spring onions or 1 bunch, sliced
3 leeks, roughly chopped
650g (1lb 7oz) potatoes, washed but not peeled, cut into 2cm (¾in) cubes
sea salt

1 litre (1¾ pints) vegetable stock
100g (3½oz) young nettles or nettle tips (about ¼ carrier bag full), washed
juice of half a lemon
freshly ground black pepper
plain thick yogurt, to serve

1 Heat the oil in a soup pan over a medium heat. Add the spring onions, leeks and potatoes with a little sea salt. Stir, cover, and cook for 5 minutes, stirring frequently.

2 Add the stock and bring to the boil. Add the nettles, stir, and simmer for 10 minutes, or until the potato is soft. Cool briefly, then purée with a hand blender until completely smooth. Taste for seasoning, then squeeze in a little lemon juice and grind in some pepper. Serve each bowl with a dollop of thick yoghurt and more pepper.

NETTLES
Because they grow everywhere, nettles are generally easy to find. When fresh, the stalks are firm and the young leaves are green. Wilted or yellowing leaves should be avoided. Cooked nettles lose their sting.

In Provence, they say *"aïgo boulido sauvo la vido"* – "garlic broth saves your life". Ten cloves of garlic go into this dish, yet it is not terrifyingly garlicky." **Sophie Grigson**

garlic broth

⚙ **SERVES** 4   🕐 **PREP** 15 MINS **COOK** 20 MINS   ✳ **FREEZE** NOT SUITABLE

10 garlic cloves, crushed
6 sage leaves
1 bay leaf
1 large sprig of thyme
2 tbsp extra virgin olive oil, plus extra
   to drizzle

1 litre (1¾ pints) water or light chicken stock
salt and freshly ground black pepper
8 croûtes (see p39)
1 garlic clove, halved (optional)
3 egg yolks
grated Gruyère, to serve

1 Put the garlic into a saucepan with the sage, bay leaf, thyme, oil, water or stock, and some salt and freshly ground black pepper. Bring to the boil, then simmer gently for 15 minutes. Meanwhile, rub one side of each croûte with the cut clove of garlic, if using, and place two in each bowl. Drizzle a little oil over each one.

2 Turn off the heat and pick out and discard the bay leaf and thyme (but not the sage). Whisk 3 tbsp of the hot soup into the egg yolks, then pour the whole lot back into the pan and stir. Taste and adjust the seasoning, then transfer the soup to a hot tureen. At the table, ladle the soup into the bowls, set before the diners, and pass round the Gruyère.

GARLIC
The flavour of garlic differs according to how you prepare it. Left whole and boiled, it tastes mild and sweet. When you chop it, its flavour intensifies, and the more finely it's chopped, the more pungent it becomes.

Daphne Lambert runs Greencuisine at Penrhos Court in Herefordshire. There she teaches the benefits of organic, local, and wild foods.

wild garlic soup

⊘ **SERVES** 4–6   🕐 **PREP** 10 MINS **COOK** 35 MINS   ❄ **FREEZE** UP TO 3 MONTHS

6 large handfuls of wild garlic leaves
25g (scant 1oz) butter
3 medium potatoes, diced

1 large onion, diced
600ml (1 pint) hot vegetable stock
sea salt and freshly ground black pepper

1 Bring a pan of water to the boil and immerse the garlic leaves for 30 seconds. Remove with a slotted spoon (reserving the cooking liquid) and plunge into a bowl of cold water. Leave to cool, then drain and set aside.

2 Meanwhile, melt the butter in a saucepan over a medium heat. Add the potatoes and onion and cook gently for 15 minutes. Add the stock and 600ml (1 pint) of the reserved cooking liquid, bring to the boil, then lower the heat and simmer for 15 minutes or until the potatoes are soft.

3 Remove the pan from the heat and add the garlic leaves. Whiz the mixture in a blender until smooth, then return to the pan and reheat gently. Season with salt and freshly ground black pepper and serve.

winter vegetables

Simple, affordable, and immensely satisfying, this hearty soup makes a warming meal when accompanied with some freshly baked crusty bread. **Roopa Gulati**

cream of vegetable soup

⊙ **SERVES** 6   🕐 **PREP** 15 MINS **COOK** 40–55 MINS   ❄ **FREEZE** UP TO 3 MONTHS
WITHOUT THE CREAM AND MILK

45g (1½oz) butter
2 carrots, sliced
1 leek (white part only), sliced
2 parsnips, sliced
1 onion, sliced
1 small turnip, sliced
3 celery stalks, sliced
1 potato, sliced

1.2 litres (2 pints) hot vegetable stock
2 tsp fresh thyme leaves
1 bay leaf
pinch of grated nutmeg
salt and freshly ground black pepper
3 tbsp single cream
3 tbsp milk
bunch of chives, snipped, to garnish

1 Melt the butter in a large pan, add the carrots, leek, parsnips, onion, turnip, celery, and potato, and stir to coat well. Cover the pan with a lid and cook for 10–15 minutes or until the vegetables have softened.

2 Add the stock, thyme, bay leaf, and nutmeg, then season with salt and freshly ground black pepper. Bring to the boil and simmer, uncovered, for 30–40 minutes or until the vegetables are meltingly soft. Scoop out the bay leaf and discard.

3 Whiz the soup in a blender until smooth. You may need to do this in batches. If you like the texture of your soups very smooth, strain it through a fine sieve, otherwise leave it as it is. Stir in the cream and milk, adding more milk if the consistency is still too thick. Season with salt and freshly ground black pepper, then reheat gently. Garnish with the chives and serve.

A substantial soup that is a meal in itself. Mix and match whatever vegetables are in season – courgettes, cabbage, and leek are all excellent in a minestrone.

minestrone soup

SERVES 4–6   **PREP** 20 MINS, PLUS 8 HOURS SOAKING   **FREEZE** UP TO 1 MONTH
COOK 1¾ HRS   AT THE END OF STEP 2

100g (3½oz) dried white cannellini beans
2 tbsp olive oil
2 celery stalks, finely chopped
2 carrots, finely chopped
1 onion, finely chopped
400g can chopped tomatoes

750ml (1¼ pints) hot vegetable stock
or chicken stock
salt and freshly ground black pepper
60g (2oz) small short-cut pasta
4 tbsp chopped flat-leaf parsley
40g (1½oz) Parmesan, finely grated

1 Put the dried beans in a large bowl, cover with cold water, and leave to soak in the fridge for at least 8 hours or overnight. Drain the beans, then place them in a large saucepan and cover with cold water. Bring to the boil, then boil hard for 10 minutes, skimming the surface of any scum with a slotted spoon. Lower the heat, part-cover the pan, and simmer for 1 hour or until the beans are tender. Drain and set aside.

2 Heat the oil in the rinsed-out pan over a medium heat. Add the celery, carrots, and onion, and fry, stirring occasionally, for 5 minutes or until tender. Stir in the cooked beans, then add the tomatoes and their juice, the stock, and some salt and freshly ground black pepper. Bring to the boil, stirring all the time, then cover with a lid and simmer for 20 minutes.

3 Add the pasta and simmer for 10–15 minutes or until it is cooked but still firm to the bite. Stir in the parsley and half the Parmesan, then adjust the seasoning. Serve hot, sprinkled with the remaining Parmesan.

Mounded together in the centre of the bowl, the vegetables in this soup resemble coins – which is one of the reasons it got its name. The other is that it is very inexpensive to make.

"penny" soup

⊘ SERVES 4   **🕐 PREP** 15 MINS **COOK** 30 MINS   **❅ FREEZE** UP TO 3 MONTHS
WITH ALL VEGETABLES PURÉED

1 leek
300g (11oz) potatoes
250g (9oz) large carrots
175g (6oz) small sweet potatoes
1 tbsp olive oil

15g (½oz) butter
600ml (1 pint) hot vegetable stock
1 tbsp chopped flat-leaf parsley
salt and freshly ground black pepper

1 Slice the vegetables into 3mm (⅛in) rounds. Heat the oil and butter in a large saucepan, add the leeks, and cook over a medium heat, stirring frequently, for 3–4 minutes or until soft. Add the potatoes, carrots, and sweet potatoes and cook, stirring, for 1 minute.

2 Pour in the stock, then bring to the boil, cover with a lid, and simmer for 20 minutes or until the vegetables are tender but not soft. Transfer about one-third of the vegetables to a blender or food processor with a little of the liquid and blend to a smooth purée, then return to the pan. Stir in the parsley, season to taste with salt and freshly ground black pepper, and serve, with the vegetables in a little mound in the centre.

Leftovers of this big warming soup from Tuscany are never thrown away, but used to make the sturdy Ribollita (see right). Both are frugally filling, and very good. **Sophie Grigson**

zuppa di verdure

❂ SERVES 6   **⏱ PREP** 25 MINS, PLUS OVERNIGHT SOAKING   **❄ FREEZE** UP TO 3 MONTHS
COOK 2–3 HRS   BEFORE CAVOLO NERO IS ADDED

200g (7oz) dried cannellini or haricot beans, soaked overnight in water, or 400g can cannellini beans, drained and rinsed
bouquet garni made from a sprig of rosemary, a sprig of thyme, and 2 bay leaves (see p24)
4 tbsp extra virgin olive oil, plus extra to serve
1 onion, chopped
3 carrots, diced
2 celery stalks, diced
2 leeks, very thinly sliced

3 garlic cloves, chopped
1 dried red chilli, finely chopped
3 tomatoes, skinned, deseeded, and chopped
2 tbsp tomato purée
salt and freshly ground black pepper
4 cavolo nero or curly kale leaves, or the outer leaves of a Savoy cabbage, tough stalks removed and the leaves coarsely chopped
6 slices stale bread
1 garlic clove, cut in half

1 Drain the beans and place them in a large pan with the bouquet garni and twice their volume of cold water. Bring to the boil, then boil hard for 10 minutes. Lower the heat, and simmer gently for 1–2 hours or until tender, adding more water if needed. Remove the pan from the heat, discard the bouquet garni, and leave the beans to cool in their cooking water.

2 Heat the oil in a large heavy pot, then add the onion, carrots, celery, leeks, garlic, and chilli. Cover with a lid and sweat over a low heat for 10 minutes, stirring once or twice. Add the tomatoes and tomato purée and cook over a moderate heat for 3–4 minutes. Add the beans, their cooking water and enough water to cover the vegetables generously. Season with enthusiasm. Bring to the boil and simmer gently for 20 minutes or until the vegetables are tender. Purée half the soup in a blender, then return to the pan. Add the cavolo nero and simmer for 10 minutes or until tender. Adjust the seasonings.

3 Rub the bread with the garlic and arrange in a warm shallow dish or tureen. Spoon in the soup and serve with a bottle of best olive oil out on the table for people to help themselves.

Ribollita means "reboiled" in Italian, and that is more or less what this soup is – reboiled Zuppa di verdure (see left). It is wonderful, heart-warming comfort food. **Sophie Grigson**

ribollita

SERVES 4–6　　**PREP** 10 MINS **COOK** 40 MINS　　　**FREEZE** NOT SUITABLE

1 quantity day-old Zuppa di verdure, made up to the point just before the cavolo nero is added

6 cavolo nero or curly kale leaves, or the outer leaves of a Savoy cabbage, tough stalks removed and the leaves coarsely chopped

6 slices good-quality stale bread

1 garlic clove, halved

2–3 tbsp extra virgin olive oil, plus extra to serve

½–1 red onion, very finely sliced

4 tbsp freshly grated Parmesan (optional)

1 Preheat the oven to 190°C (375°F/Gas 5). Bring the soup to the boil in a large pan, stir in the cavolo nero, and simmer for 10 minutes or until tender. Meanwhile, rub the stale bread with garlic.

2 Oil a large gratin dish or similar ovenproof dish with olive oil, then spoon about a quarter of the soup into the dish, spreading it over the base. Now, lay half the slices of bread over the soup, then spoon over half the remaining soup. Repeat these two layers one more time. Lay the red onion over the top, then scatter with the Parmesan, if using. Drizzle over a little olive oil, then bake for 30 minutes. Serve sizzling hot, with extra olive oil out on the table for those that want it.

This one-pot meal of slowly cooked vegetables flavoured with pork and confit of duck comes from southwest France. It is best made the day before and reheated. **Marie-Pierre Moine**

garbure

SERVES 4–6   **PREP** 40 MINS **COOK** 1 HR   ❄ **FREEZE** UP TO 3 MONTHS

100g (3½oz) lardons or diced pancetta
1 Spanish onion, finely chopped
3 garlic cloves, crushed
1 leg confit of duck
1.5 litres (2¾ pints) chicken stock
1 small Savoy cabbage, core removed and leaves cut into 2.5 x 7.5cm (1 x 3in) strips
1 large carrot, sliced
1 celery stalk, diced
1 leek, cleaned and sliced
1 large floury potato, cubed

sea salt and freshly ground black pepper
1 tsp pimentón picante or hot smoked paprika
½ tsp ground cumin
2–3 sprigs of fresh thyme
2–3 sprigs of flat-leaf parsley, plus 1 tbsp finely chopped parsley to garnish
250g (9oz) can haricot beans, drained, rinsed, and drained again
8–12 croûtes (see p39), rubbed with garlic and brushed with olive oil, to serve

1 Put a large, deep, heavy-based casserole pan over a moderate heat, add the lardons or pancetta, and fry, stirring frequently, for 2–3 minutes or until crisp and cooked through. Remove with a slotted spoon and drain on kitchen paper. Add the onion and garlic to the pan, reduce the heat a little, and cook, stirring frequently, for 5–8 minutes or until softened.

2 Pick the meat from the duck leg, discarding the skin and bones but reserving the fat, and cut into shreds. Stir into the onion and garlic, then add the stock, cabbage, carrot, celery, leek, and potato. Season lightly with salt and more generously with freshly ground black pepper, then add the pimentón or paprika, cumin, thyme, and parsley. Bring to a simmer, cover, reduce the heat a little, and cook, stirring occasionally, for 30 minutes.

3 Lift out the thyme and parsley. Lightly mash the beans in a bowl, then stir them into the soup and continue cooking until the vegetables are tender. Taste and adjust the seasoning. To serve, stir in the reserved lardons or pancetta along with 1 tbsp of the duck fat, then sprinkle with the parsley. Place a croûte in each bowl and ladle the piping hot soup on top.

A mixed vegetable potage (soup) like this is traditional French family fare. It is ladled out of a tureen into wide shallow bowls as a starter all over the country. **Marie-Pierre Moine**

french country soup

SERVES 4　　　**PREP** 15 MINS **COOK** 45 MINS　　　**FREEZE** UP TO 3 MONTHS
AT THE END OF STEP 2

1 tbsp sunflower oil or groundnut oil
30g (1oz) butter
3 large leeks, cleaned and chopped
1 large floury potato, roughly cubed
2 large carrots, chopped

750ml (1¼ pints) light vegetable stock
　or chicken stock
2 bay leaves
sea salt and freshly ground black pepper

1 Put the oil and half the butter in a large sauté pan over a very moderate heat. Add the leeks, potato, and carrots and cook, stirring frequently, for 5 minutes. Reduce the heat a little, add the stock and bay leaves, then season lightly with salt and freshly ground black pepper. Cover and cook gently, stirring occasionally, for 30 minutes or until the vegetables are very soft.

2 Leave to cool for several minutes, then lift out the bay leaves. Transfer the soup to a blender and whiz until smooth. Strain back into the pan through a sieve, using the back of a wooden spoon to push through as much as possible. Pour the hot water through the sieve to extract as much as you can from the vegetables.

3 Reheat gently, stirring frequently. Taste and adjust the seasoning, then stir in the remaining butter and serve very hot.

POTATOES
Getting some of the less common varieties of potato – such as Remarka or these British Queens – is one of the great benefits of shopping at farmers' markets or having a vegetable box delivered. The same goes for other vegetables.

Despite its French name, this silky-smooth, cold soup actually comes from the USA. It is also delicious served hot – simply add the cream and chives at the end of cooking.

vichyssoise

⊘ SERVES 4 **🕑 PREP** 15 MINS, PLUS 3 HRS CHILLING
COOK 45 MINS

❄ FREEZE UP TO 3 MONTHS
BEFORE THE CREAM IS ADDED

30g (1oz) butter
3 large leeks (white parts only), finely sliced
2 potatoes, about 175g (6oz) in total, chopped
1 celery stalk, roughly chopped
1.2 litres (2 pints) hot vegetable stock

salt and freshly ground black pepper
150ml (5fl oz) double cream, plus extra
 to garnish
2 tbsp finely chopped chives

1 Melt the butter in a heavy pan over a medium heat, add the leeks, and stir to coat well. Press a circle of damp greaseproof paper on top of them, cover with a lid, and cook, shaking the pan gently from time to time, for 15 minutes or until they are soft and golden. Discard the greaseproof paper.

2 Stir in the potatoes, celery, and stock, then season with salt and freshly ground black pepper. Bring to the boil, stirring all the time, then cover with a lid and simmer for 30 minutes or until the vegetables are tender.

3 Remove the pan from the heat and leave to cool slightly, then whiz the soup in a blender until very smooth. You may need to do this in batches. Season to taste with salt and freshly ground black pepper, then chill for at least 3 hours. To serve, pour into bowls, stir a little cream into each, then sprinkle with the chives and some more freshly ground black pepper.

LEEKS
Although it means trimming and cleaning them, go for organic leeks with roots and plenty of green leaves rather than the neat cylinders you see in pre-prepared packs – it's hard to tell how fresh these are. For more information, see p23.

in praise of...
leeks
Leeks are regularly
the bridesmaid in
recipes. Centre stage,
though, they are a
revelation. Choose for
tenderness and taste,
then cook until soft
but not stodgy, even
in soup.
Shaun Hill

This is a variation on leek and potato soup and was a regular item on the menu at Robert Carrier's restaurant in London, where I worked in the 1970s. It has not dated. **Shaun Hill**

saffron soup

SERVES 4   **PREP** 15 MINS **COOK** 20 MINS   **FREEZE** UP TO 3 MONTHS
BEFORE CREAM IS ADDED

1 tbsp olive oil
1 large onion, sliced
200g (7oz) leeks, cut into 2.5cm (1in) lengths
150g (5½oz) potatoes, diced
1 tsp saffron
1 tsp ground cumin

1 litre (1¾ pints) hot chicken stock
salt and freshly ground black pepper
2 tbsp dry white wine
2 tbsp double cream
1 tbsp lemon juice
snipped chives, to garnish

1 Heat the oil in a heavy-based pan and fry the onion gently for 6–8 minutes or until soft. Add the leeks, potatoes, saffron, cumin, and stock, then season with salt and freshly ground black pepper. Cover with a lid and bring to the boil, then lower the heat and simmer for 10 minutes or until the potatoes are tender. Do not let them disintegrate into the soup.

2 Transfer to a blender, add the wine, and whiz until smooth. Stir in the cream and lemon juice and season with salt and freshly ground black pepper. If the soup is too thick, dilute it with more stock or water. If it is too thin, add more olive oil. Garnish with the snipped chives and serve.

This is excellent with croûtes (see p39). Top them with grated Gruyère or Cheddar and some freshly ground black pepper, then flash them under the grill until bubbling. **Marie-Pierre Moine**

onion and garlic soup

⚙ **SERVES** 4 🕐 **PREP** 20 MINS **COOK** 40 MINS ❄ **FREEZE** NOT SUITABLE

1 tbsp light olive oil
15g (½oz) butter
1 Spanish onion, finely chopped
1 banana shallot, very finely chopped
sea salt and freshly ground black pepper
100ml (3½ fl oz) hot water
1 small head of garlic, broken up into
   individual cloves but left unpeeled

150ml (5fl oz) dry white wine
600ml (1 pint) hot vegetable stock
   or chicken stock
100ml (3½fl oz) full-fat or
   semi-skimmed milk
2 egg yolks
4 heaped tbsp double cream
1 heaped tsp Dijon mustard

1 Heat the oil and butter in a large sauté pan or other heavy-based pan over a moderate heat. Add the onion and shallot, season lightly with salt and freshly ground black pepper, and cook for 3 minutes, stirring all the time. Lower the heat, add the hot water, and cook gently, stirring frequently, for 20 minutes or until the water has evaporated and the onion mixture is very soft.

2 Meanwhile, bring some lightly salted water to the boil in a small pan. Add the garlic and bring back to the boil, then lower the heat and simmer for 10–15 minutes or until very soft. Drain, then refresh under cold running water. Pour the wine, stock, and milk into the onion mixture and bring to a simmer over a moderate heat, stirring occasionally.

3 Working over a bowl, squeeze each garlic clove between your thumb and forefinger until the flesh pops out. Add the egg yolks, then mash the garlic, stirring to make a smooth mix. Gradually whisk in the cream. Pour in 3 tbsp of the simmering soup and whisk well. Season lightly with salt and freshly ground black pepper. Whisking vigorously, pour or spoon the garlic mixture into the soup, keeping the pan over a low heat. Stir in the mustard, adjust the seasoning, and serve.

This Parisian classic is given extra punch with a spoonful of brandy in every bowl. Serve it the moment you've made it – French onion soup must be piping hot.

french onion soup

⊙ SERVES 4   **🕐 PREP** 10 MINS **COOK** 1 HR 20 MINS   **❄ FREEZE** UP TO 1 MONTH
WITHOUT THE CROÛTES AND CHEESE

30g (1oz) butter
1 tbsp sunflower oil
675g (1½lb) onions, thinly sliced
1 tsp sugar
salt and freshly ground black pepper
120ml (4fl oz) red wine

2 tbsp plain flour
1.5 litres (2¾ pints) hot beef stock
4 tbsp brandy
8 croûtes (see p39)
1 garlic clove, cut in half
115g (4oz) Gruyère or Emmental, grated

1 Melt the butter with the oil in a large, heavy pan over a low heat. Add the onions and sugar and turn to coat well. Season with salt and freshly ground black pepper, then press a piece of damp greaseproof paper on top of the onions. Cook, uncovered, stirring occasionally, for 40 minutes or until they are a rich dark brown colour. Take care not to let them stick and burn.

2 Remove the greaseproof paper and stir in the wine. Increase the heat to medium and stir for 5 minutes while the onions glaze. Sprinkle in the flour and stir for 2 minutes, then pour in the stock and bring to the boil. Reduce the heat to low, cover with a lid, and leave to simmer for 30 minutes. Taste and season with salt and freshly ground black pepper, if necessary.

3 Preheat the grill to its highest setting. Divide the soup among flameproof bowls and stir 1 tbsp of the brandy into each. Rub the croûtes with the cut garlic and place one in each bowl. Sprinkle with the cheese and grill for 2–3 minutes or until the cheese is bubbling and golden. Serve at once.

Meltingly soft onions make a flavoursome base for this lightly spiced soup enriched with almonds and sweetened with a hint of caramel. **Roopa Gulati**

onion and almond soup

⊘ SERVES 4   **⏱ PREP** 20 MINS, PLUS 2 HOURS SALTING
COOK 1 HR   **❄ FREEZE** UP TO 2 MONTHS
BEFORE CREAM IS ADDED

1 onion, very finely sliced
½ tsp sea salt flakes
vegetable oil, to deep-fry
100g (3½oz) almonds (with skins on)
750ml (1¼ pints) hot chicken stock
60g (2oz) butter
¼ tsp nigella seeds

4 large onions, diced
1 red chilli, chopped
1 tsp muscovado sugar
2 tbsp balsamic vinegar
120ml (4fl oz) single cream
salt and freshly ground black pepper

1 For a fried onion garnish, put the onion slices in a shallow dish, sprinkle with the sea salt, then set to one side for at least 2 hours. Using your hands, squeeze out the liquid, then pat dry with kitchen paper. Deep-fry in hot oil for 1–2 minutes or until golden, then drain on kitchen paper.

2 Bring a small pan of water to the boil, add the almonds, turn off the heat, and cover with a lid. Leave to soak for 15 minutes, then drain and slip off the skins once the nuts are cool enough to handle. Transfer to a food processor with 100ml (3½fl oz) of the stock, then whiz to a paste and set aside.

3 Meanwhile, melt the butter in a large pan, add the nigella seeds, and fry over a gentle heat for 1 minute. Stir in the diced onions and chilli, cover, and cook over a very low heat for 20–30 minutes or until soft but not brown, then turn up the heat and remove the lid. When the onions begin to turn a golden colour, stir in the sugar, and cook until it starts catching on the bottom of the pan. Add the vinegar and continue cooking until sticky.

4 Add the rest of the stock and the almond paste and simmer for 20 minutes. Whiz the soup until smooth in a blender, then return to the pan, stir in the cream, and season with salt and freshly ground black pepper. Reheat gently and serve garnished with the fried onions.

Combined with just a few simple ingredients, roast potatoes can quickly be transformed into a luxuriously smooth, rich, and comforting winter soup. **Angela Nilsen**

roast potato soup

◉ SERVES 4   **🕐 PREP** 15 MINS **COOK** 1 HR 15 MINS   **❄ FREEZE** UP TO 3 MONTHS
BEFORE ONION AND BACON ARE ADDED

450g (1lb) floury potatoes, such as King
   Edward, cut into 5cm (2in) chunks
2 tbsp olive oil
salt and freshly ground black pepper
3 large shallots, roughly chopped
2 garlic cloves, halved
1 large parsnip, cut into small chunks

900ml (1½ pints) hot vegetable stock
4 rashers streaky bacon, cut into thin strips
   and rinds discarded
1 onion, halved lengthways and thinly sliced
100ml (3½fl oz) double cream
large knob of butter

1 Preheat the oven to 200°C (400°F/Gas 6). Put the potatoes and 1 tbsp of the oil into a small roasting tin and toss to coat well. Season with freshly ground black pepper, then roast for 45 minutes or until golden. Turn occasionally to ensure even roasting. Transfer to a large pan and add the shallots, garlic, and parsnip. Add the stock, bring to the boil, then cover with a lid and simmer for 20 minutes or until the parsnip is tender.

2 Meanwhile, heat the remaining oil in a frying pan, add the bacon, and fry for 5 minutes or until crisp. Remove with a slotted spoon and drain on kitchen paper. Add the onion to the pan, along with a pinch of salt, and fry over a medium heat for 8–10 minutes or until dark golden brown and well caramelized. Set to one side and keep warm.

3 Remove the soup from the heat, add the cream and butter, and stir until the butter has melted. Whiz in a blender or food processor until smooth. You may need to do this in batches. Add a little more stock if the soup is too thick. For an extra smooth soup, press the mixture through a fine sieve. Season to taste with salt and freshly ground black pepper, then reheat gently and serve topped with the crispy onion and bacon.

Broccoli and shallot add colour and freshness to this rich combination of potato and cheese. You can use Caerphilly or Wensleydale in place of the mascarpone. **Marie-Pierre Moine**

potato soup with broccoli, shallot, and mascarpone

SERVES 4　　**PREP** 20 MINS **COOK** 40 MINS　　**FREEZE** UP TO 3 MONTHS

1 tbsp olive oil
10g (¼oz) butter
2 large banana shallots, finely chopped
350g (12oz) floury potatoes, chopped
　into 2.5cm (1in) chunks
sea salt and freshly ground black pepper

1 large head of broccoli, cut into florets
4 tbsp mascarpone
4 croûtes (see p 39)
30g (1oz) creamy, strong-flavoured blue
　cheese, such as Roquefort, fourme
　d'Ambert, or Gorgonzola piquante

1 Heat the oil and butter in a sauté pan over a moderate heat, add the shallots and potatoes and cook for 5 minutes, stirring often. Meanwhile, boil 1.5 litres (2¾ pints) water in the kettle.

2 Pour 1.35 litres (2½ pints) boiling water into the pan and stir well. Season lightly with sea salt and freshly ground black pepper and bring to a simmer. Lower the heat, cover with a lid, and simmer for 10 minutes. Add the broccoli, stir, cover again, and continue cooking for 10–15 minutes or until the vegetables are tender. Leave to cool for several minutes, then transfer the contents of the pan to a blender and whiz until smooth. Strain the soup back into the pan through a sieve, using a wooden spoon to push as much of the mixture through as possible.

3 Pour in the rest of the hot water. Place the pan over a moderate heat, stir in the mascarpone, and keep stirring until it has blended in. Season with salt and freshly ground black pepper. Spread the croûtes with the blue cheese, ladle the soup into bowls, and float a piece in the centre of each one.

If you can't get hold of fresh chanterelle mushrooms for this, you can use jarred or canned. Drain, rinse, and then drain them again before you fry them.

german potato soup

⦿ **SERVES** 6   🕐 **PREP** 25 MINS **COOK** 45 MINS   ❄ **FREEZE** UP TO 3 MONTHS
WITHOUT THE FRIED ONION
OR CHANTERELLES

75g (2½oz) butter
¼ celeriac, diced
250g (9oz) carrots, diced
675g (1½lb) floury potatoes, diced
1 onion, studded with a bay leaf and a clove
1.5 litres (2¾ pints) hot vegetable stock
200g (7oz) leeks, sliced
1 onion, diced

200g (7oz) chanterelles, large ones halved
120ml (4fl oz) whipping cream or
    150g (5½oz) crème fraîche
salt and freshly ground black pepper
pinch of dried marjoram
pinch of freshly grated nutmeg
2 tbsp chopped flat-leaf parsley, chervil,
    or chives

1 Melt two-thirds of the butter in a large pan, add the celeriac and carrots, and cook, stirring frequently, for 6–8 minutes or until light brown. Add the potatoes, onion, and stock and bring to the boil. Lower the heat, cover with a lid, and simmer for 20 minutes or until tender. Add the leeks, cover again, and cook for 10 minutes more.

2 Meanwhile, melt the rest of the butter in a frying pan, add the diced onion, and fry, stirring continuously, for 4–5 minutes or until soft but not brown. Add the chanterelles and fry, stirring frequently, for 5 minutes.

3 Remove the whole onion from the soup and discard. Transfer about one-third of the contents of the pan to a blender and whiz until smooth. Stir in the cream and return to the pan. Season with salt and freshly ground black pepper, then add the marjoram, nutmeg, and the fried onion and chanterelles, and reheat gently. Serve sprinkled with the herbs.

The scallops are a counterpoint to the distinctive taste of the Jerusalem artichoke purée in this traditional soup menu pairing. **Shaun Hill**

scallop and artichoke soup

⊚ SERVES 4   **🕐 PREP** 20 MINS **COOK** 25 MINS   **✳ FREEZE** UP TO 3 MONTHS
AT THE END OF STEP 2

100g (3½oz) unsalted butter
1 onion, chopped
1 garlic clove, chopped
1kg (2¼lb) Jerusalem artichokes, peeled
  or scrubbed and cut into small dice
1.5 litres (2¾ pints) hot chicken stock
  or water
100ml (3½fl oz) double cream

salt and freshly ground black pepper
a pinch of freshly grated nutmeg
4 rashers streaky bacon, cut into small
  dice, rinds discarded
4 scallops (white part only)
2 tbsp sunflower oil
few drops of lemon juice
snipped chives, to garnish

1 Melt half the butter in a large pan and fry the onion gently. Add the garlic and artichokes and sweat over a low heat for 3 minutes. Add the stock or water, cover with a lid, and simmer until the artichokes are completely cooked and soft. Purée in a blender with the cream and the remaining butter. You may need to do this in batches. Return to the pan and season with salt and freshly ground black pepper, then sprinkle in the nutmeg and keep warm.

2 Fry the bacon in a frying pan until crisp, then spoon on to kitchen paper to drain. Cut the scallops into large discs, season with salt and freshly ground black pepper, then fry in the sunflower oil – they will be ready almost as soon as they are sealed by the heat. Squeeze over a few drops of lemon juice.

3 Divide the artichoke purée among four bowls, spoon the bacon and scallops on top, then garnish with the chives and serve.

Use whatever proportion of carrots and Jerusalem artichokes you have, adding up to 700g (1lb 9oz) in total. The carrots enhance the colour and sweetness of the soup. **Celia Brooks Brown**

jerusalem artichoke soup with saffron and thyme

SERVES 4–6   **PREP** 15 MINS **COOK** 35–45 MINS   **FREEZE** UP TO 3 MONTHS

2 tbsp virgin rapeseed oil or olive oil, plus extra to garnish
2 medium onions, chopped
3 garlic cloves, chopped
350g (12oz) Jerusalem artichokes, scrubbed and roughly chopped
350g (12oz) carrots, scrubbed and roughly chopped

sea salt and freshly ground black pepper
1.2 litres (2 pints) hot vegetable stock
1 tbsp fresh thyme leaves or 1½ tsp dried thyme
large pinch (about 30 strands) of saffron
juice of ½ lemon

1 Heat the oil in a large pan over a medium heat, add the onions, and fry for 5–10 minutes or until soft and translucent. Add the garlic and fry for 30 seconds or until fragrant. Stir in the artichokes, carrots, and a little salt, then cover with a lid and sweat, stirring frequently, for 10–15 minutes or until the vegetables are softened.

2 Add the stock, thyme, and saffron, bring to the boil, then lower the heat to a simmer and cook for 20 minutes or until the vegetables are thoroughly soft. Cool briefly, then whiz until smooth in a blender. Stir in the lemon juice and season to taste with salt and freshly ground black pepper. Serve in warm bowls, with a drizzle more oil on top.

Make the effort to brew up your own stock, as the flavour of the celeriac and hazelnuts in this soup is not domineering enough to disguise any shortcomings. **Sophie Grigson**

celeriac and hazelnut soup

SERVES 6   **PREP** 15 MINS **COOK** 40 MINS   ✱ **FREEZE** UP TO 3 MONTHS
BEFORE THE CREAM IS ADDED

100g (3½oz) shelled hazelnuts
45g (1½oz) butter
1 medium/large celeriac, roughly diced
1 onion, chopped
2 tbsp long-grain rice or pudding rice

1 litre (1¾ pints) hot chicken stock
salt and freshly ground black pepper
juice of ½ lemon
90ml (3fl oz) double cream

1 Preheat the oven to 190°C (375°F/Gas 5). Spread the hazelnuts out on a baking tray and roast for 5–10 minutes or until they turn a shade darker and the skins flake off easily. Check regularly to prevent burning. Allow to cool slightly, then rub off the skins.

2 Melt the butter in a large pan over a low heat. Add the celeriac, onion, rice, and hazelnuts and turn to coat well, then slam on the lid and leave to sweat gently for 10–15 minutes, stirring once or twice. Pour in half the stock, season well with salt and freshly ground black pepper, and bring to the boil. Simmer gently for 15 minutes or until the celeriac and rice are good and tender.

3 Let the soup cool for a few minutes, then whiz until completely smooth in a blender, adding the remaining stock to thin the soup down. Return to the pan, stir in the lemon juice and then the cream, and reheat, being sure to taste and balance the seasoning. Serve totally hot and steaming.

A light, colourful soup with quite a chilli kick. Larger turnips have a stronger flavour, which is perfect for this dish. Don't use the delicate baby ones. **Carolyn Humphries**

turnip soup with pimento, chilli, and noodles

🍽 **SERVES** 4–6   🕐 **PREP** 10 MINS **COOK** 30 MINS   ❄ **FREEZE** UP TO 3 MONTHS
AT THE END OF STEP 1

4 spring onions, chopped
2 good-sized turnips, diced
½ tsp crushed dried chillies
1 green jalapeño chilli, deseeded
  and cut into thin rings
2 star anise
2 tsp tomato purée

900ml (1½ pints) hot vegetable stock
  or light chicken stock
1 slab dried thin Chinese egg noodles
1 preserved pimento, drained and diced
soy sauce
freshly ground black pepper
small handful of coriander leaves, torn

1 Put the spring onions, turnips, chillies, star anise, tomato purée, and stock in a saucepan and bring to the boil. Lower the heat, part-cover, and simmer gently for 30 minutes or until the turnips are really tender. Discard the star anise.

2 Meanwhile, put the noodles in a bowl, cover with boiling water, and leave to stand for 5 minutes, stirring to loosen, then drain. Stir the noodles into the soup, along with the pimento. Season to taste with soy sauce and freshly ground black pepper, then stir in half the coriander. Ladle into warm soup bowls, top with the remaining coriander, and serve.

TURNIPS
Choose organic turnips for the sweetest, most mustardy flavour. To prepare, top and tail. Small turnips then need only the thinnest layer of skin peeling off. Larger turnips usually have a thicker layer of hard woody skin to peel.

Alice Waters of Chez Panisse restaurant in California writes "Young turnips with their greens are in the markets in spring and fall. Together they make a delicious soup."

turnip soup

SERVES 4–6   **PREP** 20 MINS **COOK** 40 MINS   **FREEZE** UP TO 3 MONTHS

2 bunches of young turnips with greens, about 675g (1½lb) total in weight
3 tbsp butter or olive oil
1 onion, thinly sliced
1 bay leaf

2 sprigs of thyme
salt
1.2 litres (2 pints) well-flavoured chicken stock

1 Remove the greens from the turnips, then trim and discard the stems. Rinse and drain the leaves and cut into 1cm (½in) strips. Trim the roots from the bases and, if the skins are tough (taste one to see), peel before slicing thinly. Heat the butter or oil in a heavy pot over a low heat, add the onion, and cook very gently for 12 minutes or until soft.

2 Stir in the turnip bases, along with the bay leaf and thyme, and season with salt. Cook for 5 minutes, stirring occasionally, then pour in the stock and bring to the boil. Lower the heat to a simmer, cover, and cook for 10 minutes. Add the turnip greens and cook for another 5–10 minutes or until tender. Remove the bay leaf, check the seasoning and serve. This is excellent with a little grated Parmesan on top.

This is the original curried parsnip soup recipe created by Jane Grigson in the 1970s. Radical at the time, it has now become part of the general range of British soups. **Sophie Grigson**

curried parsnip soup

SERVES 4   **PREP** 25 MINS **COOK** 30 MINS   ❄ **FREEZE** UP TO 3 MONTHS
BEFORE CREAM IS ADDED

1 heaped tbsp coriander seeds
1 tsp cumin seeds
1 dried red chilli or ½ tsp chilli flakes
1 rounded tsp ground turmeric
¼ tsp ground fenugreek
1 medium onion, chopped
1 large garlic clove, split in half
675g (1½lb) parsnips, cored and diced

30g (1oz) butter
1 tbsp plain flour
1 litre (1¾ pints) vegetable stock, beef stock, or chicken stock
salt and freshly ground black pepper
150ml (5fl oz) cream
chopped chives or parsley, to garnish

1 Whiz the first five ingredients in a coffee mill, or pound the whole spices in a mortar, then mix with the ground. Put the mixture into a small jar – you will not need it all for this recipe.

2 Cook the onion, garlic, and parsnips gently in the butter, lid on the pan, for 10 minutes. Stir in the flour and 1–2 tbsp of the spice mixture. Cook for 2 minutes, giving the whole thing a turn round from time to time. Pour in the stock gradually, stirring constantly. Bring to the boil and leave to simmer gently for 10–15 minutes or until the parsnips are really tender.

3 Purée until smooth in a blender, then dilute to taste with water. Season to taste with salt and freshly ground black pepper, then reheat. Add the cream and serve scattered with the chives or parsley.

PARSNIPS
Widely produced organically, choose parsnips that are heavy for their size, with a firm, unblemished skin. To prepare, top and tail, then peel thinly. Baby parsnips can be cooked whole, while larger ones should be sliced and diced.

The sweetness of parsnip is balanced by mild curry powder and sharp green apple in this easy-to-prepare and warming, smooth winter soup. **Marie-Pierre Moine**

parsnip and apple soup

SERVES 4   **PREP** 20 MINS **COOK** 30 MINS   **FREEZE** UP TO 3 MONTHS
BEFORE CREAM IS ADDED

1 tbsp olive oil
10g (¼oz) butter
½ Spanish onion, finely chopped
1 garlic clove, crushed
2 tsp mild curry powder
1kg (2¼lb) parsnips, chopped
sea salt and freshly ground black pepper

1 large Bramley apple, peeled, cored,
  and chopped
1 litre (1¾ pints) hot vegetable stock
  or light chicken stock
6 tbsp single cream
2 tbsp lemon juice

1 Heat the oil and butter in a large sauté pan over a gentle heat. Add the onion, garlic, and curry powder and sweat gently, stirring frequently, for 2–3 minutes or until the onion has softened. Add the parsnips and season lightly with salt and freshly ground black pepper. Turn up the heat a little and fry, stirring frequently, for 5 minutes or until the parsnips are golden.

2 Add the apple, stir for 1 minute, then pour in the stock and bring to the boil. Lower the heat and simmer for 10–12 minutes or until the parsnips are tender. Take off the heat and leave to cool for several minutes, then transfer to a blender or food processor and whiz until smooth and creamy.

3 Pass the soup through a sieve placed over the pan, then rinse out the blender or food processor with 100ml (3½fl oz) hot water and stir this into the soup. Reheat gently, then stir in the cream and lemon juice. Adjust the seasoning and serve piping hot.

The vegetables for this soup are cooked in the oven, which brings out their naturally sweet flavour. This is delicious served with warm pitta bread. **Angela Nilsen**

moroccan roasted sweet potato soup

⊘ **SERVES** 4   ⏱ **PREP** 20 MINS **COOK** 50 MINS   ❄ **FREEZE** UP TO 3 MONTHS
BEFORE THE YOGURT IS ADDED

675g (1½lb) sweet potatoes, cut into
   big chunks
6 large shallots, quartered
3 plump garlic cloves, unpeeled
1 carrot, cut into big chunks
1 tbsp harissa, plus extra to serve
2 tbsp olive oil

salt and freshly ground black pepper
900ml (1½ pints) hot vegetable stock
1 tsp runny honey
generous squeeze of lemon juice
natural yogurt, to serve
warm pitta bread, to serve

1 Preheat the oven to 200°C (400°F/Gas 6). Put the sweet potatoes, shallots, garlic, and carrot in a roasting tin. Mix the harissa with the oil, then pour over the vegetables and toss together so they are all well coated. Season with freshly ground black pepper, then roast, turning occasionally, for 40 minutes or until tender and turning golden. Remove from the oven.

2 Squeeze the garlic cloves out of their skins into the roasting tin. Stir in the stock and honey, then scrape up all the bits from the bottom of the tin. Carefully transfer to a blender and whiz until smooth. You may need to do this in batches. Pour into a saucepan and reheat gently.

3 Add a good squeeze of lemon juice and season to taste with salt and freshly ground black pepper. Swirl the yogurt with a little harissa and top each bowl with a spoonful. Serve with warm pitta bread.

This recipe is based on a classic African soup that is hot and spicy and full of flavour. The peanut butter lends a rich, satisfying earthiness. **Angela Nilsen**

african sweet potato soup

⊘ **SERVES** 4 ● **PREP** 20 MINS **COOK** 20–25 MINS ❋ **FREEZE** UP TO 3 MONTHS

2 tbsp olive oil
1 onion, chopped
2 garlic cloves, finely chopped
2 tsp finely grated root ginger
¼ tsp dried crushed chillies
450g (1lb) sweet potatoes, cut into
 small chunks
1 red pepper, deseeded and chopped
230g can tomatoes

1 tsp cumin seeds, dry-roasted
 and crushed (see p25)
1 tsp coriander seeds, dry-roasted
 and crushed
900ml (1½ pints) hot vegetable stock
2–3 tbsp smooth or crunchy peanut butter
few drops of Tabasco (optional)
chilli oil, to serve

1 Heat the oil in a large pan, add the onion, and fry for 3 minutes. Stir in the garlic, ginger, and chillies and fry for 1 minute, then stir in the sweet potatoes, pepper, tomatoes, and crushed spices and fry for 2 minutes. Pour in the stock, bring to the boil, then simmer for 12–15 minutes or until the sweet potatoes are tender.

2 Remove from the heat and whiz in a blender until smooth. You may need to do this in batches. Pass the soup through a sieve to remove the pepper skin and then stir in the peanut butter, tasting to decide the amount you like. If you want to add more heat, splash in some Tabasco. Reheat gently, then drizzle a little chilli oil over each bowlful to serve.

As a strictly cold-season vegetable, swede stores up lots of starch in the edible root base. It is this that gives this rich, wintry soup its velvety texture. **Celia Brooks Brown**

creamy swede soup

SERVES 4–6   **PREP** 10 MINS **COOK** 40–50 MINS   **FREEZE** UP TO 3 MONTHS
BEFORE CREAM IS ADDED

25g (scant 1oz) butter
2 medium onions, chopped
750g (1lb 10oz) swede (trimmed weight),
   cut into cubes
sea salt and freshly ground black pepper

1 litre (1¾ pints) hot vegetable stock
1 tbsp honey
½ nutmeg
150ml (5fl oz) single cream, plus
   extra to garnish

1 Melt the butter in a large pan over a medium heat. Add the onions, and fry for 6–8 minutes or until lightly golden. Stir in the swede and a pinch of salt, cover with a lid, and cook for 10 minutes, stirring frequently. Pour in the stock, add the honey, and bring to the boil, grating in the nutmeg as you do so. Simmer for 20–30 minutes or until the swede is completely soft.

2 Cool briefly, then whiz in a blender until smooth and velvety. You may need to do this in batches. Season with salt and freshly ground black pepper, then stir in the cream. Serve each bowlful with a swirl of cream and a good grinding of black pepper.

SWEDE
Local soil variations produce different flavours of swede, though smaller generally equals sweeter. Choose swede that are heavy for their size, but not too large. They should be firm, with an unblemished skin.

If you are a fan of smooth soups, you can whiz this in a blender at the end of step 1 and then swirl the pesto through the resulting delicate light green purée.

kohlrabi soup with pesto

SERVES 6　　**PREP** 5 MINS **COOK** 15 MINS　　**FREEZE** UP TO 3 MONTHS

25g (scant 1oz) butter
3–4 kohlrabi, cut into bite-sized dice
1 litre (1¾ pints) hot vegetable stock

2 tbsp crème fraîche
salt and freshly ground black pepper
6 tsp pesto, to garnish

1 Melt the butter in a frying pan, add the kohlrabi, and fry for 5 minutes or until light golden brown. Pour in the stock and bring to the boil. Add the crème fraîche and season with salt and freshly ground black pepper. Cook for 8–10 minutes or until the kohlrabi is tender but not mushy.

2 Taste and adjust the seasoning, then ladle the soup into warm bowls and garnish each with a teaspoon of pesto.

KOHLRABI
Go for kohlrabi that are somewhere between a golf ball and a tennis ball in size. If they are any larger than this, they will be very tough. Store them in a biodegradable plastic bag in the chiller box of the fridge for up to 3 weeks.

Clodagh McKenna, chef, journalist and television presenter, has been a driving force behind the Slow Food movement in Ireland and the country's farmers' markets.

butternut squash soup

🍲 **SERVES** 4 ⏱ **PREP** 10 MINS **COOK** 25 MINS ❄ **FREEZE** UP TO 3 MONTHS
WITHOUT THE CREAM

20g (¾oz) butter
500g (1lb 2oz) butternut squash, deseeded
  and chopped into 2.5cm (1in) pieces
1 medium onion, chopped
1 garlic clove, crushed

a generous grating of nutmeg
500ml (16fl oz) hot chicken stock
100ml (3½fl oz) single or double cream
salt and freshly ground black pepper

1 Melt the butter in a heavy-bottomed saucepan. Add the squash, onion, and garlic, cover with a lid, and cook for 15 minutes, stirring occasionally. Grate in the nutmeg and sweat with the lid on for a further 5 minutes.

2 Stir in the stock and bring to the boil. When the squash is tender, add the cream, and simmer for 1 minute. Transfer the soup to a blender and whiz until smooth. You may need to do this in batches. Season with salt and freshly ground black pepper and serve.

Roasting the squash concentrates and develops its flavour beautifully, and leaves you free to get on with making a chilli-hot rouille sauce, which gives this soup its vigour. **Sophie Grigson**

roast squash soup

SERVES 6   **PREP** 30 MINS **COOK** 50 MINS   ❄ **FREEZE** UP TO 3 MONTHS
AT THE END OF STEP 2

675–900g (1½–2lb) winter squash, such
   as onion squash, red kuri, crown prince,
   or pumpkin, peeled and cut into chunks
450g (1lb) good tomatoes
6 garlic cloves, unpeeled
1 sprig of rosemary
2 sprigs of thyme
1 red onion, cut into 8 wedges
4 tbsp extra virgin olive oil
1.2 litres (2 pints) hot vegetable stock
   or chicken stock

salt and freshly ground black pepper
small pinch of saffron
1 garlic clove, chopped
1 red chilli, deseeded and roughly chopped
1 egg yolk
1 tbsp red wine vinegar
90ml (3fl oz) sunflower oil
4 tbsp extra virgin olive oil
12 croûtes (see p39)
freshly grated Comté or Gruyère, to serve

1 Preheat the oven to 220°C (425°F/Gas 7). Put the first seven ingredients into a roasting tin and turn to coat in oil. Roast, turning occasionally, for 45 minutes or until everything is very tender. Discard the herb stalks, and scrape the rest into a blender. Add the stock and whiz until smooth. You may need to do this in batches. Pour into a large pan and season with salt and freshly ground black pepper.

2 Meanwhile, make a rouille. Soak the saffron in 1 tbsp warm water. Pound the garlic, chilli, and a pinch of salt to a paste in a mortar, then work in the egg yolk and vinegar. Mix the two oils, then drip them in, whisking constantly. When one-third of the oil has been incorporated, increase the flow to a slow trickle. Stir in the saffron in its water, then adjust the seasonings.

3 To serve, reheat the soup, then ladle into bowls. Pass the croûtes, the rouille, and the grated cheese around separately, so everyone can smear the croûtes liberally with rouille, float them in the steaming soup, and then finish with a flurry of grated cheese.

The sharp basil and lime cream melting into this soup is a perfect finish for smart occasions. But for a more everyday supper, you can leave it out. **Sophie Grigson**

winter squash soup with basil and lime cream

◎ **SERVES** 6–8 ● **PREP** 25 MINS **COOK** 35 MINS   ❄ **FREEZE** UP TO 3 MONTHS
WITHOUT BASIL AND LIME CREAM

5 garlic cloves
1 large onion, chopped
2.5cm (1in) piece root ginger, peeled
  and chopped
3 tbsp sunflower oil
1.5 kg (3lb 3oz) winter squash, such as onion
  squash, red kuri, crown prince, or pumpkin,
  seeds and rind removed, roughly cubed
2 sprigs of parsley
1 sprig of thyme
1 bay leaf

3 star anise
350g (12oz) tomatoes, skinned, deseeded,
  and roughly chopped
2 litres (3½ pints) hot vegetable stock
  or chicken stock
salt and freshly ground black pepper
300ml (10fl oz) whipping cream
juice of 1–2 limes
a small handful of basil leaves,
  chopped, to serve

1 Chop two of the garlic cloves, but leave the rest whole. Put the chopped garlic and the whole garlic into a large pan with the onion, ginger, oil, and squash. Tie the herbs together in a bundle and throw those in too. Cover with a lid and sweat over a low heat for 10 minutes, stirring once or twice.

2 Add the star anise, tomatoes, and stock, then season with salt and freshly ground black pepper and bring to the boil. Simmer for 20 minutes or until the squash is tender. Pick out and discard the bundle of herbs and the star anise. Whiz the soup in a blender until smooth and then pass it through a sieve. Alternatively, you can work it through a food mill. Taste and adjust the seasoning, then reheat gently.

3 Meanwhile, pour the cream into a bowl, add the lime juice, and whisk. Once the cream holds its shape loosely, fold in the basil. As you ladle the soup into bowls, top with a floating crown of basil and lime cream.

Monty Don, TV presenter and Soil Association president, says, "This creamy soup is an amazing orange colour. If you use a stock powder or cube, taste before adding extra salt."

pumpkin soup

SERVES 6   **PREP** 10 MINS **COOK** 20 MINS   ❄ **FREEZE** UP TO 3 MONTHS
AT THE END OF STEP 2

1 small pumpkin (or part of a large one),
   about 750g (1lb 10oz) in total, skinned
   and cubed
2 potatoes, peeled and cubed
1 tbsp olive oil
600ml (1 pint) vegetable stock
2 tomatoes, chopped

4 fresh sage leaves
sea salt and freshly ground black pepper

for the garnish
olive oil, for frying
18 large fresh sage leaves

1 Heat the oil in a saucepan and sweat the pumpkin and potatoes
for 5 minutes. Add the stock, chopped tomatoes and the sage leaves.
Cover and simmer for about 10 minutes, until the vegetables are soft.

2 Using a blender, whiz the soup until smooth, then gently reheat.
Season with salt and pepper, to taste.

3 For the garnish, heat a little oil in a frying pan and, once hot, fry the
large sage leaves until crisp. Scatter the crispy leaves over the soup
and serve immediately.

This recipe first appeared in *Fork to Fork* by Monty and Sarah Don,
published by Conran Octopus and reproduced by kind permission

Jeanette Orrey inspired Jamie Oliver's school dinner campaign and is now Advisor to the Soil Association on improving school dinners.

pumpkin and apple soup

⊘ **SERVES** 6   🕐 **PREP** 20 MINS **COOK** 40 MINS   ❄ **FREEZE** UP TO 3 MONTHS

60g (2oz) unsalted butter
1 medium onion, finely chopped
200g (7oz) pumpkin flesh, diced
2 sharp-tasting apples such as
   Granny Smith, diced

150ml (5fl oz) hot water
1.2 litres (2 pints) cold vegetable stock
   or chicken stock
salt and freshly ground black pepper
30g (1oz) toasted pumpkin seeds, to garnish

1 Melt the butter in a large saucepan, add the onion, and cook very gently, stirring often, for 10 minutes or until soft. Do not let it brown. Add the pumpkin and apples and stir to coat well. Pour in the hot water, cover with a lid, and leave on a very, very low heat for 30 minutes, stirring from time to time. If the liquid evaporates, pour in a little more hot water. The vegetables and fruit should be very soft at the end of cooking.

2 Stir in the stock, then blend the soup in batches. As each batch is done, pour it into a sieve set over a clean saucepan. Press the contents through with the back of a ladle, a wooden spoon, or a pestle.

3 When all the soup has been sieved, reheat it very gently, then season to taste with salt and freshly ground black pepper. Serve garnished with the toasted pumpkin seeds.

This chunky country soup takes minutes to prepare and makes a good supper or lunch dish. For a vegetarian option, leave out the lardons. **Marie-Pierre Moine**

french cabbage soup

SERVES 4   **PREP** 15 MINS **COOK** 30 MINS   **FREEZE** UP TO 3 MONTHS
WITHOUT THE LARDON GARNISH

1 tbsp olive oil
100g (3½oz) small lardons, or diced bacon
1 Spanish onion, finely chopped
1 garlic clove, crushed
1 large Savoy cabbage, halved, core
 discarded, and leaves cut into shreds

sea salt and freshly ground black pepper
3 sprigs parsley
croûtons (see p39), to garnish (optional)

1 Heat the oil in a large heavy casserole over a medium heat. Add the lardons (setting aside 2 tbsp to finish), onion, and garlic. Fry, stirring frequently, for 3–4 minutes or until the onion and garlic start to colour. Add the cabbage shreds, reserving a handful to finish. Stir well and season lightly with sea salt and generously with pepper. Continue frying for 2–3 minutes, stirring occasionally.

2 Bring about 850ml (about 1½ pints) water to the boil in a kettle. Pour the boiling water over the vegetables and lardons, stir well, and add the parsley. Cover, lower the heat a little, and simmer gently for about 20 minutes, stirring occasionally.

3 Meanwhile, place a non-stick frying pan over a medium heat. Add the reserved lardons and fry until crisp and golden. Then add the reserved cabbage shreds and fry them until they have wilted, stirring frequently. Season with a little pepper.

4 Taste the soup and adjust the seasoning. Lift out the parsley. Ladle into individual bowls and scatter over the fried bacon and cabbage mixture. A few croûtons scattered across the surface provide a nice finishing touch.

Both soup and meatballs can be prepared ahead of time, but should be stored separately. Allow approximately 30 minutes to reheat and finish off the cooking. **Marie-Pierre Moine**

cabbage and tomato soup with meatballs

SERVES 4 · **PREP** 40 MINS **COOK** 1 HOUR · **FREEZE** UP TO 3 MONTHS
SOUP AND MEATBALLS SEPARATELY

for the meatballs
1 garlic clove, crushed
½ Spanish onion, finely chopped
½ tsp hot smoked paprika
½ tsp ground cumin
1 tsp dried thyme (or fresh leaves)
2 tbsp freshly grated Parmesan cheese
breadcrumbs made from 2 slices bread
400g (14oz) minced steak
1 large egg
sea salt and freshly ground black pepper
3 tbsp plain flour
3 tbsp vegetable oil
15g (½oz) butter

for the soup
2 tbsp vegetable oil
½ Spanish onion, coarsely chopped
1 garlic clove, crushed
250g (9oz) tomatoes, deseeded and chopped
1 large Savoy cabbage, halved, core and ribs
    discarded, and leaves sliced into
    bite-sized pieces
sea salt and freshly ground black pepper
1 litre (1¾ pints) light beef stock
2 tbsp finely chopped parsley, to finish
3 tbsp grated or shaved Parmesan cheese

1 For the meatballs, put the first nine ingredients in a bowl, season, and mix well. Shape into walnut-sized balls and refrigerate for 30 minutes.

2 Put a large deep pan over a medium heat. Add the oil. Tip in the onion, garlic, and tomatoes. Fry for 3–5 minutes, stirring. Add the cabbage, and stir for 3 minutes. Stir in the stock and simmer for 15–20 minutes.

3 Meanwhile, sift the flour onto a plate and coat the meatballs. Heat the oil and butter in a pan over a medium-high heat. Add the meatballs and cook for 3 minutes until they are a rich brown all over. Add to the soup and simmer for 15–20 minutes. Serve scattered with parsley and Parmesan.

Many variations on this Polish dish exist. Bacon, sauerkraut, and smoked Polish sausage are essential, but you could try lamb or beef instead of the duck or venison. **Marie-Pierre Moine**

bigos

SERVES 4   **PREP** 40 MINS **COOK** 2 HRS   **FREEZE** UP TO 3 MONTHS

A small Savoy cabbage, cored, ribs removed, leaves shredded
salt and freshly ground pepper
500g (1lb 2oz) sauerkraut, drained
100g (3½oz) smoked bacon, cubed
200g (7oz) smoked Polish sausage, sliced
200g (7oz) duck breast or lean venison, cubed
1 large red onion, diced
1 clove garlic, crushed

150g (5½oz) brown mushrooms, sliced
½ tsp smoked paprika
1 bay leaf
½ tsp juniper berries
1 tsp dried marjoram
½ tsp caraway seeds, crushed using a pestle and mortar
200ml (7fl oz) red wine
250ml (8fl oz) beef stock

1 Put a large casserole over a medium heat. Add the cabbage, and cover with boiling water. Season lightly. Return to a simmer and cook for 10 minutes. Drain and reserve. Repeat with the sauerkraut but simmer for only 5 minutes. Drain, reserving the sauerkraut as well as the cooking liquid.

2 Put a non-stick frying pan over a medium heat. Fry the bacon until crisp. Spread over a platter lined with kitchen paper. Fry the sausage and duck or venison for 5 minutes, stirring. Then add to the platter with the bacon. Set aside. Now fry the onion, garlic, and mushrooms in the same pan until softened. Then add to the casserole, along with the fried meats.

3 Put the casserole over a medium heat. Stir in the paprika, bay leaf, juniper berries, marjoram, and caraway seeds. Pour in the wine and stock. Bring to a simmer, stirring. Cover, reduce the heat a little, and simmer for 1 hour, stirring from time to time.

4 Add the boiled cabbage, stir, cover, and cook for 10 minutes, and then stir in the sauerkraut. Add some or all of the reserved cooking liquid (the mixture should be a thick soup rather than a stew). Simmer for a further 15 minutes. Taste, adjust the seasoning and serve very hot.

Sauerkraut is an excellent source of vitamin C. This hearty soup is redolent of Eastern Europe, though Chinese cooks were pickling cabbage in wine as early as 200BCE.

sauerkraut soup

⊘ **SERVES** 4 🕐 **PREP** 10 MINS **COOK** 30 MINS ❄ **FREEZE** NOT SUITABLE

2 tablespoons vegetable oil
1 onion, finely chopped
100g (3½oz) bacon, diced
400g (14oz) jar or can sauerkraut,
   roughly chopped

400g (14 oz) can chopped tomatoes, peeled
2 tsp sugar
600ml (1 pint) hot vegetable or chicken stock
200ml (7fl oz) double cream
freshly ground black pepper

1 Heat the vegetable oil in a large saucepan over a low heat. Add the chopped onion and fry gently until softened but not browned. Then add the diced bacon and fry for another 3 minutes. Finally add the chopped sauerkraut, cover, and continue to cook for another 5 minutes, stirring from time to time.

2 Increase the heat under the saucepan slightly and add the chopped tomatoes, sugar, hot stock, double cream, and freshly ground black pepper and stir well. Bring to a simmer over a medium heat for 15 minutes until the sauerkraut is tender. Ladle the soup into bowls to serve and eat with toasted rye bread.

Start off with a good-quality stock for this fragrant, light, refreshing soup, then serve it piled high with fresh herbs and chillies. **Angela Nilsen**

vietnamese noodle soup

⊘ SERVES 4   **⏱ PREP** 25–30 MINS PLUS SOAKING TIME   **❄ FREEZE** NOT SUITABLE
COOK 25 MINS PLUS SITTING TIME

1.2 litres (2 pints) chicken stock, preferably home-made
6 slices root ginger (no need to peel)
½ tsp coriander seeds
4 star anise
2 stalks lemongrass, sliced
2 skinless, boneless chicken breasts
100g (3½oz) rice noodles
2 pak choi, very thinly sliced

thai fish sauce
100g (3½oz) bean sprouts
small bunch coriander, about 20g (¾oz), roughly chopped
small handful mint leaves, finely shredded
2 spring onions, thinly sliced
1 large fresh red chilli, deseeded (unless you like it hot) and thinly sliced
lime wedges

1 Pour the stock into a large saucepan, and tip in the ginger, coriander seeds, star anise, and lemongrass. Simmer gently for 10 minutes. Lower the chicken breasts into the stock and continue simmering for 15 minutes. Remove from the heat and let sit for 5 minutes. Meanwhile, break the noodles (so they are easier to eat) into a large heatproof bowl and cover with boiling water. Leave to soak for the time suggested on the packet.

2 Lift the chicken from the stock with a slotted spoon and transfer it to a board. Slice the chicken into very thin bite-sized strips. Strain and discard the flavourings from the stock and return the stock to the pan. Drop in the pak choi (off the heat) and let it wilt in the warmth of the stock. Return the chicken to the stock along with a dash of fish sauce.

3 Drain the noodles and divide between 4 big bowls. Lay the bean sprouts on top. To serve, ladle the chicken and hot stock over the noodles and top each bowl with a generous scattering of the coriander, mint, and spring onions, the chilli and another splash of fish sauce. Offer lime wedges for squeezing over.

Potato and kale soup (caldo verde) is ubiquitous in Portugal, where cooks use incredibly finely shredded cabbage. Here we have to substitute our own winter greens. **Sophie Grigson**

portuguese potato and kale soup

SERVES 4　　**PREP** 15 20 MINS **COOK** 20–25 MINS　**FREEZE** UP TO 3 MONTHS

450g (1lb) potatoes, peeled and sliced
4 garlic cloves, sliced
1 small onion, finely chopped
salt and freshly ground black pepper

225g (8oz) curly kale, or cavolo nero or
 Savoy cabbage
110g (4oz) chorizo, skin removed and sliced
extra virgin olive oil, to serve

1 Place the potato slices in a large saucepan with the garlic and onion. Season with salt and pepper and add enough water to cover generously. Simmer until tender. Pass through the fine blade of a mouli-legume, or mash to a smooth purée. Add a little more water if necessary to thin to a soupy consistency. Return to the pan and adjust the seasoning, adding plenty of pepper.

2 While the potatoes are cooking, cut the stalks from the kale, then roll up the leaves, and shred very thinly – the resulting threads of cabbage should be around 3mm (⅛in) wide. Bring the soup back to the boil. Stir in the kale and sausage. Simmer for 5 minutes. Ladle into 4 soup bowls, pour a little olive oil onto each, and serve.

KALE
Intense in flavour and vibrant in colour, use locally grown kale with firm stalks and fresh, curly leaves. Or you could grow this hardy vegetable yourself. The tough central stalks should be removed before cooking.

Cauliflower is transformed when treated to gentle heat and aromatic spicing. For a vegetarian option, garnish this with croûtons and Parmesan cheese instead of bacon. **Roopa Gulati**

cauliflower soup with toasted coriander

SERVES 4–6   **PREP** 15–20 MINS **COOK** 40 MINS   **FREEZE** UP TO 1 MONTH
WITHOUT CREAM OR BACON

2 tsp coriander seeds
40g (1½oz) unsalted butter
1 onion, diced
1 potato, diced
1 head cauliflower, finely chopped
500ml (16fl oz) vegetable stock

1 bay leaf
8 streaky bacon rashers, rinds removed
200ml (7fl oz) milk
100ml (3½fl oz) single cream
salt and freshly ground black pepper

1 Heat a sturdy frying pan or small griddle and lightly roast the coriander seeds, stirring all the time, for about a minute. Grind the seeds to a coarse powder using a mortar and pestle and set aside.

2 Melt the butter in a large saucepan over a low heat. Add the onion and potato, cover and leave to soften for 10 minutes. Add the cauliflower and ground coriander, season well, cover and continue cooking for a further 10 minutes.

3 Pour over the stock, add the bay leaf, cover, and simmer for about 15 minutes, until the cauliflower has softened. Meanwhile, cook the bacon rashers under a hot grill until crisp. Drain on kitchen paper, roughly chop, and set aside.

4 Remove the bay leaf and blend the soup to a purée with a stick blender or in a liquidizer. Stir in the milk and add the cream. Reheat and season again if necessary. Ladle the soup into bowls and scatter with the chopped bacon before serving.

Make sure your cauliflower is impeccably fresh, and check that the cheese really is smoked, and not just laced with fake smoke flavouring as so many are. **Sophie Grigson**

smoked cauliflower cheese soup

SERVES 6 **PREP** 15–20 MINS **COOK** 25–30 MINS **FREEZE** UP TO 3 MONTHS
BEFORE CHEESE IS ADDED

1 cauliflower, broken into florets
1 large onion, chopped
1 medium floury potato, cut into cubes
2 garlic cloves, sliced
1 bouquet garni (see p24)
30g (1oz) butter
1 litre (1¾ pints) hot vegetable
  or chicken stock

salt and freshly ground black pepper
100g (3½oz) coarsely grated smoked cheddar
a shake of cayenne pepper, freshly chopped
  parsley or chives, croûtons, or a dollop of
  soured cream, to garnish

1 Sweat the vegetables, garlic, and bouquet garni with the butter in a covered pan over a low heat for 10 minutes, stirring once or twice. Add the stock, a little salt, and loads of freshly ground black pepper and bring to the boil. Simmer until the cauliflower and potato are just tender and no more. Remove the bouquet garni and whiz the soup in a blender until smooth, adding more stock or a little milk to thin it down as necessary.

2 Reheat the soup gently, but do not allow it to boil. Stir in two-thirds of the cheese, taste, and see if you think it needs more. Add it if it does. Taste one more time, then serve with the garnish of your choice.

CAULIFLOWER
You can find various types of organic cauliflower, including purple, orange, white, and miniature. Look for those with tight, firm heads and bright green leaves. The stalks can be used for flavouring soup or stock.

This is an unexpectedly good soup, with all the fresh, nutty flavour of Brussels sprouts tempered by the sweetness of the onion. **Sophie Grigson**

brussels sprouts soup

⊘ SERVES 4–6   **🕐 PREP** 20 MINS **COOK** 1 HR 10 MINS   **❄ FREEZE** UP TO 3 MONTHS
WITHOUT THE SOURED CREAM

450g (1lb) onions, sliced
30g (1oz) butter
1 tbsp caster sugar
450g (1lb) Brussels sprouts, trimmed
  and halved
1 generous sprig thyme

1.2 litres (2 pints) light chicken or
  vegetable stock
salt and freshly ground black pepper
soured cream, crème fraîche, or
  Greek-style yogurt, to serve
paprika or cayenne pepper, to serve

1 Put the onions into a pan with the butter. Cover and sweat over a gentle heat for about 30–40 minutes until the onions are incredibly tender and soft. Sprinkle over the sugar and cook, uncovered, for another 10–15 minutes or so until the onions are lightly coloured and jammy looking, stirring occasionally.

2 Add the sprouts and the thyme and stir. Pour in the stock and season with salt and pepper. Bring up to the boil and simmer for about 10–15 minutes until the sprouts are just tender. Cool slightly, remove the thyme, and liquidize in two batches. Reheat gently if needed, then taste and adjust the seasoning. Serve piping hot, with a spoonful of soured cream, crème fraîche, or yogurt in each bowlful, and a light dusting of paprika or cayenne.

BRUSSELS SPROUTS
Look for locally grown sprouts. They can range from the size of a thumbnail to a golf ball, but smaller equals sweeter. Before using home-grown sprouts, soak them in cold water, as they may contain a few worms.

This earthy soup combines mildly nutty celeriac and more assertive celery to create a fragrant, satisfying winter warmer. **Marie-Pierre Moine**

celery and celeriac soup

SERVES 4   **PREP** 15 MINS **COOK** 20 MINS   **FREEZE** UP TO 3 MONTHS
WITHOUT THE CHILLED BUTTER

1 tbsp sunflower, groundnut, or mild-
  flavoured olive oil
30g (1oz) butter
500g (1lb 2oz) celeriac, peeled and chopped
1 large head celery, cored and chopped
1 medium floury potato, peeled and chopped

sea salt and freshly ground black pepper
1 litre (1¾ pints) light vegetable or
  chicken stock
30g (1oz) chilled butter, diced
4 slices walnut bread, lightly toasted,
  to serve

1 Put the oil and 30g (1oz) butter in a large sauté pan over a medium heat. Add the celeriac, celery, and potato. Stir well for 2–3 minutes then reduce the heat a little. Add 3–4 tbsp water, and season lightly. Partly cover and leave to stew gently until very soft. Stir the vegetables from time to time and keep the heat low.

2 Transfer the cooked vegetables to a food processor and purée. Return to the pan and add the stock. Season, stir briskly to blend, and bring to a simmer over a medium heat, stirring frequently. Reduce the heat a little and leave to simmer gently for 10–15 minutes, still stirring occasionally. Taste and adjust the seasoning.

3 Just before serving, whisk in the chilled diced butter. Serve hot with toasted walnut bread.

CELERY
Most celery found in markets is naturally vibrantly green, but look out for the less bitter blanched white variety, too. Celery's thick outer stalks are best in stews, soups, and casseroles.

Here's a refreshing soup for a warm summer's day. You could use a romaine lettuce heart or even a bunch of watercress instead of chicory, if you prefer. **Carolyn Humphries**

chicory gazpacho

⊘ SERVES 4   **⏱ PREP** 15 MINS PLUS CHILLING   **❄ FREEZE** UP TO 3 MONTHS

1 large orange
2 heads white chicory
2 slices bread, crusts removed
1 garlic clove, roughly chopped
4 spring onions, trimmed and
   roughly chopped
1 large beefsteak tomato, skinned, quartered,
   and deseeded

450ml (15fl oz) cold vegetable stock
2 tbsp olive oil, plus extra for garnish
2 tbsp white balsamic condiment
4 large basil leaves
Salt and freshly ground black pepper

1 Thinly pare the zest of half the orange. Cut in thin strips and boil in water for 1 minute. Drain, rinse with cold water, and drain again. Set aside for garnish. Finely grate the zest from the remaining orange, squeeze the juice, and set aside.

2 Cut a cone shape out of the base of each head of chicory and discard. Separate the heads into spears. Reserve four of the smallest spears for the garnish. Roughly chop the remainder.

3 Soak the bread in water for 2 minutes. Squeeze out some of the moisture then put the bread in a blender with the chopped chicory, garlic, spring onions, tomato, stock, olive oil, white balsamic condiment, and the basil leaves, the orange juice and finely grated zest. Purée the soup in a blender or food processor then season to taste. Chill until ready to serve.

4 Ladle into four shallow soup plates, and drizzle with a little olive oil. Garnish each with a tiny chicory spear and a few strands of blanched orange zest. Serve cold.

This simple soup recipe with onion, garlic, and parsley brings out the flavour of mixed wild mushrooms beautifully. Delicious served with soured cream. **Anna Del Conte**

mixed fungi soup

◎ SERVES 4　　**◷ PREP** 15 MINS **COOK** 1 HR　　**❄ FREEZE** UP TO 3 MONTHS

75g (2½oz) unsalted butter
100g (3½oz) onion, finely chopped
1 garlic clove, finely chopped
15g (½oz) flat-leaf parsley, chopped
225g (8oz) mixed wild mushrooms, diced
4 tbsp milk

salt and freshly ground black pepper
grated nutmeg
40g (1½oz) flour
1.2 litres (2 pints) vegetable or chicken stock
4 tbsp soured cream

1 Heat half the butter with the onion, garlic, and parsley in a sauté pan and cook for 3 minutes. Add the mushrooms, and sauté for another 3 minutes. Pour in the milk, and season with salt and nutmeg. Cook for a few more minutes and set aside.

2 In another saucepan, melt the remaining butter. Remove the pan from the heat and beat in the flour. Return the pan to a low heat and cook until the mixture deepens in colour. Remove the pan from the heat once more, and add the stock gradually by the ladleful. Stir constantly to avoid lumps forming, and return the pan to a low heat.

3 When all the stock has been combined with the flour, add the mushroom mixture and the juices. Bring to the boil, and simmer for 15–20 minutes. Season with salt and pepper to taste. Spoon a tablespoon of soured cream into each bowl and serve.

MUSHROOMS
Many different varieties of wild mushrooms can be found in farmers' markets or in the wild. If you're new to foraging, or unsure about which mushrooms are safe to eat, take a good identification book, or stick to the markets.

This hearty Italian country soup has deep, earthy flavours. Check the mushrooms after soaking, as there may be bits of dirt or straw that need removing.

porcini mushroom soup

◎ SERVES 4   **🕐 PREP** 20 MINS, PLUS 30 MINS STANDING   **❄ FREEZE** UP TO 3 MONTHS
COOK 1 HR   WITHOUT THE BREAD

30g (1oz) dried porcini
3 tbsp extra virgin olive oil, plus extra
   to serve
2 onions, finely chopped
2 tsp chopped fresh rosemary leaves
1 tsp fresh thyme leaves
2 garlic cloves, finely sliced

115g (4oz) chestnut mushrooms, sliced
2 celery sticks with leaves, finely chopped
400g (14oz) can chopped tomatoes
750ml (1¼ pints) vegetable stock
salt and freshly ground black pepper
½ stale ciabatta or small crusty white loaf,
   torn into chunks

1 Put the dried porcini in a heatproof bowl, pour over 300ml (10fl oz) boiling water, and leave to stand for 30 minutes. Drain, reserving the soaking liquid, then chop any large pieces of porcini.

2 Heat the oil in a saucepan, add the onions, cover, and leave to cook for 10 minutes, or until soft. Add the rosemary, thyme, garlic, chestnut mushrooms, and celery, and continue cooking, uncovered, until the celery has softened.

3 Add the tomatoes, porcini, and the stock. Strain the soaking liquid through a piece of muslin or a fine sieve into the pan. Bring the soup to the boil, then lower the heat and simmer gently for 45 minutes.

4 Season to taste with salt and pepper, and add the chunks of bread. Remove the pan from the heat. Cover and leave to stand for 10 minutes before serving. Spoon into deep bowls and drizzle each serving with a little olive oil.

in praise of...
mushrooms
Nothing is more
satisfying to a cook
than a mushroom
soup: first the foraging
in the wood or choosing
the best specimens
from the market, then
the making of the dish,
and finally the eating.
Anna del Conte

Using a selection of both wild and cultivated mushrooms produces a soup bursting with flavour. The horseradish cream provides a welcome kick.

mushroom soup

⊘ **SERVES** 4   🕐 **PREP** 10 MINS **COOK** 45 MINS   ❄ **FREEZE** UP TO 3 MONTHS

30g (1oz) butter
1 onion, finely chopped
2 celery sticks, finely chopped
1 garlic clove, crushed
450g (1lb) mixed mushrooms, roughly chopped

200g (7oz) potatoes, peeled and cubed
1 litre (1¾ pints) vegetable stock
2 tbsp finely chopped fresh parsley
salt and freshly ground black pepper
horseradish cream, to serve (optional)

1 Melt the butter in a large saucepan, add the onion, celery, and garlic, and fry for 3–4 minutes, or until softened.

2 Stir in the mushrooms and continue to fry for a further 5–6 minutes. Add the potatoes and the stock, and bring to the boil. Reduce the heat and leave to simmer gently for 30 minutes.

3 Using a blender, whiz the soup until smooth, working in batches if necessary. Sprinkle over the parsley and season to taste with salt and pepper. Serve immediately, stirring a little horseradish cream into each soup bowl, if desired, for an extra kick.

pulses
and nuts

This soup contains annatto. If you've never used the spice before, it has a sweet peppery flavour and an orangey red colour. It is widely used in Latin America. **Carolyn Humphries**

cuban black bean soup

SERVES 4   **PREP** 20 MINS, PLUS OVERNIGHT SOAKING   **FREEZE** UP TO 3 MONTHS
COOK 1¾ HRS

225g (8oz) dried black beans, soaked in cold water overnight
1 bay leaf
450ml (15fl oz) chicken stock or ham stock
1 tbsp sunflower oil
1 large onion, finely chopped
1 garlic clove, crushed
½ tsp ground cumin
½ tsp ground annatto

pinch of ground cloves
1 beefsteak tomato, skinned and chopped
1 tsp white wine vinegar
115g (4oz) cooked ham, diced
1½ tsp light brown sugar
salt and freshly ground black pepper
a few torn coriander leaves, to garnish
corn tortilla chips, crushed, to serve
grated Cheddar, to serve

1 Drain the soaked beans and put in a large saucepan with enough water to cover by 5cm (2in). Add the bay leaf, bring to the boil, then boil rapidly for 10 minutes. Reduce the heat, cover loosely with a lid, and simmer gently for 1 hour or until really tender. Drain, reserving the liquid. Add enough stock to the cooking liquid to make 900ml (1½ pints) in all.

2 Discard the bay leaf and coarsely purée the beans and some of the stock in a blender – the mixture should not be completely smooth. Alternatively, crush with a potato masher, then set aside.

3 Heat the oil in the rinsed-out pan, add the onion, and fry gently, stirring, for 3–4 minutes or until softened but not browned. Add the garlic and fry for 1 minute, then add the spices and fry for 30 seconds. Add the tomato and vinegar and cook, stirring, for 3–5 minutes or until pulpy.

4 Add the beans, the remaining stock, and the ham. Bring to the boil, reduce the heat, and simmer gently for 20 minutes or until thickened. Season with salt and freshly ground black pepper, then ladle into bowls, garnish with the coriander, and sprinkle with tortilla chips and cheese.

If you can, make this soup in advance and let it stand for a while before reheating – it will be even better. It's also good made with overgrown runner beans, podded. **Celia Brooks Brown**

black-eyed bean soup

⊘ SERVES 4–6　　**⏱ PREP** 15 MINS **COOK** 40 MINS　　**❄ FREEZE** UP TO 3 MONTHS

1 tbsp virgin rapeseed oil or sunflower oil
3 leeks, cleaned and sliced
1 small red pepper, chopped
1 small yellow pepper, chopped
3 garlic cloves
5cm (2in) piece fresh ginger, peeled and
　grated or roughly chopped
1 small red chilli
1 tsp cumin seeds

sea salt and freshly ground black pepper
2 x 400g cans black-eyed beans, drained,
　rinsed, and drained again
400ml (14fl oz) coconut milk
500ml (16fl oz) hot vegetable stock
1 tsp brown sugar
fresh coriander leaves, to garnish
lime wedges, to serve

1 Heat the oil in a saucepan over a medium heat, add the leeks and peppers, cover, and cook, stirring frequently, for 5–7 minutes or until soft. Meanwhile, put the garlic, ginger, chilli, cumin, and 1 tsp salt in a blender with 4 tbsp water and whiz until completely smooth. Add to the pan, using a little more water to rinse out every last bit. Cook, stirring, for 2–3 minutes or until most of the liquid has evaporated.

2 Add the beans, coconut milk, stock, sugar, and a good grinding of black pepper and bring to the boil. Reduce the heat to a simmer and cook gently for 30 minutes, stirring frequently. Taste for seasoning, then serve each bowlful garnished with fresh coriander and a lime wedge.

BLACK-EYED BEANS
So called because of the "black eye" where the bean was originally joined to the pod, black-eyed beans have a creamy, pea-like flavour. When shopping for them, choose organic beans that have been canned without sugar and salt.

This hearty, substantial soup improves with reheating, so it benefits from being made a day in advance. Reheat gently over a low heat.

tuscan bean soup

⊘ **SERVES** 4   🕐 **PREP** 15 MINS **COOK** 1 HR 20 MINS   ❄ **FREEZE** UP TO 3 MONTHS
AT THE END OF STEP 2

4 tbsp extra virgin olive oil, plus extra
   for drizzling
1 onion, chopped
2 carrots, sliced
1 leek, sliced
2 garlic cloves, chopped
400g (14oz) can chopped tomatoes
1 tbsp tomato purée
900ml (1¾ pints) chicken stock

salt and freshly ground black pepper
400g (14oz) can borlotti beans, flageolet
   beans, or cannellini beans, drained
   and rinsed
250g (9oz) baby spinach leaves or spring
   greens, shredded
8 slices ciabatta bread
grated Parmesan cheese, for sprinkling

1 Heat the oil in a large saucepan and fry the onion, carrot, and leek over a low heat for 10 minutes, or until softened but not coloured. Add the garlic and fry for 1 minute. Add the tomatoes, tomato purée, and stock. Season to taste with salt and pepper.

2 Mash half the beans with a fork and add to the pan. Bring to the boil, then lower the heat and simmer for 30 minutes. Add the remaining beans and spinach to the pan. Simmer for a further 30 minutes.

3 Toast the bread until golden, place 2 pieces in each soup bowl, and drizzle with olive oil. To serve, spoon the soup into the bowls, top with a sprinkling of Parmesan, and drizzle with a little more olive oil.

Robust, garlicky, and fragrant with rosemary and sage, this is a hearty, satisfying soup. Serve it with some fresh crusty bread and a drizzle of good-quality olive oil.

bean and rosemary soup

⊘ SERVES 8   **🕙 PREP** 15 MINS **COOK** 40 MINS   **❄ FREEZE** UP TO 3 MONTHS

2 tbsp olive oil
2 onions, finely chopped
salt and freshly ground black pepper
1 tbsp finely chopped fresh rosemary leaves
a few fresh sage leaves, finely chopped
4 celery stalks, finely chopped

3 garlic cloves, grated or finely chopped
2 tbsp tomato purée
2 x 400g cans borlotti beans, drained, rinsed, and drained again
1.2 litres (2 pints) hot chicken stock
2.5kg (5½lb) potatoes, cut into chunky pieces

1 Heat the oil in a large pan, add the onions, and cook over a low heat for 6–8 minutes or until soft and translucent. Season well with salt and freshly ground black pepper, then stir in the rosemary, sage, celery, and garlic and cook over a very low heat, stirring occasionally, for 10 minutes.

2 Stir in the tomato purée and beans and cook gently for 5 minutes. Pour in the stock, bring to the boil, then add the potatoes and simmer gently for 15 minutes or until cooked. Taste, season with salt and freshly ground black pepper, if needed, and serve.

This is so thick and hearty it is a meal in itself – a real family soup. For children, try topping it with some broken-up tortilla chips. **Angela Nilsen**

mexican chilli bean soup

SERVES 4 **PREP** 10 MINS **COOK** 40 MINS **FREEZE** UP TO 3 MONTHS
AT THE END OF STEP 2

2 tbsp sunflower oil
1 onion, chopped
1 small red pepper, deseeded and
   finely chopped
2 garlic cloves, finely chopped
400g (14oz) lean minced beef
1 tsp ground cumin
2 tsp medium or hot chilli powder
½ tsp dried oregano
400g (14oz) can chopped plum tomatoes

2 tbsp tomato purée
750ml (1¼ pints) hot vegetable stock
   or chicken stock
400g (14oz) can red kidney beans, drained,
   rinsed, and drained again
handful of chopped flat-leaf parsley
salt and freshly ground black pepper
soured cream or natural yogurt, to serve
grated Cheddar, to serve
4 warm tortillas (optional), to serve

1 Heat the oil in a large saucepan, add the onion, and fry for 5 minutes. Add the pepper and garlic and stir-fry for 2 minutes. Add the mince and stir-fry for 5 minutes or until it has broken up and browned. Stir in the cumin, chilli powder, and oregano and fry for another minute or so.

2 Stir in the tomatoes, tomato purée, and stock, then simmer for 20–25 minutes or until reduced slightly and a good soupy consistency. Add the beans and simmer for another 5 minutes. Stir in half the parsley and season with salt and freshly ground black pepper.

3 Ladle into bowls and serve topped with a spoonful of soured cream or yogurt, a scattering of Cheddar, and the rest of the parsley.

RED KIDNEY BEANS
Valued for their colour and the robust, sweet flavour they acquire during cooking, red kidney beans are otherwise known as chilli beans. When buying them canned, go for organic beans preserved without salt or sugar.

This hearty, wholesome soup takes the edge off chilly winter weather. It's worth using dried beans, which have a much fuller flavour than the canned variety. **Roopa Gulati**

creamy kidney bean soup

SERVES 6 | **PREP** 20 MINS **COOK** 3¼ HRS
OR 40 MINS IN A PRESSURE COOKER | **FREEZE** UP TO 3 MONTHS
AT THE END OF STEP 3

225g (8oz) dried kidney beans, soaked
   overnight in cold water
2 red onions, diced
400g can chopped tomatoes
1 tbsp tomato purée
5 garlic cloves, halved
5cm (2in) fresh root ginger, roughly chopped
3 large green chillies
salt and freshly ground black pepper

150ml (5fl oz) single cream
squeeze of fresh lime juice, to taste

for the garnish
1 small mouli, coarsely grated, or 4–6 red
   radishes, sliced
1 large green chilli, finely chopped
2 tbsp chopped fresh coriander leaves
squeeze of fresh lime juice, to taste

1 Drain the kidney beans, discarding the soaking liquid. Put the beans in a very large heavy-bottomed pan and cover with 1.7 litres (3 pints) of water. Add the onions, tomatoes, tomato purée, garlic, ginger, and chillies.

2 Cover the pan and simmer for about 3 hours, until the beans are just breaking up. Top up the liquid if required during cooking. Alternatively, use a pressure cooker – the beans will be tender in about 30 minutes.

3 Once the beans have cooled slightly, scoop out the chillies. Using a blender, whiz the soup until smooth in batches, then sieve to remove the skins. Season well with salt and pepper, stir in the cream and reheat. Add lime juice to taste.

4 For the garnish, combine the grated mouli or sliced radish with the green chilli and coriander leaves. Sharpen with a squeeze of lime, then top each bowl of soup with a small heap of the herby mouli.

A quick homemade version of pesto is spooned on top of this butter bean soup, giving it extra flavour, colour, and texture – perfect for serving at a supper party. **Angela Nilsen**

butterbean soup with rocket pesto

🍲 **SERVES** 4   🕐 **PREP** 20 MINS **COOK** 20 MINS   ❄ **FREEZE** UP TO 3 MONTHS
SOUP AND PESTO SEPARATELY

2 tbsp olive oil
1 onion, chopped
2 celery sticks, halved lengthways, sliced
2 garlic cloves, chopped
4 slices prosciutto, chopped
pinch dried crushed chillies
handful basil leaves, shredded
900ml (1½ pints) vegetable or chicken stock
50g (1¾oz) spaghetti, broken into pieces
400g (14oz) can butter beans, drained

for the pesto
25g (scant 1oz) rocket, very finely chopped
2 tbsp very finely chopped basil
25g (scant 1oz) Parmesan cheese, grated
25g (scant 1oz) pine nuts, toasted, very
  finely chopped
1 small garlic clove, finely chopped
3 tbsp olive oil
salt and freshly ground back pepper

1 Heat the oil for the soup in a large saucepan. Add the onion and celery and fry for 4–5 minutes until the onion is soft but not brown. Add the garlic and fry for 1 minute. Stir in the prosciutto and chillies and fry another 1–2 minutes until the prosciutto is starting to go crisp. Stir in the basil, stock, and spaghetti. Bring to the boil. Simmer for about 10 minutes or until the spaghetti is al dente. Tip in the butter beans and warm through.

2 Spoon 3 ladlefuls of the soup into a food processor or blender and whiz until smooth. Stir it back into the rest of the soup and season to taste.

3 Mix all the ingredients for the pesto together in a bowl or roughly chop in a small blender. Season it with pepper and a pinch of salt. Reheat the soup and serve with a spoonful of pesto on top.

Livia Firth, wife of actor Colin, is founder of the ethical homeware store ECO. "I use leeks as the base of my soups as they are sweeter than onions."

cannellini bean and carrot soup

SERVES 4-6   **PREP** 10 MINS **COOK** 1 HR   **FREEZE** UP TO 3 MONTHS

3–4 leeks, finely sliced
1 tbsp olive oil
20g (¾oz) butter
410g tin cannellini beans, drained and rinsed, then drained again

3 medium carrots, finely chopped
salt and freshly ground black pepper
1 tsp medium curry powder (optional)
750ml (1¼ pints) cold water
extra virgin olive oil, to serve

1 Warm the oil and melt the butter in a large, deep pan over a very low heat. Add the leeks and cook for at least 10 minutes, adding a tiny bit of water when the leeks start to stick to the bottom of the pan.

2 Add the cannellini beans and carrots, then turn up the heat and stir well with a wooden spoon to mix the vegetables and flavours together. Allow it to simmer for 5–6 minutes. Season the soup with salt, and stir in the curry powder, if using. Add the water and bring to the boil. Cover with a lid, and simmer for 45 minutes.

3 Transfer the mixture to a blender and whiz till smooth, then ladle into serving bowls. Encourage your guests to add a bit of olive oil and some freshly ground black pepper to their soup – it makes a wonderful finishing touch.

This thick soup from northern Italy is guaranteed to keep out the winter chills. Soak the beans overnight to rehydrate them and cut down on the cooking time.

white bean soup

SERVES 4   **PREP** 30 MINS **COOK** 2 HRS   ✳ **FREEZE** UP TO 3 MONTHS
AT THE END OF STEP 3

3 tbsp olive oil
2 onions, finely chopped
2 garlic cloves, crushed
225g (8oz) dried cannellini beans,
   soaked overnight
1 celery stick, chopped
1 bay leaf
3–4 parsley stalks, without leaves

1 tbsp lemon juice
1.2 litres (2 pints) vegetable stock
salt and freshly ground black pepper
3 shallots, thinly sliced
60g (2oz) pancetta, chopped (optional)
85g (3oz) fontina cheese or Taleggio cheese,
   chopped into small pieces

1 Heat 2 tbsp olive oil in a saucepan, add the onions, and fry over a low heat for 10 minutes, or until softened, stirring occasionally. Add the garlic and cook, stirring, for 1 minute.

2 Drain the soaked beans and add to the pan with the celery, bay leaf, parsley stalks, lemon juice, and stock. Bring to the boil, cover, and simmer for 1½ hours, or until the beans are soft, stirring occasionally.

3 Remove the bay leaf and liquidize the soup in batches in a blender, or through a hand mill. Rinse out the pan. Return the soup to the pan and season to taste with salt and pepper.

4 Heat the remaining olive oil in a small frying pan, and fry the shallots and pancetta (if using) until golden and crisp, stirring frequently to stop them sticking to the pan. Reheat the soup, adding a little stock or water if it is too thick. Stir the fontina into the soup. Ladle into individual bowls, and sprinkle each serving with the shallots and pancetta.

Flageolet beans give texture while rosemary and dried mushrooms provide loads of flavour for this rustic Italian-style soup. **Angela Nilsen**

rosemary's bean soup with italian cheese crisps

SERVES 4 **PREP** 10 MINS PLUS 20 MINS SOAKING **COOK** 15–20 MINS **FREEZE** UP TO 3 MONTHS WITHOUT CHEESE CRISPS

12g (½oz) dried porcini mushrooms, covered in water to soak
50g (1¾oz) Grana Padano, pecorino, or Parmesan cheese, grated
1½ tsp very finely chopped rosemary
2 tbsp olive oil
1 onion, chopped

2 garlic cloves, chopped
3 rosemary sprigs
2 400g (14oz) cans flageolet beans, drained and rinsed
600ml (1 pint) vegetable stock
extra virgin olive oil, for drizzling
ciabatta loaf cut into chunks, to serve

1 Preheat the oven to 200°C (400°F/Gas 6). Let the mushrooms soak for 20 minutes. Meanwhile make the cheese crisps. Line a baking sheet with parchment. Scatter the cheese and half the rosemary in a thin, even layer on the sheet in an 18cm (7in) circle. Bake for 8 minutes or until it starts to turn golden round the edges. Remove and leave to cool and firm on the sheet. Now strain the mushrooms and chop them. Reserve the liquid.

2 Heat the oil in a large saucepan, add the onion, and soften for 4–5 minutes. Stir in the garlic, chopped mushrooms, and rosemary. Fry for 2–3 minutes. Add the beans, stock, and 6 tbsp of the reserved mushroom liquid. Simmer for 10 minutes. Remove the rosemary. Roughly purée about three-quarters of the soup. Pour this back into the pan with the rest of the soup. Season to taste then warm through.

3 Break the cheese crisps into large pieces. For each serving, sprinkle with the rest of the chopped rosemary, drizzle with the oil and accompany with the cheese crisps and ciabatta.

Lime gives a distinctive, vibrant twist to this clean-tasting, healthy soup from New Mexico. It has the added advantage of being very quick and easy to prepare. **Marie-Pierre Moine**

green lentil soup with lime

SERVES 4   **PREP** 5 MINS **COOKING** 30 MINS   ❄ **FREEZE** UP TO 3 MONTHS
AT THE END OF STEP 3

1 litre (1¾ pints) light chicken stock
2–3 sprigs fresh thyme
300g (10oz) green lentils

sea salt and freshly ground black pepper
grated zest and juice of 1 organic lime

1 Pour the stock into a saucepan over a medium heat. Add the thyme and bring to a simmer.

2 Add the lentils, and season lightly. Return to a simmer, cover, reduce the heat a little. Cook for 20–25 minutes until the lentils are very soft.

3 Turn off the heat and leave to cool for several minutes. Transfer to a blender or food processor, and whiz until just smooth.

4 Pour the soup back into the saucepan and stir in the lime zest and juice. Reheat gently, taste, and adjust the seasoning. Serve very hot.

This hearty vegetarian soup has just a touch of spice and is quick and easy to prepare. Serve with plain, low-fat yogurt and good crusty bread.

lentil soup

SERVES 4 **PREP** 20 MINS **COOK** 35 MINS **FREEZE** UP TO 3 MONTHS

1 tbsp olive oil
2 onions, finely chopped
2 celery sticks, finely chopped
2 carrots, finely chopped
2 garlic cloves, crushed

1–2 tsp curry powder
150g (5½oz) red lentils
1.4 litres (2½ pints) vegetable stock
120ml (4fl oz) tomato juice or vegetable juice
salt and freshly ground black pepper

1 Heat the oil in a large pan over a medium heat, then add the onions, celery, and carrots. Cook, stirring, for 5 minutes, or until the onions are soft and translucent.

2 Add the garlic and curry powder and cook, stirring, for a further 1 minute, then add the lentils, stock, and tomato juice.

3 Bring to the boil, then lower the heat, cover, and simmer for 25 minutes, or until the vegetables are tender. Season to taste with salt and pepper, and serve hot.

This Moroccan bean and lentil soup is a meal in a bowl often eaten for breakfast during Ramadan, to keep people going right through a day of fasting. **Sophie Grigson**

harira

⊘ **SERVES** 6-8   🕐 **PREP** 15 MINS **COOK** 1 HR 5 MINS   ❄ **FREEZE** UP TO 3 MONTHS

1 large onion, chopped
2 tbsp olive oil
300-500g (10oz–1lb 2oz) shoulder
  of lamb on the bone
1 tsp ground ginger
1 tsp ground cinnamon
leaves of 1 small bunch parsley,
  finely chopped
leaves of 1 small bunch coriander,
  finely chopped

150g (5½oz) brown lentils, rinsed
400g can chopped tomatoes
2 tbsp tomato purée
salt and pepper
100g (3½oz) vermicelli
400g can chickpeas, drained,
  or 400g (14oz) cooked chickpeas
30g (1oz) plain flour
lemon wedges, to serve

1 Cook the onion gently in the oil until tender and translucent. While it cooks, cut the meat from the lamb bones in 3cm (1¼in) cubes. Do not throw out the bones.

2 Once the onions are tender, stir in the spices, half the parsley and half the coriander, then add the meat and bones and turn to coat evenly. Add the lentils, tomatoes and tomato purée and season. Mix well and simmer for a few minutes, then add 1.7 litres (3 pints) of water. Leave to simmer for 45 minutes. Remove the lamb bones and add the vermicelli and chickpeas.

3 Put the flour in a small bowl with a ladleful of the cooking liquid and stir to make a smooth paste the consistency of thick cream, adding more liquid if needed. Stir this back into the soup and simmer for 3-4 minutes until it has thickened and the vermicelli is cooked.

4 Just before serving, stir in the remaining herbs and adjust the seasoning. Serve with wedges of lemon.

This vegetable and lentil dish is best served piping hot, in cavernous bowls. You can find pink lentils (*masoor dal*) in Asian food stores. **Roopa Gulati**

kichidi

⊘ **SERVES** 6-8   🕐 **PREP** 15 MINS **COOK** 50 MINS   ❋ **FREEZE** UP TO 3 MONTHS
WITHOUT THE LIME AND CORIANDER

1 butternut squash, about 700g (1lb 9oz)
½ tsp garam masala
salt and pepper
2 tbsp olive oil
100g (3½oz) basmati rice
100g (3½oz) pink or red lentils
5cm (2in) ginger, peeled and finely grated

2 tbsp ghee or clarified butter
2 tsp cumin seeds
½ tsp red chilli flakes
juice of 1 lime
3 tbsp chopped coriander
2 tbsp unsalted butter

1 Preheat the oven to 200°C (400°F/Gas 6). Halve the squash lengthways and scoop out the seeds and fibres. Put it in a roasting tin, cut side up, sprinkle with the garam masala, season and drizzle with the oil. Cover with foil and roast for 45 minutes, or until meltingly tender. Leave to cool slightly then scoop out the flesh, lightly crush it with a fork and set aside.

2 Meanwhile, combine the rice and lentils in a large saucepan and cover with 2 litres (3½ pints) of water. Add the ginger, bring to the boil, then reduce the heat and simmer for about 30 minutes until the rice grains have lost their texture and broken down. Add more hot water to loosen the texture if needed. Stir in the lightly crushed squash.

3 Heat the ghee in a separate pan and fry the cumin and chilli for about 30 seconds, until aromatic and darker in colour. Tip the spices and ghee into the rice and lentils and stir well, seasoning with plenty more salt and pepper. Stir in the lime juice and coriander.

4 Divide between deep bowls and finish with a generous dollop of butter in the centre of each helping.

Small, dark green, and with a distinctive earthy flavour, puy lentils are less floury than paler or red lentils, and they cook quickly without disintegrating. **Marie-Pierre Moine**

puy lentil soup

SERVES 4   **PREP** 20 MINS **COOK** 45 MINS   **FREEZE** UP TO 3 MONTHS
AT THE END OF STEP 2

3 tbsp fruity olive oil, plus extra for serving
1 Spanish onion, finely chopped
1 garlic clove, crushed
400g (14oz) puy lentils, rinsed and drained
salt and freshly ground black pepper
2 thick gammon steaks, 100g (3½oz) each

2 sprigs of fresh thyme
2 sprigs of flat leaf parsley
1 tbsp finely chopped parsley, to serve
1 tsp grated zest of an unwaxed lemon, to serve

1 Put 1½ tbsp oil in a large, heavy saucepan over a moderate heat. Fry the onion and garlic for 2–3 minutes until golden and softened, stirring frequently. Stir in the lentils and season with salt and pepper. Put one of the gammon steaks on top of the lentils and add the thyme and parsley. Pour in enough cold water to cover the lentils and gammon with an extra 3cm (1¼in) water on top. Bring gently to a simmer, partially cover and cook for 25–30 minutes until the lentils are cooked through.

2 Lift out the cooked gammon and chop into small pieces. Discard the parsley and thyme. Reserving 3 ladlefuls of soup, put the contents of the pan with the chopped gammon in a blender or food processor and whiz until smooth. Return to the pan and stir in the reserved mixture.

3 Gently reheat until piping hot. Meanwhile, using the rest of the oil, fry the second gammon steak in a non-stick frying pan over a moderately high heat for 4–5 minutes, turning after 3 minutes, until cooked through and crisp and golden on both sides. Cut into small chunky pieces.

4 Taste and adjust the seasoning. Stir the soup and ladle into warmed bowls. Scatter the crispy gammon over the top and add a drizzle of extra virgin olive oil. Finish with a little chopped parsley and lemon zest, mixed together.

This chunky vegetable soup owes much of its appeal to the robust nature of homemade harissa, which can be made in advance and stored in the refrigerator. **Roopa Gulati**

harissa and chickpea soup

⊘ **SERVES** 4   🕒 **PREP** 25 MINS **COOK** 45 MINS   ❄ **FREEZE** UP TO 3 MONTHS

for the harissa paste
1 red pepper
2 tbsp olive oil
½ tsp coriander seeds
2 tsp cumin seeds
1 tsp caraway seeds
2 tsp tomato purée
3 garlic cloves, roughly chopped
4 red chillies, seeds removed, roughly
  chopped
1 tsp smoked paprika
juice of 1 lemon

for the soup
1 tbsp olive oil
100g (3½oz) smoked pancetta, cubed
2 red onions, diced
1 potato, peeled and diced
3 sticks celery, diced
1 small fennel, thinly sliced
3 tbsp oregano leaves, chopped
400g (14oz) can chopped tomatoes
750ml (1¼ pints) vegetable stock
400g (14oz) can chickpeas, drained
1 bay leaf

1 To make the harissa, rub the red pepper with olive oil and cook under a hot grill for 10–15 minutes, turning frequently, until the skin is blackened and charred. Remove to a bowl, cover with cling film, and leave to cool. Peel away the skin, discard the seeds, and roughly chop the flesh.

2 Heat a small frying pan over a low heat and roast the coriander, cumin and caraway seeds for about a minute, stirring. Using a mortar and pestle, pound the spices to a powder. Transfer to a food processor and add the red pepper along with the tomato purée, garlic, red chillies, paprika, and lemon juice. Process until smooth, gradually adding the remaining olive oil.

3 For the soup, heat the olive oil in a large saucepan and fry the pancetta until golden, then remove. Add the onion, potato, celery, fennel, and oregano to the pan. Cover and soften over a low heat for 10 minutes. Stir in 1–2 tbsp of the harissa paste and the tomatoes and continue cooking for 5 minutes. Add the stock, pancetta, chickpeas, and bay leaf. Season well and simmer in a half-covered pan for 20 minutes. Remove the bay leaf and serve.

Shaun Hill of The Walnut Tree, near Abergavenny, says, "The drumstick makes this a questionable dish for your vegetarian friends – unless you are an accomplished liar."

chickpea soup

SERVES 6   **PREP** 15 MINS, PLUS OVERNIGHT SOAKING   **FREEZE** UP TO 3 MONTHS
COOK 1 HR 40 MINS

200g (7oz) chickpeas, soaked in water
overnight, then drained
2.5 litres (4¼ pints) cold water
1 chicken drumstick
4 tbsp olive oil
2 celery stalks, chopped
1 medium onion, chopped

1 medium leek, chopped
3 garlic cloves, finely sliced
salt and freshly ground black pepper
100ml (3½fl oz) dry white wine
1 tbsp lemon juice
6 tbsp extra virgin olive oil, to serve
2 tbsp chopped chives and parsley, to garnish

1 Put the chickpeas in a saucepan with plenty of cold water and bring to the boil. Skim away any foam with a slotted spoon, then drain and return to the pan. Add the cold water and chicken, bring to the boil, and skim again. Cover with a lid and simmer for 1½ hours or until the peas are done. Lift out the chicken after 45 minutes, remove the meat, and set to one side.

2 Heat 1 tbsp of the oil in a frying pan, add the celery, onion, and leek, and cook for 5–10 minutes or until soft. Add the garlic, season with salt and freshly ground black pepper, then fry for another minute. Add the contents of the frying pan to the chickpeas, then stir in the cooked chicken. Pour in a little water if the mixture seems too thick to blend.

3 Transfer the soup to a blender and whiz in batches until smooth, adding the wine, lemon juice, and the remaining 3 tbsp olive oil in three or four stages. Season with salt and freshly ground black pepper, then return to the pan and heat through. Divide the soup among six bowls, float 1 tbsp of extra virgin olive oil on the top of each one, then serve garnished with the chopped chives and parsley.

If chervil isn't available, you can replace it with a few leaves of fresh mint to finish. You can also use frozen baby peas if fresh peas in the pod are out of season. **Marie-Pierre Moine**

potage saint germain

⚫ **SERVES** 4   🕐 **PREP** 15 MINS **COOK** 1 HR   ❄ **FREEZE** UP TO 3 MONTHS
BEFORE MADEIRA IS ADDED

1 tbsp sunflower, groundnut, or
  mild-flavoured olive oil
15g (½oz) butter plus 25g (scant 1oz)
  chilled butter, diced
4 large spring onions (white parts only),
  chopped
1.5 litres (2¾ pints) hot chicken or
  light vegetable stock
150g (5½oz) split green peas, rinsed
  and drained

sea salt and freshly ground black pepper
500g (1lb 2oz) shelled garden peas
  (about 800g/1¾lb unshelled)
1 small head soft lettuce, leaves snipped
1 large egg yolk
3 tbsp crème fraîche
1–2 tbsp Madeira or port
few sprigs of chervil

1 Put a large sauté pan over a medium heat. Add the oil and 15g (½oz) butter. Tip in the spring onions. Reduce the heat a little and sweat for 5 minutes, stirring frequently. Pour the hot stock into the pan, and then add the split peas. Season it lightly, and bring back to a simmer. Reduce the heat a little, cover, and cook for another 20 minutes, stirring occasionally.

2 Add the garden peas and the lettuce, stir, and cook for 5 minutes. Leave to cool a little, then pour the contents of the pan into a blender or food processor and whiz until smooth. Push the soup back into the pan through a fine sieve, mashing the vegetables with the back of a spoon to extract as much as possible. Pour 100ml (3½fl oz) water through the sieve to thin down the soup. Reheat gently over a low heat.

3 In a cup or small bowl combine the egg yolk and the crème fraîche with 2–3 tablespoons of the hot soup. Whisk this into the pan a little at a time. Continue cooking until the soup is piping hot. Adjust the seasoning. Just before serving, stir in the Madeira or port. Whisk in the diced butter and snip over a little chervil.

Be careful when seasoning this hearty soup, as the bacon means that little, if any, extra salt will be needed. Try this dish with olive oil croûtons.

split pea and bacon soup

⊘ SERVES 6   **🕐 PREP** 30 MINS **COOK** 1 HR 10 MINS   **❄ FREEZE** UP TO 3 MONTHS

250g (9oz) dried split green peas, rinsed and drained
1.5 litres (2¾ pints) water
250g (9oz) piece smoked streaky bacon
¼ celeriac, peeled and diced
1 large carrot, diced
1 small leek, diced

1 medium floury potato, peeled and diced
1tsp dried marjoram
15g (½oz) butter
1 onion, diced
freshly ground black pepper
3–4 tsp chopped chives, to garnish

1 Put the peas in a large saucepan with the water and bring to the boil. Add the bacon, cover, and cook for about 40 minutes over a medium heat. Add the celeriac, carrot, leek, and potato, and stir in the marjoram. Bring to the boil again, cover, and cook for another 20 minutes.

2 Melt the butter in a pan, and add the onion. Brown slightly, stirring continuously, then set aside.

3 Remove the bacon from the soup. Discard the excess fat and rind. Shred the meat and return it to the soup together with the fried onion. Season it with pepper. Sprinkle with chopped chives to serve.

You can use vacuum-packed cooked chestnuts for this Italian soup, but fresh ones have a more velvety texture, though you need to allow time for peeling. **Sophie Grigson**

piedmont chestnut soup

SERVES 6   **PREP** 5 MINS USING COOKED CHESTNUTS   **FREEZE** UP TO 3 MONTHS
COOK 1 HR 55 MINS   BEFORE RICE IS ADDED

225g (8oz) fresh chestnuts or 180g (6oz)
   cooked peeled chestnuts
2 sprigs thyme
1 bay leaf
1.2 litres (2 pints) chicken stock

salt and freshly ground black pepper
60g (2oz) risotto rice
30g (1oz) butter
300ml (10fl oz) milk
a little truffle oil, to serve

1 If using fresh chestnuts, score each one with a small sharp knife (see below), then put half a dozen at a time into a microwaveproof bowl. Cover tightly with cling film and cook on full power for 20–30 seconds or until the skins have split, then peel. Put the peeled chestnuts in a pan with the herbs, stock, and a little salt and freshly ground black pepper, bring to the boil, then simmer for 1½ hours.

2 Add the rice and simmer for 10 minutes. Stir in the butter and the milk and simmer for a final 10 minutes. Remove the bay leaf and thyme, taste, and adjust the seasonings, if necessary. Serve, with a few drops of truffle oil in each bowlful to turn this peasant soup into a major treat.

PEELING FRESH CHESTNUTS

Score a deep cross in the skin of each chestnut with a sharp knife, to stop it exploding as it cooks.

After cooking, the shells will have split. Peel off the outer and inner skin with your fingers.

If fresh chestnuts aren't in season, use canned whole unsweetened chestnuts or dried peeled ones. You could also use pancetta or lardons instead of ham. **Marie-Pierre Moine**

chestnut soup with ham

SERVES 4   **PREP** 30 MINS **COOK** 45 MINS   **FREEZE** UP TO 3 MONTHS
WITHOUT THE HAM GARNISH

600g (1lb 5oz) fresh chestnuts
1½–2 tbsp sunflower, groundnut or
   mild-flavoured olive oil
20g (¾oz) butter
½ Spanish onion, finely chopped
1 garlic clove, crushed
3 bay leaves

2 tsp dried fennel seeds, plus 1 heaped tsp,
   to garnish
sea salt and freshly ground black pepper
1.2 litres (2 pints) light vegetable stock
100g (3½ oz) slice of cooked ham, diced
1½ tbsp mascarpone, to finish (optional)

1 Score each chestnut with a small sharp knife (see below left), then place in a saucepan, cover with cold water, and bring to the boil. Drain, leave until cool enough to handle, then peel and set aside. (You could also peel them using the microwave method on the opposite page.)

2 Place a large, heavy-based saucepan over a medium heat. Add the oil and half the butter. Fry the onion and garlic until golden and softened, about 2–3 minutes, stirring frequently. Add the peeled chestnuts, the bay leaves, and the 2 tsp fennel seeds. Stir and season. Pour in the stock. Bring to a gentle simmer, partly cover, and cook for 20–30 minutes, stirring occasionally until the chestnuts are soft.

3 Leave to cool. Discard the bay leaves. Transfer the soup to a blender or food processor and whiz until smooth. Strain the soup through a sieve back into the pan, pushing with the back of a spoon. Gently reheat the soup.

4 Meanwhile, place a non-stick frying pan over a fairly low heat. Add the reserved butter, and then add the diced ham and the extra fennel seeds. Fry gently, stirring a few times. Taste and adjust the seasoning. Stir the soup and ladle it into bowls. Scatter over a little of the diced ham and fennel seeds. If you like, add a small dollop of mascarpone to each serving.

As delicate as it is delicious, this pretty, pastel-green soup is scented with citrussy cardamom notes, which make a marvellous marriage with the pounded pistachios. **Roopa Gulati**

creamy pistachio soup

SERVES 2–3   **PREP** 40 MINS **COOK** 20 MINS   **FREEZE** UP TO 2 MONTHS
WITHOUT CREAM AND CORIANDER

125g (4½oz) (shelled weight) unsalted pistachio nuts
1 green chilli, cut in half and deseeded
120ml (4fl oz) hot water
6 green cardamom pods, crushed and seeds extracted
1 small blade of mace
½ tsp coriander seeds, dry-roasted (see p25)
25g (scant 1oz) butter
2 large garlic cloves, finely chopped

small bunch of spring onions (white parts only), finely chopped
2.5cm (1in) piece of root ginger, peeled and finely chopped
½ tsp garam masala
450ml (15fl oz) hot vegetable stock
100ml (3½fl oz) single cream
1 tbsp chopped coriander leaves
salt and freshly ground black pepper

1 Bring a pan of water to the boil, add the pistachios, and cook for 2–3 minutes. Drain in a colander and refresh under cold running water. Pat the nuts dry with kitchen paper, then turn out on to a tea towel. Give them a vigorous rub with the towel – the skins should slip off easily. Reserve a generous tablespoon for garnishing and put the rest in a food processor. Add the chilli and hot water and process to a rough paste, then set aside.

2 Grind the cardamom seeds, mace, and coriander to a powder with a pestle and mortar. Melt the butter in a saucepan over a medium heat, add the garlic, spring onions, and ginger, and soften for 2–3 minutes. Stir in the ground spices and garam masala and cook for a few seconds, then add the pistachio paste and stock. Simmer, without a lid, for 10–15 minutes, stirring occasionally.

3 Blend in batches until smooth. Stir in the cream and coriander leaves, then season with salt and freshly ground black pepper. Serve the soup garnished with the reserved pistachio nuts roughly chopped.

Josephine Fairley, co-founder of Green & Blacks Chocolate, now runs Judges Bakery, an organic bakery in Hastings, East Sussex. "This Spanish soup is heavenly in summer."

white gazpacho

⊘ SERVES 4   **◷ PREP** 20 MINS   **✷ FREEZE** NOT SUITABLE

85g (3oz) white bread (crusts removed),
    cut into cubes
500ml (16fl oz) iced water
250g (9oz) whole blanched almonds
6 garlic cloves, roughly chopped

3 tbsp olive oil
3 tbsp sherry vinegar or white
    balsamic vinegar
salt and freshly ground black pepper
150g (5½oz) seedless white grapes

1 Soak the bread in all but 3 tbsp of the iced water for 10 minutes. Meanwhile, place the almonds in a food processor and whiz until ground as finely as possible. Add the remaining 3 tbsp iced water and blend to a paste. Remove the bread from the water (reserving the water) and add to the processor, along with the garlic, and blend again.

2 With the motor running, gradually add the water the bread soaked in, followed by the oil. Keep pulsing until the mixture is absolutely smooth. Add the vinegar and season to taste with salt and freshly ground black pepper. To serve, place a handful of grapes in the bottom of each bowl, ladle the soup on top, then drizzle with a little olive oil, if desired.

fish and shellfish

Originally nothing more than a humble fisherman's soup using the remains of the day's catch, bouillabaisse has evolved into one of the great Provençal dishes.

bouillabaisse

SERVES 4   **PREP** 20 MINS **COOK** 45 MINS   **FREEZE** NOT SUITABLE

4 tbsp olive oil
1 onion, thinly sliced
2 leeks, thinly sliced
1 small fennel bulb, thinly sliced
2–3 garlic cloves, finely chopped
4 tomatoes, skinned, deseeded, and chopped
1 tbsp tomato purée
250ml (8fl oz) dry white wine
1.5 litres (2¾ pints) fish stock or chicken stock
pinch of saffron threads
strip of orange zest
1 bouquet garni
salt and freshly ground black pepper
2 tbsp Pernod

1.35kg (3lb) mixed white and oily fish and shellfish, such as gurnard, John Dory, monkfish, red mullet, prawns, and mussels, heads and bones removed
8 croûtes, to serve

for the rouille
125g (4¼oz) mayonnaise
1 bird's-eye chilli, deseeded and roughly chopped
4 garlic cloves, roughly chopped
1 tbsp tomato purée
½ tsp salt

1 Heat the oil in a large pan over a medium heat. Add the onion, leeks, fennel, and garlic and fry, stirring, for 5–8 minutes, or until the vegetables are soft but not coloured. Stir in the tomatoes, tomato purée, and wine.

2 Add the stock, saffron, zest and bouquet garni. Season with salt and pepper, and bring to the boil. Reduce the heat, partially cover, and simmer for 30 minutes, stirring occasionally. Whiz the rouille ingredients in a blender until smooth. Transfer to a bowl, cover, and chill until required.

3 Just before the liquid finishes simmering, cut the fish into chunks. Remove the zest and bouquet garni and add the firm fish. Reduce the heat to low and simmer for 5 minutes. Add the delicate fish and simmer for 2–3 minutes, or until it is cooked through and flakes easily. Stir in the Pernod and season to taste. To serve, spread the croûtes with rouille and place 2 in the bottom of each bowl. Ladle the soup on top.

The seafood must be just-cooked, so cut dense fish in small pieces or add it earlier. Try red mullet, bass, haddock, cod, salmon, turbot, raw shrimps or shelled scallops. **Shaun Hill**

north sea fish soup

SERVES 4   **PREP TIME** 20 MINS **COOK** 20 MINS   **FREEZE** NOT SUITABLE

500g (1lb 2oz) mixed fish fillets and shellfish
salt and pepper
1 tbsp lemon juice
600ml (1 pint) fish or chicken stock
60ml (2fl oz) white wine
2 shallots, chopped

1 egg yolk
1 tbsp double cream
1 tomato, skinned, seeded and chopped
1 tbsp chopped parsley
croûtons, to serve

1 Skin the fish, if necessary, and cut into 2.5cm (1in) pieces. Season and add the lemon juice. Bring the stock, white wine and shallots to the boil in a large saucepan.

2 Add the fish in the order it takes to cook: red mullet or bass first, 2 minutes later the turbot, if using, followed by any haddock, cod or salmon and, finally, shrimps or scallops. Simmer uncovered until all the fish is just cooked.

3 Stir the egg yolk and cream together in a bowl. Take the soup from the heat, stir in the egg mixture, then add the tomato and parsley. Serve with croûtons.

This soup from Brittany was originally a way to use the leftover catch of the day. Try it with haddock, smoked haddock, pollock or cod. **Marie-Pierre Moine**

cotriade

⚙ **SERVES** 4   🕐 **PREP** 20 MINS **COOK** 30 MINS   ❄ **FREEZE** NOT SUITABLE

2 large floury potatoes, peeled
2 tbsp groundnut, sunflower or mild olive oil
30g (1oz) butter
2 Spanish onions, coarsely chopped
1 litre (1¾ pints) light fish stock
3 sprigs of thyme
3 bay leaves
3 sprigs of flat-leaf parsley
sea salt and freshly ground black pepper
800g (1¾lb) mixed fish, skinned, cut into
   large chunks
4 thick slices country bread, to serve

for the dressing
5–6 tbsp groundnut, sunflower or mild
   olive oil
½ tsp Dijon mustard
sea salt and freshly ground black pepper
1 tbsp white wine or cider vinegar
2 tbsp finely chopped parsley

1 Cut the potatoes in half then cut each half into four and set aside. Put the oil and butter in a large, heavy sauté pan. Add the onions and soften over a moderate heat until just golden, stirring frequently. Add the stock then tip in the potatoes and herbs. Season lightly, stir, cover and cook for 12–15 minutes or until the potatoes are almost cooked.

2 Place the fish in the pan and season lightly. Gently stir then cook for 10 minutes, or until the fish just starts to flake when pierced with a fork. If you are freezing this soup, cool and do so now. Meanwhile, make the dressing. In a cup or small jug, mix together the oil and mustard and season, then whisk in the vinegar until emulsified. Stir in the parsley.

3 Remove the soup from the heat and adjust the seasoning. Lift out the herbs. Put the bread in 4 warm bowls and moisten with a little dressing. Ladle over the soup and drizzle on the remaining dressing. Serve hot.

This flavourful soup needs no accompaniment, but croûtes rubbed with garlic, spread with rouille (see p234), or topped with Gruyère cheese are a welcome addition. **Marie-Pierre Moine**

soupe de poissons

⊘ **SERVES** 6   🕐 **PREP** 20 MINS **COOK** 1 HOUR   ❄ **FREEZE** UP TO 2 MONTHS

5 tbsp olive oil
4 medium onions, chopped
2 leeks, chopped
1.5–2kg (3lb 3oz–4½lb) mixed fish
  and seafood
4 pieces dried fennel stalks, 5cm (2in) long
4 medium, ripe tomatoes, quartered
9 garlic cloves, crushed

5 sprigs of fresh flat-leaf parsley
3 bay leaves
15cm (6in) strip dried orange peel
1 tbsp tomato purée
salt and freshly ground black pepper
pinch of saffron threads
6 croûtes, to serve

1 Put the oil in a large, heavy saucepan. Add the onions and leeks, and soften over a moderate heat until just golden.

2 Gut the larger fish. Rinse all the fish and seafood. Add to the pan and stir, then add the fennel, tomatoes, garlic, parsley, bay leaves, orange peel, and tomato purée. Stir and cook for 8–10 minutes until the fish is just beginning to flake when pierced with a fork. Pour in 2.5 litres (4 pints) hot water and season lightly with salt and pepper. Reduce the heat and simmer gently for 20 minutes.

3 Remove from the heat. Leave to cool a little, stirring and mashing down the soft fish pieces with the back of a large wooden spoon. Remove the fennel, orange peel, and bay leaves. If you like, whiz the soup to a rough purée in a blender. Push the soup through a chinois or a very fine sieve into a clean saucepan. Return the soup to a simmer over a moderate heat.

4 Soften the saffron in a ladleful of the soup, then stir into the rest of the soup in the pan. Adjust the seasoning. Ladle the soup into bowls. Serve hot, with croûtes.

This rustic, Mediterranean-style fish soup – robustly flavoured with brandy, orange, and fennel – is simple to prepare and sure to please.

fish soup with fennel

⊘ **SERVES** 4–6   🕐 **PREP** 10 MINS **COOK** 1 HR   ❋ **FREEZE** NOT SUITABLE

30g (1oz) butter
3 tbsp olive oil
1 large fennel bulb, finely chopped
2 garlic cloves, crushed
1 small leek, sliced
4 ripe plum tomatoes, chopped
3 tbsp brandy
¼ tsp saffron threads, infused in a little hot water
zest of ½ orange
1 bay leaf

1.7 litres (3 pints) fish stock
300g (10oz) potatoes, diced and parboiled for 5 minutes
4 tbsp dry white wine
500g (1lb 2oz) fresh black mussels, scrubbed and debearded
salt and freshly ground black pepper
500g (1lb 2oz) monkfish or firm white fish, cut into bite-sized pieces
6 raw whole tiger prawns
parsley, chopped, to garnish

1 Heat the butter with 2 tbsp of the oil in a large, deep pan. Stir in the fennel, garlic, and leek, and fry over a moderate heat, stirring occasionally, for 5 minutes, or until softened and lightly browned.

2 Stir in the tomatoes, add the brandy, and boil rapidly for 2 minutes, or until the juices are reduced slightly. Stir in the saffron, orange zest, bay leaf, fish stock, and potatoes. Bring to the boil, then reduce the heat and skim off any scum from the surface. Cover and simmer for 20 minutes, or until the potatoes are tender. Remove the bay leaf.

3 Meanwhile, heat the remaining oil with the wine in a large, deep pan until boiling. Add the mussels, cover, and continue on high heat for 2–3 minutes, shaking the pan often. Discard any mussels that do not open. Strain, reserving the liquid, and set the mussels aside. Add the liquid to the soup and season to taste. Bring to the boil, add the monkfish and prawns, then reduce the heat, cover, and simmer gently for 5 minutes, or until the fish is just cooked and the prawns are pink. Add the mussels to the pan and bring almost to the boil. Serve the soup sprinkled with chopped parsley.

A German soup, from the region of Schleswig-Holstein on the North Sea coast. You can use any white fish, so choose whatever is freshest.

büsumer fish soup

SERVES 6–8   **PREP** 15 MINS **COOK** 20 MINS   **FREEZE** NOT SUITABLE

2 large carrots, chopped
1 large potato (King Edward or Maris Piper), peeled and diced
1 large onion, diced
1 litre (1¾ pints) hot vegetable stock
1 bay leaf
salt and freshly ground black pepper
500g (1lb 2oz) white fish fillets (pollock or haddock), skinned, boned, and cut into bite-sized pieces

juice of 1 lemon
200g (7oz) button or chestnut mushrooms, sliced
100g (3½ oz) raw peeled king prawns
120ml (4fl oz) double cream
½ bunch of dill, chopped

1 Put the carrots, potato, and onion into a saucepan, add the hot stock and bay leaf, and bring to the boil. Reduce the heat and simmer for 10 minutes.

2 Sprinkle a little salt and pepper, and half the lemon juice, over the fish pieces, then add these to the stock along with the mushrooms and simmer for another 5 minutes at a low heat.

3 Add the prawns to the pan along with the remaining lemon juice, and cook for 3 minutes, or until the prawns turn pink. Remove the bay leaf and season with salt and pepper, to taste. Stir in the cream and half the dill and serve immediately, using the remaining dill to garnish.

If you enjoy the intense salty-sweetness of eel, you'll love this German-style soup. Contact your fishmonger in advance to order a fresh eel, asking for it to be prepared.

hamburg eel soup

⊘ SERVES 6   **⏱ PREP** 15 MINS **COOK** 1 HR 20 MINS   **❄ FREEZE** UP TO 2 MONTHS

750 ml (1¼ pints) Riesling wine
2 tbsp white wine vinegar
2 tbsp chopped fresh parsley
1 onion, sliced
2 carrots, diced
1 bay leaf
salt and freshly ground black pepper

1 prepared eel (cleaned, skinned, and cut
  into 5cm (2in) pieces)
30g (1oz) butter
1½ tbsp plain flour
2 litres (3½ pints) hot vegetable stock
bouquet garni (see p24)

1 Pour the wine and 500ml (16fl oz) of water into a large saucepan with the vinegar, then add the chopped parsley, onion, carrots, and bay leaf, and season with salt and pepper. Bring to the boil and cook for 4–6 minutes. Add the eel pieces and simmer at a low heat for 10 minutes, or until the flesh is tender, then leave to cool.

2 Melt the butter in a saucepan, add the flour, and cook, stirring, until blended. Stir in the stock a little at a time. Add the bouquet garni to the pan, and cook slowly for 1 hour.

3 To serve, remove the eel pieces from the cooking liquid. Stir half the cooking liquid into the vegetable stock, divide the eel pieces among six bowls, and ladle the soup over.

Henningsvaer is a picturesque little port right up north in Norway's Lofoten Islands and this soup is the speciality of a small restaurant there. **Sophie Grigson**

henningsvaer fish soup

SERVES 6-8　　**PREP** 15 MINS **COOK** 45 MINS　　**FREEZE** UP TO 2 MONTHS
WITHOUT THE CRÈME FRAÎCHE

1.5 litres (2¾ pints) good fish stock
350g (12oz) cod fillet
60g (2oz) butter
1 onion, finely chopped
1 large carrot, finely chopped
1 large leek, finely chopped

2 tsp caster sugar
2 tbsp white wine vinegar
salt and pepper
300ml (10fl oz) crème fraîche
chopped parsley, to serve

1 Bring the stock to the boil. Add the cod, bring gently back to the boil then remove from the heat. When cool enough to handle, lift out the cod and flake, discarding skin and stray bones. Set aside the fish and stock.

2 Melt the butter in a large pan and add the vegetables. Stir to coat in the fat, then cover the pan, reduce the heat to very low and leave to sweat for 20 minutes, stirring once or twice. Add the stock, sugar and vinegar, season and bring to the boil. Simmer for 10 minutes. Stir in the crème fraîche and flaked fish. Taste and adjust the seasoning, then reheat gently without boiling. Serve immediately, sprinkled with the parsley.

Replace the mussels with shell-on prawns in this Flemish soup if you prefer; peel, and add the empty shells to the reduced stock for 3 minutes before straining. **Marie-Pierre Moine**

waterzooi

🍽 **SERVES** 4   🕐 **PREP** 20 MINS **COOK** 30 MINS   ❄ **FREEZE** NOT SUITABLE

1 large waxy potato, peeled
1 large carrot, peeled
1 medium-large courgette
400g (14oz) asparagus
300g (10oz) monkfish
1 sole, filleted and skinned
600ml (1 pint) light chicken or fish stock

100ml (3½fl oz) dry white wine
3 large spring onions, finely chopped
500g (1lb 2oz) mussels, rinsed and scrubbed
100ml (3½fl oz) whipping cream
salt and pepper
1 tbsp finely chopped tarragon, to serve

1 Cut the potato and carrot in 1 x 5cm (½ x 2in) batons. Slice the courgette on the diagonal. Cut off the asparagus tips, then chop the spears into 5cm (2in) lengths. Cut the monkfish into 4cm (1½in) chunks and cut each sole fillet crossways in half. Set the vegetables and fish aside separately.

2 Put the stock, wine and spring onions (reserving a few to serve) in a casserole dish. Bring to the boil over a moderate heat. Add the potato, reduce the heat to a simmer and cook for 5 minutes, then add the carrot and cook for 5 minutes. Add the courgette and asparagus and cook for 1–2 minutes, or until all is al dente. Lift out the vegetables and set aside.

3 Bring the stock to the boil over a high heat and reduce by a third. Reduce the heat to a simmer, tip in the mussels, cover and cook for 3–4 minutes. Strain through a muslin-lined sieve into a bowl, leave to cool briefly, then discard any mussels that haven't opened. Shell the rest and set aside. Return the stock to the pan and simmer over a moderate heat, then stir in the cream and season to taste. Add the monkfish, cook for 2–3 minutes, then the sole for 1 minute, then the vegetables and mussels for a final 2 minutes.

4 Using a slotted spoon, distribute the vegetables between the bowls. Place the fish on top, ladle over the broth and scatter with mussels. Sprinkle with chopped tarragon and the reserved spring onion. Serve hot.

This combination of South Indian and South East Asian flavours is a marvellous match for any firm-fleshed fish or seafood. Prawns are a good alternative to cod. **Roopa Gulati**

pineapple broth with cod

◉ SERVES 4   **◷ PREP** 30 MINS **COOK** 40 MINS   **❄ FREEZE** UP TO 2 MONTHS

1 onion, diced
50g (1¾oz) raw peanuts, skinned
2 tbsp desiccated coconut
3cm (1¼in) piece of root ginger, chopped
1 tsp coriander seeds
2 tsp sesame seeds
1 tsp cumin seeds
1 tsp poppy seeds
3 tbsp tamarind pulp
½ tsp turmeric
¾ tsp chilli powder

salt and freshly ground black pepper
2 tbsp vegetable oil
1 tsp date palm sugar
400ml (14fl oz) fish stock
200ml (7fl oz) pineapple juice
400ml (14fl oz) coconut milk
200g (8oz) line-caught cod, chopped
juice of 1 lime
125g (4½oz) fresh pineapple pieces, chopped
2 tbsp mint leaves, roughly torn
2 tbsp raw peanuts, toasted and chopped

1 Heat a cast-iron frying pan. Add the onion, peanuts, coconut, ginger, and all the seeds. Stir over a low heat until the coconut darkens and spices are aromatic, about 5 minutes. Transfer to a bowl to cool, then place in a food processor and process to a coarse paste. Add the tamarind pulp, turmeric, chilli powder and seasoning, and process to a smooth paste.

2 Heat the vegetable oil in a large saucepan and fry the paste for about 10 minutes on a low heat. Stir in the sugar and continue cooking until the paste begins to catch on the bottom of the pan. Pour in the stock and pineapple juice and simmer for 20 minutes, partially covered.

3 Remove the soup from the heat and, using a stick blender or liquidizer, purée until smooth. Stir in the coconut milk and return the pan to the heat. Once it begins to bubble, add the fish and simmer for 3 minutes. Add the lime juice and stir in the pineapple pieces and mint leaves. Ladle into bowls and scatter over the peanuts.

Chowder makes a hearty lunchtime soup for any time of the year. Where possible, always buy your wild salmon from a sustainable source. **Angela Nilsen**

wild salmon chowder

SERVES 4   **PREP** 15 MINS   **FREEZE** NOT SUITABLE
COOK 25 MINS PLUS 5–10 MINS RESTING

2 tbsp olive oil
4 rashers streaky bacon, chopped
6 spring onions, cut into 2.5cm (1in) slices
3 sprigs thyme
2 bay leaves
600g (1lb 5oz) small waxy potatoes, such as Desirée or roseval, thickly sliced
25g (scant 1oz) butter

1 tbsp plain flour
700ml (scant 1¼ pints) fish or chicken stock
400g (14oz) salmon fillets, skinned and cut into chunks
150ml (5fl oz) single cream
2–3 tbsp snipped dill
zest of ½ lemon, finely grated
salt and freshly ground black pepper

1 Heat 1 tbsp of the oil in a wide, deep sauté pan. Add the bacon and fry until crisp. Drain on kitchen paper and set aside. Pour the remaining oil into the pan, add the spring onions, thyme, and bay leaves and stir-fry for 1 minute. Add the potatoes and fry 2–3 minutes.

2 In another saucepan, melt the butter and beat in the flour. Cook for 1–2 minutes and then gradually add the stock. Bring to the boil and then simmer gently for 3–4 minutes or until thickened slightly. Add the thickened stock to the potatoes and bring to the boil. Cook for 10 minutes without stirring, until the potatoes are just tender.

3 Reduce the heat and submerge salmon chunks into the stock. Simmer very gently for 3–5 minutes, just until the fish is cooked. Do not stir or the fish will break up.

4 Remove from the heat. Without stirring, pour the cream over, scatter with the dill and lemon zest. Let the soup sit for 5–10 minutes for all the flavours to blend. When ready to serve, warm through gently and briefly, discard the thyme and bay leaves, and add seasoning if needed. Ladle into bowls and serve scattered with black pepper and the crispy bacon.

This is a complete meal in a bowl. Raw mangoes add bite to a citrussy broth flecked with fiery red chillies. Raw mangoes are available from South Asian stores. **Roopa Gulati**

mango and snapper broth

⊘ **SERVES** 4 ⏱ **PREP** 15 MINS, PLUS 20 MINS MARINATING ❄ **FREEZE** NOT SUITABLE
COOK 15 MINS

1 tbsp light soy sauce
2 tsp fish sauce
1 tbsp toasted sesame oil
1 tbsp mirin
1 tsp sugar
juice of 1 lime
500g (1lb) red snapper fillets, skinless,
    cut into 2.5cm (1in) cubes
2 stalks lemongrass, finely chopped
2 tbsp vegetable oil
4 birds eye red chillies, finely sliced
4 spring onions, finely sliced
5cm (2in) fresh root ginger, finely shredded
4 garlic cloves, roughly chopped

4 small raw green mangoes, or under-ripe
    mangoes, peeled and finely chopped
2 tsp date palm sugar or dark muscovado sugar
2 tbsp rice wine vinegar
1 litre (2 pints) fish stock
8 lime leaves, torn in half
1 tbsp fish sauce
100g (4oz) medium egg noodles
100g (4oz) fine green beans, halved
salt to season
juice of 1 lime, to taste
2 tbsp chopped fresh coriander leaves
1 tbsp shredded fresh mint leaves

1 Combine the soy and fish sauce, sesame oil, mirin, sugar, and lime juice, and spoon over the fish. Refrigerate for 20 minutes. Pound the lemongrass to a paste with a dash of water, using a mortar and pestle. Set aside.

2 Heat the oil in a wok or large pan and fry the chillies, spring onions, ginger, and garlic for 30 seconds over a high heat. Add the mangoes and fry for 1 minute. Stir in the sugar until it begins to caramelize. Add the vinegar, lemongrass, stock, lime leaves, and fish sauce. Bring to the boil.

3 Stir in the noodles, beans, and fish pieces (not the marinating liquid). Simmer for 3–5 minutes, until the noodles are cooked and the fish flakes easily. Season with salt, sharpen with lime juice, and add the herbs.

The strong flavours of cavolo nero and smoked haddock develop in minutes, making this soup very satisfying. If you want to freeze it, do so before adding the fish. **Marie-Pierre Moine**

portuguese haddock soup

SERVES 4   **PREP** 20 MINS **COOK** 20 MINS   **FREEZE** NOT SUITABLE

300g (10oz) leaves of cavolo nero, kale, or savoy cabbage
2 tbsp mild olive oil
1 Spanish onion, finely chopped
3 garlic cloves, peeled and crushed

1 large waxy potato, peeled and diced
250ml (8fl oz) full-fat or semi-skimmed milk
salt and pepper
300g (10oz) smoked haddock fillet, skinned and flaked

1 Rinse the greens, cut out and discard the large ribs and shred the leaves finely. Put a sauté pan over a moderate heat and add the oil. Once it is hot, add the onion and garlic and stir for 4–5 minutes, or until softened.

2 Add the potato and milk, then pour in enough water to cover everything by 2–3cm (¾–1¼ in). Season generously, bring to a simmer and cook for 5 minutes, then add the cabbage and continue cooking for 10–15 minutes until the vegetables are tender.

3 Stir in the haddock and simmer for a minute, then take off the heat and cover. Leave to stand for 5 minutes before serving.

This comforting soup is based on a simple roux-based sauce, so it is vital to use very good stock to make it really sing. It makes an excellent light lunch.

creamy smoked trout soup

⊘ SERVES 6　　**🕑 PREP** 15 MINS **COOK** 10 MINS　　**❄ FREEZE** UP TO 2 MONTHS

50g (1¾oz) butter
35g (1¼oz) plain flour
750ml (1¼ pints) hot vegetable or fish stock
250ml (8fl oz) whipping cream
4 tbsp white wine
2–3 tsp Worcestershire sauce

salt and freshly ground black pepper
squeeze of lemon juice
375g (13oz) hot-smoked trout fillets,
　skinned and flaked
2 tbsp chopped parsley

1 Over a low heat, melt the butter in a pan, stir in the flour and mix until smooth. Cook for 2–3 minutes, stirring constantly. Gradually pour in the hot stock, making sure there are no lumps by whisking vigorously. Bring to the boil then cook, uncovered, over a low heat for about 3 minutes, stirring occasionally.

2 Add the cream, white wine, Worcestershire sauce, salt, pepper and a little lemon juice, then bring to the boil again. Add the fish pieces and briefly heat them through. Sprinkle the soup with parsley and serve.

TROUT
Make sure you buy hot-smoked trout for this dish, as it is already cooked. Go for whole moist fillets as pre-flaked fish can be dry. For guidelines on fish sustainability, check the Marine Conservation Society's website.

Make sure you don't boil the soup after adding the miso paste as it spoils the flavour. You'll find wakame (dried seaweed) and miso in large supermarkets. **Carolyn Humphries**

miso soup with tuna

SERVES 4   **PREP** 25 MINS **COOK** 15 MINS   **FREEZE** NOT SUITABLE

10cm (4in) piece wakame
2 tbsp dried shiitake mushrooms
2 spring onions, chopped
1 tsp grated fresh root ginger
1 long thin carrot, thinly sliced

450ml (15fl oz) chicken stock
200g (7oz) fresh tuna steak, diced
2 tbsp miso paste
soy sauce, to season
1 tbsp snipped chives

1 Put the wakame and mushrooms in a bowl and cover with cold water. Soak for 15 minutes. Drain, reserving the liquid. Lift out the wakame, remove any hard central ribs and cut into strips.

2 Put the wakame, mushrooms, spring onions, ginger and carrot into a saucepan. Make the soaking water up to 750ml (1¼ pints) with the stock and add to the saucepan. Bring to the boil, reduce the heat, cover and simmer for 10 minutes until the carrot is just tender.

3 Add the tuna and cook for a further 5 minutes. In a small bowl, blend the miso paste with 2 tbsp water and stir in to the soup. Season to taste with soy sauce. Heat through but do not boil. Ladle into warm soup cups and sprinkle with snipped chives.

A rich main meal soup, naturally thickened with okra, a classic gumbo ingredient. In its native Louisiana, they would use sweet ground sassafras leaves. **Carolyn Humphries**

mixed seafood gumbo

⊘ SERVES 6   **🕐 PREP** 20 MINS **COOK** 50 MINS   **❄ FREEZE** UP TO 2 MONTHS
AT THE END OF STEP 2

1 tbsp sunflower oil
1 onion, chopped
2 celery sticks, chopped
1 large garlic clove, chopped
115g (4oz) cooking chorizo, sliced
2 tbsp plain flour
600ml (1 pint) fish or chicken stock
400g (14oz) can chopped tomatoes
1 green pepper, diced

250g (9oz) okra, trimmed and cut
  in short lengths
¼ tsp cayenne
½ tsp dried oregano
½ tsp caster sugar
salt and pepper
200g (7oz) mixed raw seafood cocktail
225g (8oz) long-grain rice
chopped parsley, to serve

1 Heat the oil in a large pan. Add the onion and celery and fry gently, stirring, for about 5 minutes, or until lightly golden. Stir in the garlic and chorizo and cook for 2 minutes. Stir in the flour and cook for another minute. Remove from the heat and gradually blend in the stock, then the tomatoes. Return to the heat and bring to the boil, stirring. Add the remaining ingredients, except the seafood and rice, bring back to the boil, reduce the heat, part-cover and simmer gently for 30 minutes.

2 Add the seafood and simmer for a further 5 minutes, stirring occasionally. Taste and re-season.

3 Meanwhile, cook the rice in plenty of boiling, lightly salted water for 10 minutes or until just tender. Drain in a colander, rinse with boiling water and drain again.

4 Spoon some rice into each of 6 large soup bowls. Ladle the gumbo over, sprinkle with a little chopped parsley and serve hot.

in praise of...
shellfish
There are few greater
pleasures than
gathering wild mussels
from a Scottish sea loch
at low tide, and then
feasting on these
delicious fruits of
the sea.
Patrick Holden

Arthur Potts Dawson of the eco-friendly restaurant Acorn House in London writes, "This is a delicious autumn soup for all the family."

potato and clam soup

⊘ **SERVES** 4–6   🕐 **PREP** 25 MINS **COOK** 1 HR 30 MINS   ❄ **FREEZE** NOT SUITABLE

1kg (2¼lb) clams
120ml (4fl oz) dry white wine
2–3 tbsp olive oil
2 celery stalks, finely diced
1 red onion, finely chopped
1 carrot, finely chopped
4 tomatoes, skinned, deseeded, and chopped

2 medium potatoes, finely diced
1 litre (1¾ pints) cold filtered water
1 sprig of rosemary
1 tbsp finely chopped flat-leaf parsley
   or chervil
salt and freshly ground black pepper
4–6 slices country bread

1 Wash the clams thoroughly in cold running water, throwing away any with broken shells and any that are open and won't close when gently tapped. Put them in a large frying pan with the wine, cover with a lid, and place on a high heat for 5 minutes or until the shells open. Discard any that remain closed as they will not be edible. Drain, reserving the liquid. Remove the clams from their shells, place in a bowl, cover, and refrigerate until needed. Strain the cooking liquid through a fine sieve.

2 Heat the oil in a large heavy-bottomed pan, add the celery, onion, and carrot, and cook on a low heat for 10 minutes or until light brown. Add the tomatoes, potatoes, the reserved cooking liquid, and the filtered water, and bring to the boil. Add the rosemary, then lower the heat, cover with a lid, and simmer for 1 hour.

3 Stir in the clams and the parsley or chervil, then season with salt and freshly ground black pepper. Remove the rosemary, put a slice of bread in the bottom of each bowl, and ladle over the soup.

Americans often serve this traditional, creamy soup with saltine crackers, though cream crackers are also good. The clams must be cooked on the day of purchase.

new england clam chowder

⊘ SERVES 4   **🕐 PREP** 15 MINS **COOK** 35 MINS   **❄ FREEZE** NOT SUITABLE

36 live clams
1 tbsp oil
115g (4oz) thick-cut rindless streaky bacon
  rashers, diced
2 floury potatoes, such as King Edward,
  peeled and cut into 1cm (½in) cubes

1 onion, finely chopped
2 tbsp plain white flour
600ml (1 pint) whole milk
salt and freshly ground black pepper
120ml (4fl oz) single cream
2 tbsp finely chopped flat-leaf parsley

1 Discard any open clams, then shuck the rest, reserving the juices. Add enough water to the juices to make 600ml (1 pint). Chop the clams. Heat the oil in a large, heavy saucepan and fry the bacon over a medium heat for 5 minutes or until crisp. Remove and drain on kitchen paper.

2 Add the potatoes and onion to the pan and fry for 5 minutes or until the onion has softened. Add the flour and stir for 2 minutes. Stir in the clam juice and milk and season to taste. Cover with a lid, lower the heat and, simmer for 20 minutes or until the potatoes are tender. Add the clams and simmer gently, uncovered, for 5 minutes. Stir in the cream and reheat without boiling. Serve sprinkled with the bacon and parsley.

SHUCKING CLAMS

Work the tip of a knife between the top and bottom shell, then twist upwards to open the clam.

Sever the muscle at the top, then do the same at the bottom to release the clam meat.

There are several variations on Manhattan clam chowder, using vegetables such as celery and green peppers. Its defining feature is its tomato base.

manhattan clam chowder

SERVES 4   **PREP** 15 MINS **COOK** 35 MINS   **FREEZE** NOT SUITABLE

36 live clams, freshly bought
1 tbsp oil
115g (4oz) thick-cut rindless streaky bacon
   rashers, diced
1 onion, finely chopped
2 floury potatoes, such as King Edward,
   peeled and cut into 1cm (½in) cubes

2 tbsp plain white flour
2 x 400g (14oz) cans of chopped tomatoes
   with their juice
salt and freshly ground black pepper
fresh thyme, to garnish

1 Discard any clams that are open. Shuck the clams and reserve the juice, topping up with water to make 600ml (1 pint). Chop the clams.

2 Heat the oil in a large, heavy saucepan and fry the bacon over a medium heat, stirring frequently, for 5 minutes, or until it is crisp. Remove from the pan with a slotted spoon, drain on kitchen paper and set aside.

3 Add the onion and potatoes to the pan and fry for 5 minutes, or until the onion has softened. Add the flour and stir for 2 minutes.

4 Stir in the tomatoes and their juice and season to taste with salt and pepper. Cover the pan, reduce the heat and leave to simmer for 20 minutes or until the potatoes are tender. Add the clams and simmer gently, uncovered, for 5 minutes. Serve the chowder hot, sprinkled with bacon and thyme.

Rosemary Shrager is a chef, food writer, and television presenter, and also runs an acclaimed cookery school. "This is a wonderful, unusual, inspired soup."

mussel and saffron soup

⊘ SERVES 4　　**⏱ PREP TIME** 15 MINS **COOK** 35 MINS　　**❄ FREEZE** NOT SUITABLE

100ml (3½fl oz) dry white wine
500ml (16fl oz) fish or chicken stock
2kg (4½lb) mussels, scrubbed
　and de-bearded
30g (1oz) butter
125g (4½oz) onions, finely chopped
125g carrots, diced
85g (3oz) celeriac, diced

1 thin leek, finely sliced
1 garlic clove, chopped
1 tbsp curry powder
good pinch of saffron threads,
　soaked in 2 tbsp hot water
250ml (8fl oz) double cream
salt and pepper
2 tbsp parsley, finely chopped

1 Bring the wine and stock to a boil in a large sauté pan over a high heat. Add the mussels, discarding any that will not shut when tapped, and cover. As the mussels open, remove them to a bowl. When all are open, filter the liquid through muslin into another bowl. Discard two-thirds of the shells.

2 Clean the sauté pan. Melt the butter over a low heat and add the vegetables and garlic, stirring well. Cook for 10 minutes, then stir in the curry powder and add the mussel liquid and the saffron in its water. Add the cream and cook without boiling for 5 minutes. Return the mussels to the pan, heat through gently, and season well. Sprinkle over the parsley, and serve.

SCRUBBING AND DE-BEARDING MUSSELS

Scrub the mussels under cold running water, then scrape off any barnacles with a knife.

Pinch the dark stringy "beard" between forefinger and thumb and pull it firmly away.

A typical Provence concoction, this mussel and fennel soup harmoniously combines seafood and vegetables in a fragrant broth. **Marie-Pierre Moine**

mussel and fennel soup

◉ SERVES 4   **● PREP TIME** 15 MINS **COOK** 45 MINS   **❋ FREEZE** UP TO 1 MONTH

1kg (2¼lb) fresh mussels
500ml (16fl oz) dry white wine
4 medium, ripe tomatoes
3 tbsp olive oil
1 leek, chopped
2 sprigs of fresh flat-leaf parsley
2 sprigs of thyme

1 bay leaf
¼ small fennel bulb, chopped
5cm (2in) piece dried orange peel
fine sea salt and freshly ground black pepper
1 large floury potato, peeled and chopped
pinch of saffron strands

1 Rinse and debeard the mussels. Tip them into a large saucepan and add the wine. Cover the pan, put over a high heat, and cook for 5–6 minutes, shaking occasionally, until the mussels open (discard any that remain stubbornly closed). Remove from the heat. Line a sieve with muslin and place over a bowl. Tip the mussels into the sieve and leave until cool enough to handle, then remove and discard the shells. Reserve both the mussels and the cooking liquid.

2 Pierce the tomatoes with a knife, put them in a bowl and pour over boiling water to cover. Leave for 1 minute, then drain and slip off the skins. Quarter, remove and discard the seeds and chop the flesh. Heat the oil in a large sauté pan over a moderate heat. Add the tomatoes, leek, herbs, fennel and orange peel and season. Cook until softened, stirring frequently.

3 Add the mussel cooking liquid to the pan, then 500ml (16fl oz) of just-boiled water. Bring to a simmer. Add the potato and cook until soft. Remove from the heat, leave to cool a little, then remove the herbs and orange peel. Mash the potato pieces into the soup to thicken.

4 Soften the saffron in a small bowl with a spoonful of soup, then stir it back in. Taste and adjust the seasoning, add the mussels, reheat gently and serve immediately.

This aromatic soup comes from France's Atlantic coast. You can prepare it ahead but take care to reheat the mussels gently or they become tough and overcooked. **Marie-Pierre Moine**

mouclade

⊚ **SERVES** 4   🕒 **PREP** 20 MINS **COOK** 30 MINS   ✹ **FREEZE** NOT SUITABLE

1.5kg (3lb 3oz) small fresh mussels, well
   scrubbed and washed
45g (1¼oz) butter
1 large banana shallot, finely chopped
350ml (12fl oz) dry white wine
several sprigs of flat-leaf parsley
¼ small fennel bulb, chopped
1 bay leaf
sea salt and freshly ground black pepper

pinch of cayenne
1 large egg yolk
5 tbsp soured cream or crème fraîche
1 large garlic clove, crushed
½ tsp mild paprika or 1 tsp mild
   curry powder
a few strands of saffron or ¼ tsp
   ground saffron
chunks of fresh warm bread, to serve

1 Put a large sauté pan over a moderate heat. Tip in the mussels with 15g (½oz) of the butter, the shallot, wine and 350ml (12fl oz) water. Add the parsley, fennel and bay leaf, season lightly and add the cayenne. Increase the heat and bring to the boil. Cover and cook the mussels for 4–5 minutes, or until they open, shaking the pan a few times.

2 Using a slotted spoon, lift out the mussels and put in a bowl. Discard any that haven't opened and set aside the rest. Strain the liquor through a muslin-lined sieve into a bowl and set aside. In a small bowl, mix the egg yolk with the cream until smooth. In a separate bowl, using a fork, mash the remaining butter with the garlic, paprika and saffron.

3 Shell the mussels, keeping 12 in their shells and moisten them all with a little of the cooking liquid. Keep warm.

4 Put a large pan over a low heat. Add the butter and, when it bubbles, pour in the mussel liquor, stir and bring to a simmer. Remove 3 tbsp and whisk it into the egg mixture, then whisk this back into the pan and stir until hot and blended. Adjust the seasoning and divide the mussels between 4 warm bowls. Pour the broth over and serve with the bread.

These succulent mussels in their moat of gingery juices are terrific with a mound of fluffy rice on the side, but crusty bread mops up the broth just as nicely. **Roopa Gulati**

mussels in a ginger and chilli broth

⦿ **SERVES** 2–4   ⏱ **PREP** 20 MINS **COOK** 30–35 MINS   ❄ **FREEZE** NOT SUITABLE

1.5 kg (3lb) mussels, in their shells, cleaned
100g (4 oz) butter
2 onions, finely chopped
2 birds eye red chillies, finely chopped
5cm (2in) fresh root ginger, finely shredded
5 large garlic cloves, finely chopped
2 stalks lemongrass, split lengthways
   and lightly bruised

125ml (4fl oz) ginger wine
400ml (14fl oz) fish stock
150ml (5 fl oz) coconut milk
3 tbsp coconut cream
salt and freshly ground black pepper
juice of 1–2 limes, to taste
3 tbsp chopped fresh coriander leaves

1 Wash the mussels under cold running water. Give any open ones a firm tap against the counter top and discard any that don't close.

2 Melt the butter in a large pan over a low heat and gently cook the onions, chillies, ginger, garlic, and lemongrass for 10 minutes until soft but not coloured.

3 Turn the heat up high and add the ginger wine followed by the stock. Bring to the boil before tipping in the mussels. Cover the pan and cook for 5–7 minutes, until the mussel shells have opened. Discard the lemongrass along with any mussels that remain closed.

4 Pour in the coconut milk and cream, and bring to the boil. Season with salt and pepper, sharpen with lime juice, and stir in the coriander leaves before serving.

Allegra McEvedy, TV chef and food writer, was co-founder of Leon, the healthy and ethical restaurant chain. "A soup for early Spring, using foods coming in and going out of season."

soup of the first and last

SERVES 4–6   **PREP** 30 MINS **COOK** 45 MINS   **FREEZE** NOT SUITABLE

10 oysters, opened, and with juice
1 tbsp butter
1 white onion, finely diced
2 garlic cloves, finely chopped
1 celery stalk, finely diced
salt and freshly ground black pepper
200ml (7fl oz) double cream
400ml (14fl oz) cold water
½ celeriac, peeled and finely diced

200g (7oz) Jersey royals, cut into thin slices
2 small–medium turnips, cut in two, then sliced into half-moons
200g (7oz) garlic leaves, roughly cut into 4cm (1¾in) pieces (you could use baby spinach and more garlic, but it won't be quite the same)
a handful of wild garlic flowers (optional)

1 Wash 4–6 oyster shells (one per serving) to remove any grit. Cover with boiling water, to clean and keep warm. Heat the butter in a pan, add the onion, garlic, celery, and a pinch of salt, cover with a lid, and sweat over a low heat for 5 minutes or until soft. Add the cream, water, and celeriac, and simmer, covered, for 10 minutes. Add the Jersey royals and cook for 10 minutes, then add the turnips and cook for 10 more minutes.

2 Take off the heat and ladle half the soup into a blender. Add 4–6 oysters (depending on how many you need to serve) and half the garlic leaves and blend until smooth. Tip the mixture back in to the pan, rinse the blender out with 400ml (14fl oz) cold water, and add that to the pan as well. Season with salt and freshly ground black pepper, add the rest of the garlic leaves, then bring to a gentle simmer and cook for 5 minutes.

3 Meanwhile, put the remaining oysters and their juices in a pan with 2 tbsp water, and poach for 4 minutes or until firm. Turn halfway through. Stir the juice (but not the oysters) into the soup, then check the seasoning and the consistency – add a little hot water if the soup is too thick. Divide among 4–6 bowls. Drop a warm oyster shell in each, fill with a poached oyster, and garnish with wild garlic flowers if you like.

A rich broth sets off the sweetness of the scallops while the chorizo (or black pudding) adds a spicy contrast. Serve as the first course of a dinner party menu. **Marie-Pierre Moine**

creamy scallop bisque

⊘ **SERVES** 4   🕐 **PREP** 20 MINS **COOK** 40 MINS   ❄ **FREEZE** NOT SUITABLE

300ml (10fl oz) dry white wine
15g (½oz) butter
1 small onion, finely chopped
1 small shallot, very finely chopped
1 medium-sized ripe tomato, chopped
200g (7oz) prawns, shelled
100g (3½oz) cod or pollock, skinned and cut into chunks
12 small scallops (or 6 large), white parts and corals

2 tbsp chopped parsley
2 tsp dill seeds
sea salt and freshly ground black pepper
3 tbsp brandy
100ml (3½fl oz) single cream
75g (2½oz) chorizo, diced, or black pudding, minced
1 tbsp finely chopped chives, to finish

1 Boil 700ml (1¼ pints) water with the wine. Put the butter in a sauté pan over a medium heat. Add the onion and shallot and soften until golden. Add the tomato, prawns, fish, corals, parsley, and dill seeds. Stir, and cook for 5 minutes. Stir in the brandy, and cook for a minute. Pour in the boiling wine mixture and season lightly. Reduce the heat, and simmer gently for 10 minutes. Take off the heat and leave to cool. Stir and mash down the soup with the back of a spoon. Then gently heat the cream in another pan until hot.

2 Transfer the soup to a blender and purée. Strain through a sieve back into the pan and stir in the hot cream. Return to a simmer. Remove from the heat and adjust the seasoning. Cover and keep warm.

3 Put a non-stick frying pan over a medium heat. Add the chorizo or black pudding and fry for 3–5 minutes until cooked through and crispy. Set aside on a plate lined with kitchen paper and keep warm.

4 Add the scallops to the pan. Cook for 2 minutes, turn over and cook for a minute. Remove from the heat. Ladle the soup into 4 bowls and add the scallops. Scatter over the chorizo or black pudding and serve immediately.

Serve this delightful soup with some nutty rye bread and chilled unsalted butter. If you like, you can use crab for a less expensive alternative to the lobster. **Carolyn Humphries**

brandied lobster chowder

SERVES 4   **PREP** 20 MINS **COOK** 1 HR   **FREEZE** UP TO 2 MONTHS
WITHOUT CREAM OR MANGETOUT

1 small cooked lobster
850ml (scant 1½ pints) water
150ml (5fl oz) dry white wine
1 bay leaf
knob of unsalted butter
2 shallots, finely chopped
4 tbsp brandy
1 large tomato, skinned and diced

2 tsp anchovy essence
4 large new potatoes, scraped and diced
8 baby corn, cut in short lengths
salt and freshly ground pepper
60g (2oz) mangetout, cut in short lengths
5 tbsp single cream
4 thick slices lemon
4 sprigs of parsley

1 Twist the legs and claws off the lobster. Cut the body in half lengthways and remove the dark vein that runs along it. Lift out the tail meat, and cut in small pieces. Crack the large claws, remove the meat, and dice. Set all the meat aside. Leave the remaining bits of meat in the shell. Roughly chop it up and put it in a saucepan with the claws and legs. Add the water, wine, and bay leaf. Bring to the boil, reduce the heat, cover, and simmer for 30 minutes. Strain and reserve the stock.

2 Melt the butter in another large saucepan over a low heat. Add the shallots and fry gently, stirring for 1 minute. Add the brandy, ignite, and shake the pan until the flames subside. Add the tomato, anchovy essence, potatoes, and corn. Return the stock to the pan. Season and bring to the boil. Reduce the heat, cover, and simmer gently for 20 minutes until the potatoes are really tender.

3 Meanwhile, blanch the mangetout in a little boiling water for 2 minutes until just tender. Drain, rinse with cold water, and drain again. Then add to the soup along with the cream and lobster meat. Taste and season again. Reheat the soup but do not boil it. Ladle into deep soup cups. Serve with a slice of lemon and a small sprig of parsley in each bowl.

The name 'bisque' refers to a rich and luxurious shellfish soup with cream and brandy and is thought to have come from the Spanish Biscay region.

lobster bisque

SERVES 4   **PREP** 45 MINS **COOK** 1 HR 10 MINS   **FREEZE** UP TO 2 MONTHS
BEFORE CREAM IS ADDED

1 lobster, cooked, about 1kg (2¼lb) in weight
50g (1¾oz) butter
1 onion, finely chopped
1 carrot, finely chopped
2 celery sticks, finely chopped
1 leek, finely chopped
½ fennel bulb, finely chopped
1 bay leaf
1 sprig of tarragon
2 garlic cloves, crushed

75g (2½oz) tomato purée
4 tomatoes, roughly chopped
120ml (4fl oz) Cognac or brandy
100ml (3½fl oz) dry white wine or vermouth
1.7 litres (3 pints) fish stock
120ml (4fl oz) cream
salt and freshly ground black pepper
pinch of cayenne
juice of ½ lemon
chives, to garnish

1 Split the lobster in half, remove the meat from the body and chop the meat into small pieces. Twist off the claws and legs, break at the joints and remove the meat, then crack all the shells with the back of a knife. Chop the shells into rough pieces and put the meat into the refrigerator.

2 Melt the butter in a large pan over a medium heat, add the vegetables, herbs and garlic, and cook for 10 minutes, or until softened, stirring occasionally. Add the lobster shells. Stir in the tomato purée, tomatoes, Cognac, white wine and fish stock. Bring to the boil and simmer for 1 hour.

3 Leave to cool slightly, then ladle into a food processor. Process in short bursts, until the shell breaks into very small pieces. Strain through a coarse sieve, pushing through as much as you can, then pass it again through a fine sieve before returning to the heat.

4 Bring to the boil, add the reserved lobster meat and the cream, then season to taste, adding the cayenne and lemon. Serve in warm bowls, garnished with chives.

Buy your crab ready cooked or, for optimum freshness, buy it live and cook it yourself. Boiling is the most common way to cook a live crab, although they can also be steamed.

crab bisque

SERVES 4   **PREP** 45 MINS **COOK** 1 HR 10 MINS   **FREEZE** UP TO 2 MONTHS
BEFORE CREAM IS ADDED

1 cooked spider crab or velvet crab, about 1kg (2¼lb) in weight
50g (1¾oz) butter
olive oil
1 onion, finely chopped
1 carrot, finely chopped
2 celery stalks, finely chopped
1 leek, finely chopped
½ fennel bulb, finely chopped
1 bay leaf
1 sprig of tarragon
2 garlic cloves, crushed

2.5cm (1in) fresh ginger, peeled and finely chopped
75g (2½ oz) tomato purée
4 tomatoes, roughly chopped
120ml (4fl oz) Cognac or brandy
100ml (3½ fl oz) dry white wine or vermouth
1.7 litres (3 pints) fish stock
120ml (4fl oz) cream
salt and freshly ground black pepper
pinch of cayenne pepper
juice of ½ lemon
chopped chives, to garnish

1 Remove the crab meat from the shell and chop into small pieces. Chop the shell up roughly and put shell and meat to one side. Heat the butter and oil in a large saucepan over a medium heat. Add the vegetables, herbs, garlic, and ginger. Cook, stirring occasionally, for 10 minutes or until softened.

2 Add the chopped shell, then stir in the tomato purée, tomatoes, Cognac wine, and stock. Bring to the boil and simmer for 1 hour. Leave to cool slightly, then blend till smooth. Strain through a coarse sieve, pushing as much liquid through as you can with the back of a ladle, and then put through a fine sieve.

3 Return the soup to the pan and bring to the boil. Add the crab meat and cream, then season to taste with salt and pepper, and add cayenne and lemon juice to taste. Garnish with chives and serve in warm bowls.

Seafood and tomato make a flavourful pair in this delicate summer chilled soup. You can use the cooked clams or mussels in another dish, such as potato salad. **Marie-Pierre Moine**

crab gazpacho

SERVES 4   **PREP** 30 MINS   **FREEZE** NOT SUITABLE
COOK 10 MINS PLUS 2 HOURS CHILLING

500g (1lb 2oz) clams or mussels, cleaned
4 tbsp fruity olive oil
1 banana shallot, finely chopped
2 large spring onions, finely chopped
2 garlic cloves, crushed
100ml (3½oz) dry sherry
3 sprigs flat leaf parsley, plus 1 tbsp finely
   chopped parsley to finish
1 tsp fennel seeds, crushed

sea salt and freshly ground black pepper
½ tsp piquante pimenton
1kg (2¼lb) ripe tomatoes, rinsed and halved
2 eggs, hard-boiled and peeled
1 tbsp sherry vinegar
freshly cooked brown and white meat
   of 1 medium prepared crab
8 croûtes, rubbed with garlic

1 Put a sauté pan over a moderate heat. Tip in the clams or mussels along with 1 tbsp oil, the shallot, half the spring onion and garlic, the sherry, and 250ml water. Add the parsley sprigs, fennel seeds, salt, pepper, and pimenton. Bring to the boil. Cover and cook for 4–5 minutes, shaking a few times, until the shells open. Strain through a muslin-lined sieve into a bowl and leave to cool completely. Discard any unopened clams or mussels.

2 Put the tomatoes, the cold stock from the mussels, 1 tbsp olive oil, 1 hard-boiled egg yolk and the remaining spring onion and garlic in a blender and whiz until very smooth. Push through a sieve into a bowl. Rinse out the blender or food processor with 250ml (8fl oz) water mixed with the sherry vinegar. Pour through the sieve into the bowl.

3 Chill the soup for at least 2 hours. Press the remaining egg yolk through a sieve and finely chop the whites. Mix the brown crab meat with 2 tbsp oil and the egg yolk and whites. Add a little pepper and spread on the croûtes.

4 Ladle the cold soup into bowls and lightly stir in the white crab meat. Float a croûte on each helping and scatter over the chopped parsley.

This clear seafood soup uses dashi – a Japanese tuna- and seaweed-based fish stock – as its base. For those avoiding gluten in their diet, tamari may be used. **Shaun Hill**

prawn and sea bass soup

SERVES 4　　**PREP** 10 MINS **COOK** 5 MINS　　**FREEZE** NOT SUITABLE

100g (3½oz) spinach, blanched
1 litre (1¾ pints) dashi
100g (3½oz) sea bass fillet, cut into 4 cubes
4 large raw prawns, peeled and deveined
1 tsp soy sauce

½ small red chilli
1 spring onion, chopped
1 tbsp arrowroot
few drops lemon juice

1 Squeeze as much water as possible out of the blanched spinach, then cut into strips and set aside.

2 Bring the dashi to the boil in a saucepan and add the cubed fish and the prawns. Cook for a few moments, then add the soy sauce, chilli, and spring onion.

3 Whisk the arrowroot with 1 tbsp cold water in a bowl and stir into the soup. Bring to the boil and then remove the chilli. Add the lemon juice and spinach and serve.

This lively soup can be made in a jiffy, if you use tinned coconut milk and have a handy supply of chicken stock. It is filling enough to constitute lunch in itself. **Sophie Grigson**

prawn, chicken, coconut, and lemongrass soup

SERVES 4–6   **PREP** 10 MINS **COOK** 15 MINS   **FREEZE** NOT SUITABLE

2 cans coconut milk or 800ml (26fl oz) medium coconut milk
300ml (10fl oz) chicken stock
350g (12oz) chicken, cut into slivers
3 stalks lemongrass, heavily bruised (see p25)
1.5cm (½in) piece galangal or root ginger, cut into thin matchsticks

225g (8oz) uncooked prawns, shelled
1 red chilli, deseeded and diced
5 spring onions, sliced
juice of 1–2 limes
3 tbsp roughly chopped coriander
3 tbsp fish sauce

1 Put the coconut milk and stock into a pan. Bring up to the boil. Add the chicken, lemongrass, and galangal or ginger and lower the heat to a gentle simmer. Cook for 10 minutes, uncovered.

2 Add the prawns and cook for a further 2–3 minutes, then add all the remaining ingredients. Remove the lemongrass and discard. Taste and add more lime juice or fish sauce, if needed, then serve.

PEELING AND DEVEINING PRAWNS

Pull off the head, leaving the tail meat intact, then peel off the shell and legs with your fingers.

Make a shallow cut along the back of the prawn, then remove the dark vein with the knife tip.

This fragrant soup takes the best ingredients from a cottage garden in the southern Indian state of Kerala. If you are using dried curry leaves, add them with the stock. **Roopa Gulati**

keralan prawn soup

🔘 **SERVES** 4–6   🕐 **PREP** 20 MINS **COOK** 40 MINS   ✳ **FREEZE** NOT SUITABLE

1 tsp black peppercorns
¾ tsp mustard seeds
2 tsp coriander seeds
½ tsp fenugreek seeds
2–3 large red chillies
4 garlic cloves, chopped
5cm (2in) fresh root ginger, chopped
4 tbsp hot water
2–3 tbsp vegetable oil

small handful of fresh curry leaves
2 onions, finely chopped
750ml (1¼ pints) fish stock
250ml (8fl oz) coconut milk
250g (9oz) raw king prawns, shelled
1 tbsp coconut cream
2 tbsp fresh coriander leaves, chopped
juice of 1 lime, to taste

1 Heat a sturdy frying pan or small griddle over a low heat. Roast the peppercorns, mustard, coriander and fenugreek seeds for about 30 seconds, until they give off a spicy aroma and the mustard seeds start to pop. Grind the spices to a powder using a mortar and pestle, and set aside.

2 Roughly chop the chillies – if you like a mild flavour, use just 2 chillies and remove the seeds. Put the chillies in a small food processor with the garlic and ginger. Pour in the hot water and process to a paste. Set aside.

3 Heat the oil in a wok or saucepan. When hot, toss in the curry leaves and fry for 20 seconds, Be careful – curry leaves spit when added to hot oil. Add the onions, cover and soften for 10 minutes, stirring occasionally.

4 Stir in the chilli, garlic and ginger paste and fry for 2–3 minutes, until the water evaporates. Add the ground spice mixture and cook for a further 30 seconds, stirring all the time. Pour in the stock and simmer for 20 minutes or until reduced by one-third. Stir in the coconut milk and reheat before adding the prawns and cooking for a further 4–5 minutes. Add the coconut cream and finish with the coriander leaves and enough lime juice to sharpen.

poultry, game, and meat

A universal favourite, this soup has a zingy lemon and parsley finish. It can also be made with leftover meat and the carcase of a roasted chicken. **Marie-Pierre Moine**

traditional chicken soup

⊘ **SERVES** 4 🕐 **PREP** 2½ HRS **COOK** 30 MINS ❄ **FREEZE** UP TO 3 MONTHS
BEFORE CREAM IS ADDED

for the stock
1 small to medium free-range chicken
1 large carrot, chopped
1 leek, cut into segments
3 garlic cloves, unpeeled
20g (¾oz) dried mushrooms
3 celery stalks, chopped
2–3 sprigs each of parsley and thyme
sea salt and freshly ground black pepper

for the soup
1½ tbsp vegetable oil plus 10g (¼oz) butter
½ large red onion, finely chopped
2 garlic cloves, crushed
250g (9oz) button mushrooms, thinly sliced
100g (3½oz) short grain rice or pearl barley
4 tbsp single cream
2 tbsp finely chopped parsley
2 tsp finely grated zest of an unwaxed lemon

1 For the stock, put the chicken in a large saucepan over a low heat. Cover with water and bring slowly to boiling, skimming the surface as needed. Add the carrot, leek, garlic, dried mushrooms, celery, and herbs. Season lightly. Bring back to a simmer, partly cover, and cook for 1 hour.

2 Remove from the heat. Once cool, lift out the chicken, strip the meat from the carcase, and reserve. Return the carcase to the pan, and boil for 1 hour. Strain through a sieve into a bowl and allow the stock to cool.

3 Soak the rice or barley in cold water for 30 minutes. Rinse and drain. Skim the fat from the stock. You'll need 750ml (1¼ pints) of stock for the soup recipe but you can add boiling water if needed.

4 Put the oil and butter in a sauté pan over a medium heat. Add the onion, garlic, and mushrooms and fry for 3–5 minutes. Add the rice or barley and cook, stirring, for 2 minutes. Add the stock and cook for 15–20 minutes. Shred about 200g (7oz) of the reserved chicken and add to the soup. Taste, season if required, and return to a simmer. Stir in the cream, parsley, and lemon zest, and serve hot.

This version is quicker than the traditional method of slow-simmering a whole chicken. Some cock-a-leekie recipes use prunes – try adding a few with the vegetables in step 2.

cock-a-leekie soup

◉ SERVES 4   **◔ PREP** 10 MINS **COOK** 1¼ HRS   **❄ FREEZE** UP TO 3 MONTHS

450g (1lb) chicken breasts
  and thighs, skinned
2 bay leaves
1 litre (1¾ pints) chicken or
  vegetable stock
60g (2oz) long-grain rice

2 leeks, thinly sliced
2 carrots, grated
pinch of ground cloves
1 tsp sea salt
1 tbsp chopped fresh parsley

1 Place the chicken in a large pan with the bay leaves and pour over the stock. Bring to the boil, then reduce the heat, cover the pan, and simmer for 30 minutes.

2 Skim the surface of the soup and discard any scum that has formed. Add the rice, leeks, carrots, cloves, and salt. Bring back to the boil, reduce the heat, cover the pan, and simmer for a further 30 minutes.

3 Remove the bay leaves and discard. If you wish, lift out the chicken, remove the meat from the bones, then return the meat to the soup. Ladle the soup into a warm tureen or divide between individual serving bowls, and serve hot, garnished with parsley.

CHICKEN
Chickens that are afforded space to move around in, and access to the open air, are not surprisingly healthier than battery-kept birds, and this is reflected in the taste. Choose a bird with a firm, plump breast and tight skin.

This Mexican soup is made with thin *fideo* noodles, which are similar to angel-hair pasta. The avocado and soured cream offset the spiciness of the broth

sopa seca de fideos

◉ SERVES 4   **🕐 PREP** 20 MINS PLUS 30 MINS SOAKING   **❄ FREEZE** NOT SUITABLE
COOK 15 MINS

2 dried chipotle chillies
2 large ripe tomatoes, skinned and deseeded
2 garlic cloves
1 small onion, roughly chopped
900ml (1½ pints) chicken stock
3 tbsp vegetable oil

2 skinless boneless chicken breasts, diced
225g (8oz) Mexican *fideo* noodles or dried
   angel-hair pasta
4 tbsp soured cream, to serve
1 avocado, stone removed, chopped,
   to serve

1 Soak the dried chillies in water for 30 minutes, then drain, discarding the soaking water. Using a blender, whiz the tomatoes, garlic, onion, chillies, and 2 tbsp of the stock until smooth. Set aside.

2 Heat 2 tbsp of the oil in a large pan and stir-fry the chicken for 2–3 minutes, or until just cooked. Remove from the pan, drain on kitchen paper, and set aside.

3 Pour the remaining oil into the pan, add the noodles, and cook over a low heat, stirring constantly, until the noodles are golden.

4 Pour in the tomato mixture, stir until the noodles are coated, then add the remaining stock, and return the chicken to the pan. Cook for 2–3 minutes, or until the noodles are just tender. To serve, ladle into bowls, topping each with soured cream and chopped avocado.

Here, a nourishing chicken stock combines with the sweetness of sweetcorn and satisfying vermicelli to create a soothing meal in a bowl.

chinese chicken noodle soup

⊘ SERVES 4   **🕐 PREP** 10 MINS PLUS 30 MINS SOAKING   **❄ FREEZE** NOT SUITABLE
COOK 15 MINS

45g (1½oz) dried Chinese mushrooms
600ml (1 pint) chicken stock
2 skinless boneless chicken breasts

175g (6oz) dried rice vermicelli
100g (3½oz) sweetcorn kernels

1 Place the dried Chinese mushrooms in a heatproof bowl, pour over 300ml (10fl oz) boiling water, and leave to stand for 30 minutes. Reserving the mushrooms, strain the soaking water into a large saucepan and add the stock. Bring the pan to the boil.

2 Slice the mushrooms and cut the chicken breasts into bite-sized pieces or thin strips. Break the rice vermicelli into short lengths and stir into the pan. Bring to a simmer and cook for 2 minutes.

3 Add the mushrooms, chicken, and sweetcorn kernels to the pan, bring back to the boil, and simmer for a further 2 minutes, or until the vermicelli are tender. Spoon into bowls and serve at once.

The pasta and the liberal quantities of vegetables ensure that this chicken soup goes a long way. You can use whatever fresh vegetables are available.

chicken soup with pasta

⊘ SERVES 4–6   **🕐 PREP** 10 MINS **COOK** 1 HR   **❄ FREEZE** UP TO 3 MONTHS

4 chicken drumsticks
1.25kg (2¾lb) mixed vegetables, e.g. carrots (diced), kohlrabi (diced), green beans (topped and tailed; strings removed), cauliflower or broccoli (small florets), leeks (sliced), courgettes (sliced), peas

100g (3½oz) soup vermicelli
sea salt and freshly ground black pepper
2 tablespoons chopped parsley

1 Put the chicken drumsticks in a large saucepan, cover with 1.2 litres (2¼ pints) cold water and bring to the boil. Cover and cook over medium heat, skimming occasionally with a slotted spoon, for about 40 minutes. Remove from the heat and strain into a clean pan, then allow the stock to cool slightly before skimming the fat from the surface with a spoon.

2 Remove and discard the skin from the chicken drumsticks, strip the meat from the bones, shred and reserve.

3 Bring the stock back to the boil again, then add the vegetables. Add those with longer cooking times first, cover and simmer for 5 minutes; then add the remaining vegetables and the soup vermicelli and cover and cook for a further 5 minutes.

4 Season the soup with salt and pepper to taste. Add the reserved meat and heat it through. Ladle into bowls, garnish each with a little chopped parsley, and serve piping hot.

Based on a Thuringian vegetable soup, this recipe requires a good-quality, well-flavoured chicken stock, so make your own for best results.

german chicken broth

SERVES 4-6   **PREP** 10 MINS **COOK** 25 MINS   ✳ **FREEZE** UP TO MONTHS
AT THE END OF STEP 1

1.2 litres chicken stock
150g (5oz) green beans, topped, tailed,
  and strings removed
2 large carrots, peeled and sliced
200g (7oz) kohlrabi, diced

150g (5½oz) mangetout or sugar snap peas,
  topped and tailed
salt and freshly ground black pepper
single or double cream, to serve
1 bunch chervil, finely chopped

1 Bring the stock to the boil in a medium-sized saucepan, add the green beans and simmer for 5 minutes. Add the carrots and kohlrabi and cook for a further 5 minutes, then add the mangetout or sugar snap peas and cook for a further 5 minutes – be careful not to overcook these or they will lose their delightful crunchiness.

2 Season with salt and pepper and remove the pan from the heat. Ladle into serving bowls, add a swirl of cream to each, and sprinkle with chervil before serving.

SUGAR SNAP PEAS
These are most often steamed, lightly boiled or stir-fried, but they can also be enjoyed raw. The fresher the produce, the better the flavour and texture, so make sure you go for firm, smooth, bright green pods.

This is a traditional soup with a modern twist. Adding baking powder and mashed potato to the balls gives them a really light, fluffy texture. **Carolyn Humphries**

matzo ball soup

◉ SERVES 4   **🕐 PREP** 15 MINS **COOK** 1 HR 10 MINS   **❄ FREEZE** UP TO 3 MONTHS
BROTH ONLY

1 chicken leg and thigh portion
1 onion, finely chopped
1 leek, thinly sliced
1 large carrot, finely diced
1 litre (1¾ pints) water
1 sprig of fresh thyme
1 tsp celery salt
salt and freshly ground black pepper

for the matzo balls
1 potato, about 115g (4oz), cooked
  and mashed

45g (1½oz) fine matzo meal
½ tsp baking powder
½ tsp grated fresh root ginger
1 tbsp chopped fresh thyme
1 tbsp chopped fresh parsley
1 garlic clove, finely chopped
salt and freshly ground black pepper
1 tbsp sunflower oil
1 egg, beaten
4 small sprigs of fresh thyme, to garnish

1 Put the soup ingredients in a large saucepan. Bring to the boil, reduce the heat, cover, and simmer gently for 1 hour, topping up with water if it gets low. Meanwhile, mix the mashed potato with the matzo meal, baking powder, ginger, thyme, parsley, garlic, and a little salt and pepper. Add the oil then mix with the beaten egg to form a soft, slightly sticky dough. Shape into 8 balls.

2 Discard the thyme sprig from the soup. Carefully lift out the chicken and remove all meat from the bones, discarding the skin. Chop the flesh and return to the soup. Taste and adjust the seasoning, if necessary.

3 Bring the soup back to a simmer, drop in the balls, cover, and simmer gently for about 10 minutes until fluffy and cooked through. Ladle into warm soup bowls and garnish each with a small sprig of fresh thyme.

Consommé regularly has some garnish or herb to lend interest, but it is the quality and clarity of the soup itself that is at its heart. **Shaun Hill**

chicken consommé

⊘ SERVES 4   **⊕ PREP TIME** 15 MINS PLUS CHILLING   **❄ FREEZE** NOT SUITABLE
COOK 1 HR 20 MINS

2 large egg whites
1 tbsp passata or 1 tsp tomato purée
1 chicken leg, boned and minced or
   finely chopped
1 onion, chopped
1 carrot, chopped

1 leek, chopped
1 garlic clove, chopped
1 tbsp chopped parsley
2 litres (3½ pints) cold chicken stock
salt and freshly ground pepper
chervil, to garnish

1 To make the clarification mixture, whisk the egg whites just enough to loosen them and form a few bubbles. Add the passata or tomato purée and mix thoroughly.

2 Place the chicken, vegetables, garlic, and parsley in a bowl, add the egg white mixture and mix thoroughly – use an electric mixer with paddle attachment if need be. Refrigerate until well chilled.

3 Combine the stock with the clarification mixture in a deep, narrow saucepan. Heat slowly, uncovered, until the stock comes to the boil. Gently stir to stop the egg sticking. Once the stock reaches boiling point, turn the heat right down and leave to simmer gently for at least an hour, or until a white crust forms. When it is hard, poke a gap through it to check on the clarity.

4 When the consommé is clear and the clarification ingredients cooked, widen the gap and strain the consommé through a muslin-lined sieve into a clean container. Season, garnish with chervil, and serve.

This can be a simple chicken broth with just the drizzled egg, but it's more tasty and filling with the addition of vegetables and Chinese seasonings. **Carolyn Humphreys**

chinese egg drop soup

SERVES 4   **PREP** 5 MINS **COOK** 25 MINS   **FREEZE** NOT SUITABLE

1 litre (1¾ pints) chicken stock
1 garlic clove, crushed
½ tsp grated fresh root ginger
2 spring onions, chopped
2 tbsp soy sauce
½ tsp Chinese five-spice powder

2 corn on the cob or 200g (7oz)
  can sweetcorn
2 good handfuls of fresh baby leaf spinach
2 tbsp cornflour
2 eggs, beaten

1 Put the stock in a pan with the garlic, ginger, spring onions, soy sauce, and five-spice powder. If using fresh corn, place each corn on the cob on its end and slide a sharp knife down the length to remove all the kernels. Add the kernels to the pan, bring to the boil, reduce the heat, cover, and simmer gently for 20 minutes.

2 Add the canned sweetcorn if using, including any liquid, and the spinach. Bring back to the boil, reduce the heat, and simmer for 1 minute or until the spinach has just wilted. Taste and add more soy sauce if necessary.

3 Blend the cornflour with 4 tbsp water and stir in. Bring back to the boil and simmer, stirring, for 1 minute to thicken slightly. Gradually trickle in the beaten egg, stirring gently, so that it forms thin strands. Serve in warm soup bowls.

This lemon, chicken, and rice soup is claimed by countries across the eastern Mediterranean. The stock must be well flavoured, or it will not withstand the lemon juice. **Shaun Hill**

avgolemone

SERVES 4   **PREP** 5 MINS **COOK** 20 MINS   **FREEZE** NOT SUITABLE

50g (1¾oz) long-grain rice
1.2 litres (2 pints) well-flavoured
  chicken stock
3 eggs

juice of 1 large lemon
salt and freshly ground black pepper
lemon wedges, to serve

1 Bring the rice and stock to the boil in a saucepan. Simmer, uncovered, for 15 minutes, or until the rice is completely cooked.

2 Whisk the eggs and lemon juice in a bowl until the mixture becomes frothy. Add a ladleful of hot stock and continue to whisk.

3 Remove the rice and stock from direct heat. Whisk the egg, lemon, and stock mixture into it. Return to the heat and cook gently and briefly at a temperature below boiling point, whisking until the texture is velvety – do not allow to boil. Season and serve with lemon wedges.

Although this recipe uses coconut milk as its base and key Thai flavourings, it makes no pretence at authenticity. No extra salt should be necessary as nam pla is salty. **Shaun Hill**

thai chicken soup

◉ **SERVES** 4   🕐 **PREP** 10 MINS **COOK** 45 MINS   ❄ **FREEZE** NOT SUITABLE

4 stalks lemongrass, bruised and cut
   into 1cm (½in) lengths
200g (7oz) galangal, peeled and diced
5 kaffir lime leaves, bruised
1 chicken leg
500ml (16fl oz) water

2 small chillies
1 litre (1¾ pints) coconut milk
1 tbsp nam pla
juice of 3 limes
3 spring onions, finely chopped
2 tbsp chopped coriander leaves

1 Put the lemongrass, galangal, lime leaves, chicken, and water in a pan and bring to the boil. Simmer, uncovered, for 30 minutes or until the chicken is cooked. Remove with a slotted spoon, dice the flesh, discarding the skin and bones, and set aside.

2 Add the chillies to the pan and bring the soup back to the boil. Pour in the coconut milk and heat slowly – you want the soup to become hot enough for the flavours to infuse the coconut milk without coming to the boil.

3 Strain the soup into a clean pan or tureen. Remove the chillies from the sieve and cut into slivers. Add the nam pla, lime juice, spring onions, coriander, and chicken to the soup, then taste to check the seasoning. Serve garnished with the chilli slivers.

CHILLIES
Look for fresh, bright, shiny-looking chillies, and avoid any that have soft patches or look wrinkled. Wrapped in a biodegradable plastic bag, they will keep in the chiller box of the refrigerator for up to a fortnight.

This recipe depends on the quality of its few ingredients, so always try to use homemade stock, organic eggs and the best Parmesan cheese you can find.

stracciatella with pasta

SERVES 4–6   **PREP** 10 MINS **COOK** 20 MINS   **FREEZE** NOT SUITABLE

1.5 litres (2¾ pints) chicken stock
100g (3½oz) soup pasta
4 eggs
salt and freshly ground black pepper

½ tsp freshly grated nutmeg
2 tbsp grated Parmesan cheese
1 tbsp chopped parsley
1 tbsp olive oil

1 Place the stock in a large pan and bring to the boil. Add the pasta and cook according to packet directions, or until al dente.

2 Break the eggs into a small bowl, add the nutmeg, season to taste with salt and pepper, and whisk lightly with a fork to break up the egg. Add the Parmesan and parsley.

3 Add the olive oil to the simmering stock, reduce the heat to low, then stir the stock lightly to create a gentle "whirlpool". Gradually pour in the eggs and cook for 1 minute, without boiling, so they set into fine strands. Leave to stand for 1 minute before serving.

This broth is crammed with contrasting sweet, sour, hot and salty flavours, and is made in minutes. Instead of chicken, you could try using fish stock and shelled prawns. **Roopa Gulati**

hot and sour chicken broth

◎ SERVES 4　　**🕐 PREP** 15 MINS **COOK** 20 MINS　　**❄ FREEZE** UP TO 1 MONTH
AT THE END OF STEP 2

1 litre (1¾ pints) chicken stock
5cm (2in) piece galangal or ginger, sliced
8 lime leaves, shredded
5 garlic cloves, roughly chopped
2 tbsp chopped coriander stems
2 lemon grass, split lengthways and
　lightly bruised (see p25)
salt and freshly ground black pepper
2 chicken breasts, about 125g (4½oz) each,
　skinned and thinly shredded

2–3 bird's eye chillies, finely sliced
2 tsp sugar
3 small shallots, sliced
juice of 2 limes
3 tbsp fish sauce
2 tbsp sweet chilli sauce
2 small pak choi, roughly chopped
handful of bean sprouts

1 Pour the chicken stock into a large pan and add the galangal or ginger, lime leaves, garlic, coriander stems and lemon grass. Season, bring the stock to the boil, turn down the heat and simmer for 10 minutes.

2 Strain the stock into a clean pan and stir in the chicken, chillies, sugar, shallots, lime juice, fish sauce and chilli sauce. Simmer for 4–5 minutes, until the chicken is cooked.

3 Add the pak choi and cook the broth for a further minute. Stir in the bean sprouts and serve straight away.

Eric Treuille of Books for Cooks, a cookery mecca in Notting Hill, London, writes, "We use chicken, honey and herb sausages in this dish, but other types work just as well."

sausage and bean soup

SERVES 4   **PREP** 20 MINS **COOK** 30–35 MINS   **FREEZE** UP TO 3 MONTHS

250g (9oz) cherry tomatoes, halved
4 tbsp olive oil, plus extra to serve
salt and freshly ground black pepper
1 onion, finely chopped
200g (7oz) organic chicken or other good-quality pure-meat sausages or chorizo, skinned and roughly crumbled
4 garlic cloves, finely chopped

½–1 tsp crushed chilli flakes (according to taste)
400g can cannellini beans, drained, rinsed, and drained again
750ml (1¼ pints) hot chicken stock or vegetable stock
1 tbsp balsamic vinegar
1 handful flat-leaf parsley or basil, chopped

1 Preheat the oven to 180°C (350°F/Gas 4). Place the tomatoes on a baking tray, drizzle with half the oil, sprinkle with a couple of pinches each of salt and freshly ground black pepper, then turn to coat well. Roast for 15 minutes or until softened and slightly wilted, then remove from the oven and drizzle with the balsamic vinegar.

2 Meanwhile, heat the remaining oil in a heavy-bottomed pot over a medium heat. Add the onion and cook for 5 minutes or until soft. Stir in the sausagemeat, garlic, and chilli flakes, and cook, stirring, for 5–10 minutes or until the onion is pale yellow. Stir in the beans and stock, bring to the boil, adjust the heat to a steady simmer and cook for 10 minutes. Add the tomatoes and their juices and stir in half the parsley or basil.

3 Ladle out a cupful of the beans and tomatoes without too much liquid, and whiz until smooth in a blender. Stir back into the pot, then simmer the soup steadily for 10 minutes. If it is too thick, thin with a little hot stock or water. Stir in the rest of the herbs and adjust the seasoning, adding salt, freshly ground black pepper, chilli flakes, and balsamic vinegar to taste. Ladle into warmed bowls, drizzle with a little more olive oil, and serve.

You can vary this dish by substituting smoked pork sausage for pancetta or using duck instead of chicken. You may wish to add a little filé powder, if you have it. **Carolyn Humphries**

chicken and pork gumbo

SERVES 6 **PREP** 20 MINS **COOK** 1½ HRS **FREEZE** UP TO 3 MONTHS WITHOUT THE RICE

2 chicken leg and thigh portions
200g (7oz) smoked lardons or diced pancetta
2 boneless belly pork slices, rinded and diced
900ml (1½ pints) chicken stock
1 bay leaf
2 red peppers
30g (1oz) butter
1 onion, chopped
1 garlic clove, chopped
1 celery heart, sliced
3 tbsp plain flour
2 beefsteak tomatoes, skinned and chopped

2 tbsp tomato purée
115g (4oz) thin green beans, trimmed and cut in short lengths
150g (5½oz) okra, cut in short lengths
2 large sprigs of fresh thyme, chopped, plus a little extra to garnish
2 tsp sweet paprika
1 tsp smoked paprika
1 tsp light brown sugar
a few drops of Tabasco
salt and freshly ground black pepper
225g (8oz) long-grain rice, boiled

1 Put the chicken, lardons or pancetta, and belly pork in a saucepan with the stock and bay leaf. Bring to the boil, reduce the heat, cover, and simmer gently for 1 hour. Meanwhile, roast the peppers under a hot grill for 10–15 minutes until blackened. Put in a plastic bag, leave to cool then peel off the skin, discard the stalks and seeds, rinse, and dice the flesh.

2 Strain the stock through a sieve and set aside. Lift the chicken out of the sieve and place on a board. Remove all the meat from the bones and cut into neat pieces, discarding the skin. Add to the pork and set aside.

3 Melt the butter in the pan. Fry the onion, garlic, and celery for 2 minutes, stirring. Stir in the flour and cook for 3 minutes, stirring, until golden. Remove from the heat and blend in the stock. Return to the heat and bring to the boil. Add the remaining ingredients except the meat and rice. Bring back to the boil, reduce the heat, partially cover and simmer for 30 minutes. Stir in the meats, taste and season with Tabasco, salt and pepper. Remove the bay leaf. Spoon the rice into bowls, ladle the gumbo over and garnish with thyme.

An Anglo-Indian soup from colonial days, mulligatawny has many variations. For extra heat, pop a split red chilli in the pan when you pour over the stock. **Roopa Gulati**

mulligatawny

SERVES 4   **PREP** 20 MINS **COOK** 45 MINS   **FREEZE** UP TO 3 MONTHS

40g (1¼oz) butter
1 large onion, chopped
5cm (2in) fresh root ginger, finely chopped
2 garlic cloves, finely chopped
1 cox apple, unpeeled, diced, with peel
1 carrot, sliced
1 celery stick, sliced
1 heaped tbsp mild curry powder
1 tbsp gram flour or plain flour

4 tomatoes, roughly chopped
2 tsp tomato purée
500ml (16fl oz) hot chicken stock
2 bay leaves
salt and freshly ground black pepper
200ml (7fl oz) coconut milk or single cream
175g (7oz) cooked chicken meat, shredded
juice of ½ lime
2 tbsp chopped fresh coriander

1 Melt the butter in a large pan and soften the onion, ginger, and garlic for 10 minutes, without colouring. Add the apple, carrot, and celery to the pan and continue cooking, covered, for 5 minutes.

2 Stir in the curry powder and fry for 1 minute, stirring all the time. Sprinkle over the gram flour (or plain flour) and continue cooking for another 20 seconds.

3 Add the tomatoes and tomato purée followed by the chicken stock. Add the bay leaves and season with salt and pepper. Bring to the boil, stirring, then reduce the heat and simmer, half-covered for 20 minutes.

4 Remove the bay leaf and blend until smooth, using a stick blender or liquidizer. Sieve the soup to remove any fibres and skin. Reheat, stir in the coconut milk or cream, and add the diced chicken. Sharpen with a squeeze of lime and add the chopped coriander.

Make thrifty use of leftover turkey by simmering your own stock with the carcase after a roast dinner. This broth is every bit as appealing when made with chicken. **Roopa Gulati**

turkey broth

SERVES 6   **PREP** 20 MINS **COOK** 25 MINS   **FREEZE** UP TO 3 MONTHS
BEFORE CREAM IS ADDED

1 litre (1¾ pints) turkey stock or
  chicken stock
120ml (4fl oz) dry white wine
1 carrot, finely diced
1 parsnip, finely diced
2 celery stalks, finely diced
1 leek (white part only), finely diced

1 small turnip, finely diced
salt and freshly ground black pepper
225g (8oz) cooked turkey meat, finely diced
100ml (3½fl oz) single cream
2 tbsp chopped parsley
crusty bread, to serve

1 Bring the stock and wine to the boil in a large pan, then stir in the carrot, parsnip, celery, leek, and turnip. Season with salt and freshly ground black pepper, half-cover with a lid, and simmer for 20 minutes.

2 Stir in the cooked turkey, cream, and chopped parsley and reheat gently. Serve the soup with plenty of crusty bread.

This thick and creamy soup is perfect for using up leftover turkey, and tastes even richer if you have some home-made turkey stock to hand. **Angela Nilsen**

chunky turkey soup

⊘ **SERVES** 4   🕐 **PREP** 15 MINS **COOK** 30 MINS   ❄ **FREEZE** UP TO 3 MONTHS

1 tbsp olive oil
50g (1¾ oz) butter, softened
1 onion, chopped
1 large potato, peeled, cut into small chunks
2 carrots, cut into small chunks
1 leek, cut into small chunks
2 bay leaves
1 litre (1¾ pints) turkey or chicken stock,
   preferably home-made

25g (scant 1oz) plain flour
50g (1¾oz) frozen peas
200g (7oz) cooked turkey, cut in chunks
big handful of roughly chopped parsley
salt and pepper
hot garlic bread, to serve

1 Heat the oil and half of the butter in a large sauté pan. Add the onion and fry for 4–5 minutes until just starting to turn golden. Add the potato, carrots, leek, and bay leaves and fry for a few more minutes over a high heat until the vegetables are going golden and sticky on the base of the pan. With the heat still high, pour in the stock, scraping the bottom of the pan so you have a lovely golden-coloured stock. Lower the heat, cover with a lid and simmer for 15 minutes.

2 Work the rest of the butter into the flour with a spoon. Drop this in small pieces into the pan, whisking all the time after each addition with a wire whisk, until you have a thin sauce consistency. Simmer for about 10 minutes to finish cooking the vegetables, adding the peas for the last 2 minutes. Remove the bay leaves.

3 Stir in the turkey and parsley, grind in lots of black pepper and add salt if needed. Warm through then serve with slices of hot garlic bread.

This spicy soup is equally delicious made with other game birds, but if they are small, such as pigeon or partridge, use the whole bird including the breasts. **Carolyn Humphries**

pheasant and apple soup

◉ SERVES 4–6   **🕐 PREP** 20 MINS
COOK 1 HR 15 MINS PLUS REHEATING

❄ FREEZE UP TO 3 MONTHS
WITHOUT THE CREAM

1 small pheasant
15g (½oz) butter
1 onion, roughly chopped
1 small sweet potato, roughly chopped
1 small cooking apple, peeled and diced
500ml (18fl oz) medium-sweet cider
   or apple juice

450ml (15fl oz) chicken stock
5cm (2in) piece of cinnamon stick
1 bay leaf
salt and freshly ground black pepper
150ml (5fl oz) single cream
4 small fresh parsley sprigs, to garnish

1 Cut the breasts off the pheasant and reserve to cook for a separate dish. Cut the rest of the bird in pieces using a large sharp knife or poultry shears.

2 Melt the butter in a saucepan. Add the onion and fry gently, stirring, for 2 minutes until softened but not browned. Add the remaining ingredients except the cream. Bring to the boil, reduce the heat, cover and simmer gently for 1 hour.

3 Remove the pheasant and leave to cool slightly. Discard the bay leaf and cinnamon stick and purée the remaining soup in a blender or with a stick blender. Return to the rinsed-out pan and stir in the cream. Taste and adjust the seasoning if necessary.

4 Take the pheasant meat off the bones, discarding the skin, and shred it. Add half to the soup. Reheat the soup but do not boil. Remove the bay leaf and cinnamon stick. Ladle into shallow soup plates, put a small pile of the remaining diced pheasant in the centre and garnish each with a small sprig of parsley.

This is a substantial soup that is a great way to make one partridge suffice for four people. You could use any other small game bird in exactly the same way. **Carolyn Humphries**

partridge soup

SERVES 4   **PREP** 20 MINS **COOK** 65 MINS   **FREEZE** UP TO 3 MONTHS
WITHOUT THE SHERRY

1 tbsp sunflower oil
1 partridge, quartered
1 onion, unpeeled and quartered
900ml (1½ pints) chicken stock
1 bouquet garni
salt and freshly ground black pepper
1 potato, diced
1 carrot, diced

1 small turnip, diced
2 tbsp plain flour
4 tbsp water
200g (7oz) cooked peeled
  chestnuts, quartered
2 tbsp amontillado sherry
a few drops of soy sauce
a little chopped fresh parsley

1 Heat the oil in a saucepan and brown the partridge pieces all over. Add the onion, stock, bouquet garni, and a little salt and pepper. Bring to the boil, reduce the heat, cover, and simmer gently for 1 hour.

2 Strain the stock and return to the saucepan. Add the potato, carrot, and turnip. Bring back to the boil, partially cover and simmer gently for about 20 minutes until the vegetables are really tender. Meanwhile, take all the meat off the partridge, discarding the skin, and shred the meat.

3 Remove the bouquet garni from the soup and discard. Blend the flour with the water and add to the soup. Bring to the boil, stirring, until lightly thickened and simmer for 2 minutes.

4 Add the shredded meat, chestnuts, and sherry to the soup and simmer for 2 minutes. Add a few drops of soy sauce to taste. Ladle into warm soup bowls and garnish with a little chopped parsley.

You can buy ready-diced mixed game which includes furred game and pigeon, or use diced venison, rabbit or hare. Well-hung beef is another option. **Carolyn Humphries**

puff-crusted game soup

⊘ SERVES 4   **🕐 PREP** 20 MINS **COOK** 1 HR 20 MINS   **❄ FREEZE** UP TO 3 MONTHS
WITHOUT THE PASTRY LID

a large knob of butter
175g (6oz) diced game meat, thawed
   if frozen, cut into small pieces
1 red onion, chopped
2 tbsp plain flour
900ml (1½ pints) beef stock
1 tbsp redcurrant jelly

3 chestnut mushrooms, halved and sliced
1 tbsp chopped fresh sage
4 tbsp ruby port
salt and freshly ground black pepper
1 sheet ready-rolled puff pastry,
   thawed if frozen
1 egg, beaten

1 Melt the butter in a saucepan and fry the meat and onion for 5 minutes, stirring, until browned.

2 Blend in the flour and cook for 1 minute. Remove from the heat, gradually stir in the stock, add the redcurrant jelly and bring to the boil, stirring. Add the mushrooms, sage, port and some seasoning. Bring back to the boil, reduce the heat, cover, and simmer very gently for 1 hour, stirring occasionally until rich and really tender. Taste and adjust the seasoning if necessary.

3 Meanwhile, preheat the oven to 220°C (425°F/Gas 7). Cut four circles from the pastry slightly larger than deep oven-proof soup cups and brush with beaten egg. Stand the soup cups on a baking sheet. Brush the edges with beaten egg. Ladle in the soup. Top with the circles of pastry, pressing down lightly with a fork around the edge to secure. Make a small slit in the top of each pie lid with a sharp knife to allow the steam to escape. Bake in the oven for about 15 minutes or until puffy, crisp and golden brown. Allow to cool for 3–5 minutes before serving.

This classic French soup takes time to make, but is well worth waiting for. Try serving this with coarse-grained mustard, gherkins and creamed horseradish. **Marie-Pierre Moine**

pot au feu

◉ SERVES 4   **🕐 PREP** 40 MINS **COOK** 2 HRS   **❄ FREEZE** NOT SUITABLE

a few beef bones, if possible
1kg (2¼lb) braising steak cut into 5–6cm (2–2½in) pieces
salt and freshly ground black pepper
1 large carrot, thickly cut on the diagonal
2 turnips, thickly sliced
1 medium-to-large waxy potato, cut into 8 pieces

1 Spanish onion, halved
2 garlic cloves, crushed
3 cloves
1 large leek, thickly sliced
3 celery sticks, chopped
3 bay leaves
several sprigs each of thyme and parsley

1 Put any bones in a large, deep, heavy casserole pan. Place the meat on top of the bones. Cover with plenty of cold water, at least 6cm (2½in) above the meat, and very slowly bring to a simmer over a low heat. Season lightly. Skim off any scum that rises to the surface with a slotted spoon. Cover and let simmer very gently for 1 hour, while you prepare the vegetables. Cut one half of the onion into slices and push the cloves into the other half.

2 Skim the meat again. Add the prepared vegetables to the pan, with the bay leaves, thyme and parsley. Bring back to a simmer and skim again. Season lightly. Reduce the heat, partially cover and cook gently for at least 45 minutes, until the meat and vegetables are tender.

3 Skim again if necessary then lift out the meat and vegetables and put in a large shallow bowl or in individual bowls. Discard the bones, the half onion stuck with cloves, bay leaves, thyme and parsley.

4 Strain the stock into a saucepan through a muslin-lined sieve. Bring to a simmer and season if required. Ladle sufficient over the meat and vegetables. Leave the remaining stock to cool. There should be plenty left for you to use in other dishes (keep refrigerated for up to 3 days, or freeze).

Warming and hearty, this soup is great served with tortillas and with some guacamole (avocado mashed with lime juice) on hand to spoon in. **Carolyn Humphries**

beef chilli soup

🍲 **SERVES** 4   🕐 **PREP** 10 MINS **COOK** 35 MINS   ❄ **FREEZE** UP TO 3 MONTHS

1 tbsp olive oil
1 onion, chopped
225g (8oz) lean minced beef
½ tsp crushed dried chillies
1–2 fresh red chillies, seeded and chopped
1 tsp ground cumin
1 tsp dried oregano
450ml (15fl oz) passata

450ml (15fl oz) beef stock
400g (14oz) can red kidney beans, drained
   and rinsed
1 tbsp tomato purée
½ tsp caster sugar
salt and freshly ground black pepper
1 tbsp chopped fresh coriander or parsley
grated Manchego or Cheddar cheese, to serve

1 Heat the olive oil in a large saucepan, add the onion and fry for 4–5 minutes or until softened but not coloured. Add the mince and fry, stirring, until the grains of meat are separated and no longer pink.

2 Stir in the chillies and cumin and fry for 30 seconds, stirring. Add the oregano, passata, stock, red kidney beans, tomato purée, sugar, and salt and pepper. Bring to the boil, stirring. Reduce the heat, partially cover, and simmer gently for 30 minutes, stirring occasionally. Taste and adjust the seasoning if necessary.

3 Ladle into warm soup bowls and sprinkle with the coriander or parsley. Serve topped with grated Manchego or Cheddar cheese.

The warming flavours of steak and onions make this soup a rich and satisfying meal. For an authentic touch, use Hungarian paprika – it is fairly readily available these days.

hungarian goulash soup

SERVES 6–8   **PREP** 15 MINS **COOK** 2 HRS   **FREEZE** UP TO 3 MONTHS
AT THE END OF STEP 2

120ml (4fl oz) olive oil
675g (1½lb) onions, thinly sliced
2 garlic cloves, crushed
675g (1½lb) chuck steak, cut into
  5cm (2in) cubes
salt and freshly ground black pepper

2 tbsp paprika
1 tsp caraway seeds
1 tsp cayenne pepper, plus extra to garnish
4 tbsp tomato purée
1 litre (1¾ pints) beef stock
soured cream, to garnish

1 Heat 3 tbsp of the olive oil in a large casserole over a medium heat, add the onions, and cook, stirring occasionally, for 10 minutes or until they are golden brown. Add the garlic for the final 2 minutes, then remove the casserole from the heat.

2 Heat the remaining oil in a frying pan, add the steak, and cook, stirring often, for 5 minutes or until brown on all sides. Season with salt and add to the onions, along with the spices and tomato purée. Return the casserole to the heat and cook for 5 minutes, stirring all the time, then pour in the stock. Cover with a lid and simmer gently for 1¾ hours.

3 Season to taste with salt and freshly ground black pepper, then serve the soup garnished with soured cream, a sprinkling of cayenne, and some more freshly ground black pepper.

Choose firm, waxy potatoes that will keep their shape and texture in this deliciously savoury soup. Cooking the beans until just al dente retains maximum taste and colour.

beef and green bean soup

⊘ SERVES 6   **⏱ PREP** 20 MINS **COOK** 1 HR   **❄ FREEZE** UP TO 3 MONTHS

2 tbsp sunflower oil
500g (1lb 2oz) braising beef, eg from the
   shoulder, diced into 2cm (¾in) cubes
salt and freshly ground black pepper
1 onion, chopped
2–3 sprigs of thyme

1 litre (1¾ pints) vegetable stock
1 large potato, peeled and diced
250g (9oz) green beans, trimmed and cut into
   small pieces
1–2 tbsp chopped fresh parsley (optional)

1 Heat the oil in a pan, season the cubed meat with salt and pepper, and add half the meat to the hot oil. Brown the meat until golden all over. Remove from the pan and repeat with the rest of the meat. Remove the meat from the pan, add the onion, and fry until softened.

2 Transfer the browned meat back to the pan, tie the thyme sprigs together with kitchen string, and add them to the pan with the stock. Bring to the boil, cover, and cook over a medium heat for about 40 minutes.

3 Add the potato, bring back to the boil, cover, and cook for 10–15 minutes, or until just tender. Add the chopped beans and cook for 4–5 minutes, or until the beans are al dente.

4 Remove the thyme. Season to taste with salt and pepper, break up the meat pieces slightly, and sprinkle with parsley, if using, before serving.

Enriched with sherry, this slow-cooked soup is a classic for flavourful comfort eating. If you prefer a chunky texture, the soup also tastes good unblended.

oxtail soup

◉ SERVES 6   **◷ PREP** 20 MINS, PLUS 1 HR CHILLING   **❄ FREEZE** UP TO 3 MONTHS
                COOK 4 HRS 45 MINS   BEFORE THE SHERRY IS ADDED

2 tbsp vegetable oil
salt and freshly ground black pepper
600g (1lb 5oz) ox tails, disjointed, available
    from your butcher
1 onion, sliced
2 carrots, diced
2 celery sticks, diced

400g (14oz) tin chopped tomatoes
¼ bunch of parsley
1 bay leaf
2 sprigs of fresh thyme
1 tbsp plain flour
1 tbsp butter
150ml (5fl oz) dry sherry

1 Heat the oil in a large saucepan, season the ox tails with salt and pepper, add them to the hot oil, and fry until golden on all sides. Add the onion and fry until softened slightly. Add 2 litres of water, season with salt and pepper, and simmer, uncovered, for about 2 hours. Cover and continue to simmer for a further 2 hours. Check to see if the liquid needs topping up during cooking.

2 Add the carrots, celery, and tomatoes. Tie the parsley, bay leaf, and thyme sprigs together with kitchen string, and place in the pan. Bring to the boil and simmer for 30 minutes, or until the vegetables are tender.

3 Remove the herb bundle and discard. Scoop out the meat, remove from the bones, and discard the skin and bones. Strain the stock, reserving the vegetables. Refrigerate the stock for an hour or more. Using a blender, whiz the meat and vegetables and set aside.

4 Once the stock is chilled, remove the fat from the top and discard. Reheat the stock. In a large, dry frying pan, brown the flour over a high heat. Cool slightly. Add the butter and blend. A little at a time, stir in the stock and the meat–vegetable purée. Season with salt and pepper to taste, and add the sherry just before serving.

A favourite from Goa in southern India, the vindaloo is Portuguese in heritage and notable for its garlicky masala, spiked with wine vinegar and softened with sugar. **Roopa Gulati**

pork vindaloo broth

SERVES 6   **PREP** 35 MINS PLUS OVERNIGHT CHILLING   **FREEZE** UP TO 3 MONTHS
COOK 3 HRS   WITHOUT THE GARNISH

6 dried red chillies
650g (1½lb) boneless pork belly with rind,
    cut into 2.5 x 5cm (1 x 2in) chunks
1 tsp cumin seeds
½ tsp black peppercorns
6 garlic cloves, roughly chopped
5cm (2 in) fresh root ginger, roughly chopped
1 tsp sweet paprika
3 tbsp tamarind pulp
3 tbsp white wine vinegar
4–6 tbsp vegetable oil

5cm (2in) cinnamon stick
2 star anise
3 onions, finely chopped
175ml (6 fl oz) white wine
1.7 litres (3 pints) chicken stock
2–3 tsp date palm sugar or dark
    muscovado sugar, to taste
salt
1 red chilli, deseeded and cut into
    strips, to serve
2 tbsp fresh coriander leaves, to serve

1 Soak the chillies in hot water for 10 minutes (for a mild flavour, remove the seeds first). Put the pork in a pan, cover with boiling water, bring to the boil and simmer for 5 minutes. Drain, discard the liquid, and set aside.

2 Dry-roast the cumin and peppercorns (see page 25) and grind using a mortar and pestle. In a small food processor, process the ground spices, drained red chillies, garlic, ginger, paprika, tamarind, and vinegar. Set aside.

3 Heat the oil in a pan. When hot, fry the cinnamon and star anise for 30 seconds. Add the onions and fry for 10–15 minutes. Add the spice paste and cook for 1 minute. Pour in the wine and stock and bring to the boil. Add the pork, turn the heat down low, and simmer for 2 hours. Chill overnight.

4 Next day, scoop out the meat, strip away the rind, and dice. Skim the fat from the stock and strain the liquid into a clean pan. Bring to a fast boil over a high heat and cook for 5–10 minutes. Sweeten with sugar and season with salt. Before serving, stir in the pork and garnish with the chilli strips and coriander leaves.

The Italian name for this soup is *Minestra Maritata*, which simply means the flavours marry well together. Recipes vary, but it is always a robust, rustic mixture. **Carolyn Humphries**

italian wedding soup

◉ **SERVES** 4–5　　🕐 **PREP** 10 MINS **COOK** 1 HR 40 MINS　　❄ **FREEZE** 3 MONTHS

150g (5½oz) stewing beef, diced
1 boneless belly pork slice, rinded and diced
115g (4oz) piece of salami, diced
1 chicken portion
1 large onion, chopped
1 litre (1¾ pints) beef stock
1 sprig of fresh rosemary
1 bay leaf

salt and freshly ground black pepper
¼ head spring greens or 4–6 cavolo nero leaves, shredded
1 head of green or red chicory
60g (2oz) soup pasta shapes
freshly grated Parmesan cheese
crusty bread, to serve

1 Put all the meats in a large pan with the onion, stock, rosemary and bay leaf. Season well. Bring to the boil, skim the surface, reduce the heat, cover, and simmer very gently for 1½ hours until the meat is meltingly tender. Discard the herbs.

2 Lift out the chicken, discard the skin, remove all flesh from the bones, cut into neat pieces and return to the pot. Add the greens, chicory, and pasta. Bring back to the boil, reduce the heat, and simmer for 10 minutes. Taste and adjust the seasoning, if necessary. Ladle into large open soup plates, sprinkle with grated Parmesan cheese and serve with crusty bread.

CAVOLO NERO
This dark green cabbage almost looks black. It is popular in Italy, but you can easily grow it yourself in your garden or allotment. It has a strong, rich flavour, and the best ones have firm stalks and fresh-looking leaves.

Thick and hearty, this German meat and vegetable soup is as filling as a stew. It is versatile enough to work with pork or beef instead of lamb.

pichelsteiner

⊘ **SERVES** 6   🕐 **PREP** 20 MINS **COOK** 1 HR 10 MINS   ❄ **FREEZE** UP TO 3 MONTHS
BEFORE CABBAGE IS ADDED

2 tbsp sunflower oil
500g (1lb 2oz) lamb from shoulder or neck,
   cut into 2cm (¾in) cubes
salt and freshly ground black pepper
2 onions, halved and sliced
pinch of dried marjoram
pinch of dried lovage or thyme

1.5 litres (2¾ pints) vegetable stock
2 medium carrots, diced
1 leek, diced
2 medium potatoes, peeled and diced
½ Savoy cabbage, finely shredded
2 tbsp chopped fresh parsley

1 Heat the oil in a large pan, season the cubed meat with salt and pepper, and add half the meat to the hot oil. Brown the meat lightly, stirring continuously. Remove from the pan and repeat with the rest of the meat. Remove the meat from the pan, add the onions and fry for 2–3 minutes or until softened slightly.

2 Transfer the browned meat back to the pan and add the marjoram, lovage or thyme, and more black pepper. Add the stock, bring to the boil, cover, and cook over a medium heat for about 40 minutes.

3 When the meat is tender, add the carrots, leek, and potatoes. Bring to the boil, season with salt and pepper to taste, cover, and cook for a further 15 minutes. Add the shredded cabbage and cook for 5 minutes, or until just tender. Sprinkle with parsley before serving.

This light version of Irish stew has a richly aromatic broth. Middle neck cutlets – good value and meaty, with just enough flavourful fat – are best for this soup. **Marie-Pierre Moine**

traditional lamb broth

SERVES 4   **PREP** 20 MINS **COOK** 1 HR 45 MINS   **FREEZE** UP TO 3 MONTHS

6 middle neck lamb cutlets
1 celery stalk, including leaves, cut into chunks
1 parsnip, cut into chunks
1 large carrot, cut into chunks
1 large floury potato, peeled and chopped
3 large spring onions, chopped

3 large sprigs of flat-leaf parsley plus 2 tbsp finely chopped parsley, to finish
sea salt and freshly ground black pepper
1 small green cabbage, cored, leaves shredded
a few allspice berries
a few black peppercorns
Irish soda bread, heated in a low oven, to serve

1 Put the lamb in a large saucepan or stockpot. Cover it with cold water to 5cm (2in) above the meat. Add the celery, parsnip, carrot, potato, spring onions and 3 sprigs of parsley. Season with salt and pepper. Bring to the boil over a medium heat, reduce the heat, part-cover, and simmer gently for about 1 hour. Skim any foam from the surface with a slotted spoon. Remove from the heat, lift out the meat, and leave until cool enough to handle. Separate the meat from the bones, reserving the meat.

2 Skim any surface fat from the broth. Lift out and discard the parsley stalks. Add the meat, cabbage, allspice berries, and peppercorns. Cover and return to a simmer over a low heat for about 5 minutes. Taste, season if required and stir in the chopped parsley. Serve very hot with warm Irish soda bread.

SPRING ONIONS
In the summer months you will find wonderful fresh spring onions at farmers' markets. Buy crisp onions with firm stalks. Avoid if dry and brown on the outer skin, or if the green tops are browning or yellowing.

This broth is best with a puff-pastry lid on each bowl. As you break the lid, the spicy aroma is unleashed. The broth itself is best if you make it the day before. **Roopa Gulati**

spiced lamb broth

SERVES 4   **PREP** 30 MINS **COOK** 2 HRS 30 MINS   **FREEZE** UP TO 3 MONTHS
WITHOUT THE PASTRY LID

1.5 litres (2¾ pints) chicken stock
350g (12oz) lamb shank
250g (9oz) lamb neck fillet, cut into 4cm
 (1¾in) pieces
2 onions, roughly chopped
5cm (2in) piece of root ginger, peeled
 and chopped
5 garlic cloves, halved
1 tsp cumin seeds, dry-roasted (see p25)
½ tsp cloves
2 bay leaves

5cm (2in) cinnamon stick
8 green cardamoms, crushed
1 large brown cardamom, crushed
¼ tsp black peppercorns
1 blade mace
salt
1 tbsp vegetable oil
250g (9oz) chestnut mushrooms, sliced
1 green chilli, deseeded and shredded
375g (13oz) ready-rolled puff pastry
1 egg, beaten

1 Pour the stock into a large pan with the lamb, onions, ginger, garlic, and spices. Season with salt and bring to the boil. Partly cover, then simmer for 2 hours or until the meat is tender and the broth reduced by one third. Cool, then remove the lamb with a slotted spoon and cut into small pieces.

2 Strain the broth through a sieve into a clean pan, pressing the ingredients against the sides of the sieve to extract maximum flavour. Bring to a fast boil and season with salt. Meanwhile, heat the oil in a frying pan and cook the mushrooms and chilli for 5 minutes or until just starting to colour. Add to the broth, along with the lamb. If you're working a day ahead, leave to cool, then chill in the fridge. Remove the fat from the surface the next day.

3 Preheat the oven to 220°C (425°F/Gas 7). Almost fill four ovenproof bowls with broth. Cut four circles – about 2.5cm (1in) wider than the bowls – from the pastry. Brush the lip and edge of the bowls with egg and cover with the pastry lids. Each should have an overhang – press this down the sides of the bowl to seal. Brush the top and sides of the lid with egg, make a small hole in the top of each one, and bake for 15–20 minutes or until golden and crisp.

fruit

This is a soup to make in a hurry. All that's needed to bring out its fruity flavour is a seriously good chill – and a perfectly ripe melon. **Roopa Gulati**

chilled melon and ginger soup

SERVES 4   **PREP** 15 MINS   ❄ **FREEZE** UP TO 1 MONTH
AT THE END OF STEP 3

1 ripe Galia melon, peeled and deseeded
2.5cm (1in) fresh root ginger
1 tsp fennel seeds
200g (7oz) white seedless grapes
juice and grated zest of 1 lime
1 tsp dried mint
4 tbsp Greek yogurt, beaten
salt and freshly ground black pepper

for the garnish
2 tbsp fresh mint leaves
pinch of sugar
25g (1oz) crystallized ginger, finely chopped

1 Roughly chop three quarters of the melon flesh into bite-sized chunks. Finely chop the remainder and set aside. Coarsely grate the root ginger and squeeze any juice over the melon chunks. Discard the leftover ginger.

2 Heat a sturdy frying pan or griddle over a gentle heat and lightly toast the fennel seeds for about 30 seconds, until you smell an aniseed-like aroma. Grind the seeds to a coarse powder using a mortar and pestle.

3 Put the ground fennel seeds into a blender with the roughly chopped melon and ginger juice. Add the grapes, lime juice and zest, and dried mint. Whiz until smooth and push through a sieve to remove the skins.

4 Stir in the yogurt, season and chill thoroughly – it's best to half-freeze this soup, then give it a good whisk just before serving. Spoon into bowls, adding a small pile of the reserved melon to each one. Shred the fresh mint with the sugar, mix with the crystallized ginger and scatter over the soup, then serve immediately.

This soup provides an unexpected, beautiful finale to a meal on a summer's day. It comes into its own when a ripe orange charentais or canteloupe is used. **Sophie Grigson**

jane grigson's melon and wine soup

SERVES 6   **PREP** 10 MINS PLUS 1–2 HRS CHILLING TIME   **FREEZE** NOT SUITABLE

1 melon weighing a generous 1kg (2¼lb)
150g (5½oz) sugar
250ml (8fl oz) dry white wine

lemon juice
150ml (5fl oz) crème fraîche

1 Discard the pips and scoop the flesh from the melon. Ideally you should have 750g (1½lb) weight, but don't worry if you have more or less. The other quantities can be adjusted to your taste and this will depend more on the strength of the melon's flavour than on its bulk.

2 Dissolve the sugar in 600ml (1 pint) of water over a low heat, then simmer for 4–5 minutes. Remove the pan from the heat and allow to cool completely.

3 In a food processor or blender, process the melon with the wine until smooth, then gradually add the cool syrup. Stop when the mixture tastes just a little sweeter than you would ideally like it. Now mix in a few good squeezes of lemon juice and the crème fraîche. Serve chilled, with tiny almond biscuits or meringues.

This unusual chilled soup is extraordinarily good, bursting with health and vitality, and is made in seconds. What's not to like? **Sophie Grigson**

mango, coriander, and pomegranate soup

⊘ SERVES 4   **◔ PREP** 5 MINS   **✳ FREEZE** NOT SUITABLE

1 large or 2 small ripe mangoes
1 red chilli, seeded and roughly chopped
1cm (½in) fresh ginger, peeled and finely chopped
1 tbsp roughly chopped coriander leaves
juice of 1–1½ limes

salt
300ml (10fl oz) pomegranate or cranberry juice
roughly chopped coriander, to serve
a few pomegranate seeds, to serve (optional)

1 Peel the mango and cut off all the flesh. Drop into a blender or food processor along with the chilli, ginger, coriander, lime juice, pomegranate juice and a little salt and blend to a purée. Taste and add a little more salt if needed.

2 Pour into small bowls or shot glasses, top with a little more chopped coriander and a few pomegranate seeds (if using) and serve at once.

PREPARING MANGO

Halve the mango, cutting slightly off-centre to miss the stone in the middle. Repeat on the other side.

Slice the flesh in a lattice, then push the cubes of fruit out, using a knife if necessary.

Alfonso mangoes, renowned for their fragrant flesh and creamy texture, have a short season from early April until the end of May. Other varieties work well too. **Roopa Gulati**

mango and curry leaf soup

SERVES 4   **PREP** 15 MINS **COOK** 20 MINS   ❄ **FREEZE** UP TO 1 MONTH
AT THE END OF STEP 3

for the garnish
small handful of curry leaves
vegetable oil for deep frying

for the soup
4 ripe mangoes, Alfonso if in season,
    available from South Asian stores
2 tbsp vegetable oil
1 tsp black mustard seeds
handful of fresh curry leaves

1 red chilli, deseeded, finely chopped
2 tsp date palm sugar or dark muscovado
    sugar
½ tsp turmeric
2 tsp rice flour
300–400ml (10–14fl oz) vegetable stock
300ml (10fl oz) coconut milk
juice of 1 lime, to taste
salt and freshly ground black pepper
2 tbsp chopped fresh coriander leaves

1 First make the garnish: deep-fry the curry leaves in hot oil until crisp – it only takes a few seconds. Drain on kitchen paper and set aside.

2 Roughly chop the flesh of 3 mangoes into small pieces and finely dice the fourth. Set aside. Heat the oil in a medium pan and, when hot, fry the mustard seeds for a few seconds before adding the curry leaves and chilli. Continue frying for 30 seconds, until the leaves stop spluttering.

3 Add the 3 roughly chopped mangoes to the pan, reserving the diced mango. Turn the heat down low and simmer the fruit until softened. Stir in the sugar and cook until the mango begins to caramelize. Sprinkle over the turmeric and rice flour and fry for 30 seconds, stirring all the time. Pour over 300ml (10fl oz) of the stock and simmer for 10 minutes.

4 Add the coconut milk and simmer for 2–3 minutes. Sharpen with lime juice, season with salt and pepper, and stir in the coriander leaves and diced mango. If the soup is too thick, add a little hot vegetable stock. Divide the soup between the bowls and sprinkle with a few crisp-fried curry leaves.

in praise of...
berries

In the summer, freshly picked berries are ideal for making wonderful chilled soups in a matter of minutes. All you need is a little sugar, lemon, and a smoothing touch of yogurt or cream.
Marie-Pierre Moine

Rosehip soup is very popular in Scandinavia where it is served both chilled and hot. Fresh rosehips are best but you can make it with pre-soaked dried rosehips. **Marie-Pierre Moine**

rosehip soup

⊘ **SERVES** 4   🕐 **PREP** 30 MINS   ❄ **FREEZE** NOT SUITABLE
COOK 1 HR PLUS 1 HR CHILLING

500g (1lb 2oz) ripe rosehips, rinsed
1 vanilla pod, split lengthways
caster sugar to taste
50g (1¾oz) slivered almonds, toasted and
   sprinkled with sugar

100ml (3½fl oz) whipping cream
3 tbsp natural yoghurt
2 tbsp lemon juice
Amaretti biscuits, to serve

1 Put the rosehips in a large saucepan, and pour over boiling water to cover generously. Add the vanilla pod. Simmer over a low heat for about 20–30 minutes until soft. Strain over a bowl, but reserve and set aside the cooking liquid as well as the vanilla pod.

2 Place the sieve of rosehips over a second bowl. Press out the rosehips to extract a purée and set aside. Tip what's left in the sieve into the saucepan. Add the reserved cooking liquid and the vanilla pod. Return to a simmer, and cook for 20 minutes. Strain enough of the mixture into the reserved purée to produce a smooth soup. Stir in sugar to taste. Chill for one hour or until ready to serve.

3 Just before serving, whisk the cream and yoghurt together, and sweeten to taste. Stir the lemon juice into the chilled soup, and pour or spoon into glass coupes or bowls. Add a sprinkling of almonds, a dollop of whisked cream, and serve chilled.

ROSEHIPS
Rich in vitamin C, rosehips have an excellent nutritional profile and a distinctive flavour. Make sure you forage for the wild rosehips that grow on hedgerows, rather than picking those from the garden.

This Hungarian soup is meant to taste fresh rather than sweet. The ratio of lemon to sugar is a guideline only – it depends on how ripe the cherries are. **Shaun Hill**

cherry soup

SERVES 4   **PREP TIME** 5 MINS **COOK** 15 MINS   **FREEZE** UP TO 6 MONTHS

300g (10oz) morello cherries, fresh or canned
500ml (16fl oz) white wine
200ml (7fl oz) water

55g (scant 2oz) sugar
1 lemon, zest and juice
300ml (10fl oz) soured cream

1 Stone the cherries and reserve the fruit. Add the stones, stalks, and any juice to the wine and water in a saucepan. Bring to the boil. Simmer, uncovered, for 10 minutes.

2 Strain the liquid into a clean pan and add the reserved fruit, sugar, and lemon. Bring to the boil then, away from direct heat, whisk in the soured cream. Chill well before serving.

CHERRIES
Look for reddish-purple, sweet cherries that are firm but give a little when squeezed. If they are underripe, store them in a fruit bowl to allow them to ripen. When ripe, they can be stored in the refrigerator for a few days.

cheese

Rich and fragrant, this characterful soup should be served in small portions. Play around with the quantities of pear and Stilton to find the right balance for you. **Sophie Grigson**

pear and stilton soup

SERVES 4   **PREP** 10 MINS **COOK** 20 MINS   **FREEZE** UP TO 3 MONTHS
AT THE END OF STEP 1

1 onion, chopped
15g (½oz) unsalted butter
4 ripe pears, cored, quartered and chopped
750ml (1¼ pints) chicken stock

salt and pepper
125g (4½oz) Stilton, crumbled
juice of ½–1 lemon, to taste
fresh chives, chopped, to serve

1 In a large pan, cook the onion gently in the butter without browning. Add the pears and the stock and season lightly. Simmer until the pears are very tender. Pass through the fine blade of a mouli-legumes, or process in a blender until smooth. If making this soup in advance, cool it now and continue when you want to serve.

2 Return to the pan and reheat, without boiling. Add the Stilton and stir until melted. Sharpen with lemon juice to taste and adjust the seasoning. Sprinkle the chives over the top and serve.

STILTON
The smell of Stilton is strong, but it should still be pleasant. Try another organic blue cheese in place of Stilton, if you wish. Whatever blue you choose, it should be fresh and moist, but not wet. Cut off any rind before cooking.

Use well-flavoured Cheddar and serve the soup with plenty of warm, crusty bread. Use blue cheese if you prefer, but crumble it rather than try to grate it! **Carolyn Humphries**

cheddar and chive soup

SERVES 4 **PREP** 10 MINS
COOK 30 MINS PLUS REHEATING

FREEZE UP TO 3 MONTHS
WITHOUT THE CRÈME FRAÎCHE

large knob of butter
¼ small celeriac, chopped
1 onion, chopped
1 carrot, chopped
1 potato, chopped
750ml (1¼ pints) vegetable or chicken stock

1 bay leaf
salt and freshly ground black pepper
small handful of fresh chive stalks
150ml (5fl oz) milk
115g (4oz) Cheddar cheese, grated
4 tbsp crème fraîche, plus extra to serve

1 Melt the butter in a large saucepan. Add all the prepared root vegetables and fry gently, stirring, for 2 minutes, or until softened but not browned. Add the stock and bay leaf and season. Bring to the boil, reduce the heat, cover and simmer gently for 30 minutes. Remove the bay leaf, purée the soup in a blender or food processor then return to the rinsed-out pan.

2 Reserving 4 chive stalks for garnish; snip the remainder finely. Add to the soup with the milk, cheese and crème fraîche. Heat through gently, stirring, until the cheese melts and the soup is piping hot. Do not allow to boil.

3 Taste and adjust the seasoning, then ladle into warm, shallow soup bowls, adding a dollop of crème fraîche to each. Break the reserved chive stalks in half and gently lay them, slightly crossed, on top.

German-style cheese soups are often flavoured with beer, sometimes using lager or pilsner. This version uses wheat beer, and is thick and rich with a good blend of flavours.

emmental and beer soup

SERVES 6   **PREP** 10 MINS **COOK** 30 MINS   **FREEZE** NOT SUITABLE

25g (scant 1oz) butter
2 onions, finely chopped
1 clove garlic, chopped
45g (1½oz) plain flour
750ml (1¼ pints) chicken stock

150ml (5fl oz) German wheat beer
150g (5½oz) Emmental, finely grated
150g (5½oz) Gruyère, finely grated
freshly ground white pepper
1 tbsp fresh thyme leaves, to serve

1 Melt the butter over a low heat in a large, heavy pan. Add the onion and garlic and sauté for 10 minutes until soft but not coloured. Gradually stir in the flour, then add the stock a little at a time, stirring constantly until smooth. Bring to the boil, then keep at a gentle bubbling boil for 10 minutes or until the liquid begins to thicken slightly. Stir regularly to ensure the mixture doesn't start to stick to the pan. Then add the wheat beer and return to a gentle boil.

2 Remove from the heat and very gradually add the two cheeses, adding a handful at a time and stirring constantly. Season to taste with pepper, pour into warm soup bowls and top with fresh thyme. Serve with German bread and beer.

A great way to use up any white-rinded soft cheese, even if it's smelling a bit strong. If you don't have celeriac, use a large potato and season with celery salt. **Carolyn Humphries**

camembert and celeriac soup with cranberry swirl

⊘ SERVES 4   **⊙ PREP** 10 MINS **COOK** 25 MINS   **❀ FREEZE** UP TO 3 MONTHS
BEFORE CREAM IS ADDED

knob of butter
1 onion, chopped
½ small celeriac, about 225g (8oz) prepared
   weight, roughly diced
450ml (15fl oz) chicken or vegetable stock
1 bouquet garni
salt and freshly ground black pepper

450ml (15fl oz) milk
115g (4oz) ripe Camembert, diced
4 tbsp double cream
4 tsp cranberry sauce
4 tsp orange or cranberry juice
4 tsp sunflower oil

1 Melt the butter in a saucepan. Add the onion and fry gently, stirring, for 2 minutes, or until softened but not browned. Add the celeriac, stock, bouquet garni and a little seasoning (go easy on the salt). Bring to the boil, reduce the heat, cover and simmer gently for 15 minutes, or until the celeriac is tender. Remove and discard the bouquet garni.

2 Purée in a blender or food processor, adding the milk and cheese. Return the soup to the rinsed-out pan, stir in the cream and reheat, but do not boil. Taste and adjust the seasoning.

3 Meanwhile, whisk the cranberry sauce with the juice and oil until thoroughly blended. Ladle the soup into warm, shallow soup plates. Whisk the cranberry mixture again and, using a teaspoon, swirl a little of the cranberry mixture in the centre of each bowl and quickly draw a cocktail stick from the centre to the edge all round to form a Catherine wheel shape. Serve immediately.

breads

This basic white loaf is soft on the inside, with a light texture. If you have any left the day after you've baked it, use it for croûtons (see p39).

crusty white loaf

⊘ **MAKES** 1 LOAF   ◷ **PREP** 35 MINS, PLUS 1½ HRS RISING   ❉ **FREEZE** UP TO 6 MONTHS
COOK 40 MINS

450g (1lb) strong plain flour,
   plus extra to dust
1½ tsp fast-action dried yeast
1 tsp salt

1 tsp sugar
1 tbsp vegetable oil, sunflower,
   or light olive oil, plus extra to oil
300ml (10fl oz) lukewarm water

1 Stir the flour and yeast together in a large bowl, then mix in the salt and sugar. Make a well in the middle and pour in the oil and water. Mix to form a soft dough, adding more water if required. Turn out on to a lightly floured work surface and knead the dough for 5–10 minutes or until smooth and elastic. Shape into a round by tucking the edges into the middle, then place it smooth side up in a large oiled bowl. Cover loosely with oiled cling film and leave in a warm place for 1 hour or until doubled in size.

2 Oil and flour the inside of a 900g (2lb) loaf tin, tapping out any excess flour. Lightly knead the dough and press it into a rough rectangle. Tuck the shorter ends in, followed by the longer edges, then lay it seam side down in the loaf tin. Cover loosely with oiled cling film and leave for 30 minutes or until risen.

3 Preheat the oven to 220°C (425°F/Gas 7). Dust the top of the loaf with a little flour, then slash it with a sharp knife. Bake for 20 minutes, lower the oven temperature to 200°C (400°F/Gas 6), then bake for another 20 minutes or until risen with a golden crust. Turn the loaf out and check that it is cooked – it will sound hollow when tapped on the base. Transfer to a wire rack to cool completely.

The mix of white and wholemeal flours in this loaf makes it lighter and moister. If the recipe seems complicated, it is actually much easier and quicker than it sounds.

wholemeal loaf

MAKES 1 LOAF **PREP** 35 MINS, PLUS 1 HR 40 MINS RISING **FREEZE** UP TO 6 MONTHS
COOK 40 MINS

225g (8oz) strong white flour,
   plus extra to dust
225g (8oz) strong wholemeal flour,
   plus extra to decorate
1½ tsp fast-action dried yeast
1 tsp salt

1 tbsp vegetable oil, sunflower oil,
   or light olive oil, plus extra to oil
1 tbsp honey
200ml (7fl oz) lukewarm milk
150ml (5fl oz) lukewarm water
1 egg, beaten, to glaze

1 Mix the flours, yeast, and salt in a large bowl, then make a well in the centre. Stir the oil, honey, milk, and water together in a jug until the honey has dissolved, then pour into the well. Mix to form a slightly sticky dough, then leave to stand for 10 minutes.

2 Dust the work surface lightly with flour, then knead the dough for 5–10 minutes or until it is smooth and springs back when pressed gently. Shape into a ball and place in a large oiled bowl. Cover loosely with oiled cling film and leave in a warm place for 1 hour or until doubled in size. Meanwhile, oil and flour a 900g (2lb) loaf tin, tapping out any excess flour.

3 Turn the dough out on to a lightly floured surface and knead briefly. Shape into a rough rectangle, then tuck the shorter ends in, followed by the longer edges. Lay it seam side down in the tin, cover loosely with oiled cling film, and leave for 30 minutes or until doubled in size.

4 Preheat the oven to 220°C (425°F/Gas 7). Sift a little wholemeal flour, leaving the bran in the sieve. Brush the top of the loaf with the beaten egg, sprinkle with bran, then slash the surface with a sharp knife. Bake for 20 minutes, lower the heat to 200°C (400°F/Gas 6), then bake for another 20 minutes or until risen with a dark golden crust. Turn the loaf out on to a wire rack to cool completely.

Use only a small amount of flour on your hands and work surface when you're kneading and shaping the dough for these rolls – too much will make it dry and stiff.

soft white rolls

MAKES 16   **PREP** 25 MINS, PLUS 1½ HRS RISING   **FREEZE** UP TO 6 MONTHS
COOK 20 MINS

500g (1lb 2oz) strong white flour,
   plus extra to dust
2 tsp light soft brown sugar
7g sachet fast-action dried yeast

2 tsp salt
250–300ml (8–10fl oz) lukewarm water
a little vegetable oil

1 Sift the flour into a large mixing bowl. Add the sugar, yeast, salt, and enough of the water to form a soft, pliable dough. Dust a work surface lightly with flour and knead the dough for 10 minutes. Transfer to a lightly oiled bowl and cover loosely with oiled cling film. Leave in a warm place to rise for 1 hour or until doubled in size.

2 Turn the dough out on to the floured work surface and knead again briefly. Divide into 16 equal pieces and shape into balls. Smooth the tops and place on two lightly oiled baking trays, leaving enough space between the balls for them to spread out without touching. Leave to rise in a warm place for 30 minutes or until doubled in size.

3 Preheat the oven to 200°C (400°F/Gas 6). Bake the rolls for 20 minutes or until they are light brown on top and sound hollow when tapped on the bottom. Transfer to a wire rack and leave to cool completely.

These rolls are perfect with hearty soups. For a special occasion, you could roll each piece of dough into a long rope and then wind it in a spiral or tie it in a figure-of-eight knot.

wholemeal rolls

MAKES 16   **PREP** 20–25 MINS, PLUS 1½ HRS RISING   **FREEZE** UP TO 6 MONTHS
COOK 15–20 MINS

225g (8oz) strong white flour,
   plus extra to dust
225g (8oz) strong wholemeal flour
7g sachet fast-action dried yeast
1 tsp salt
1 tbsp sunflower oil, plus extra to oil

1 tbsp honey
200ml (7fl oz) lukewarm milk
150ml (5fl oz) lukewarm water
1 egg, beaten, to glaze
oats, to decorate

1 Mix the flours, yeast, and salt in a large mixing bowl, then make a well in the centre. Stir the oil, honey, milk, and water together in a jug until the honey has dissolved. Pour into the well and mix to form a slightly sticky dough. Dust a work surface lightly with flour, then knead the dough for 10 minutes or until no longer sticky. Shape into a ball and place in an oiled bowl. Cover loosely with oiled cling film and leave to rise in a warm place for 1 hour or until doubled in size.

2 Knead the dough lightly again, then divide into 16 equal pieces. Roll each into a ball and place on two oiled baking trays, leaving enough space between the balls for them to spread out without touching. Cover loosely with oiled cling film and leave to rise for 30 minutes or until they have doubled in size.

3 Preheat the oven to 200°C (400°F/Gas 6). Brush the rolls with the beaten egg and scatter a few oats on top. Bake for 15–20 minutes or until they sound hollow when tapped on the base. Transfer to a wire rack to cool.

These simple yeast-raised breads are cooked in a frying pan. If you would like to make them in advance, simply wrap them in foil, then reheat in the oven just before serving.

easy flatbreads

◯ MAKES 8   **◷ PREP** 10 MINS, PLUS 55 MINS RISING
                          COOK 40 MINS   **❄ FREEZE** UP TO 6 MONTHS

500g (1lb 2oz) strong white flour,
   plus extra to dust
2 tsp salt

7g sachet fast-action dried yeast
3 tbsp olive oil, plus extra to oil
250–300ml (8–10fl oz) lukewarm water

1 Mix the flour, salt, yeast, and oil in a large mixing bowl, then add enough of the water to make a soft dough. Dust a work surface lightly with flour and knead the dough well. Place in a lightly oiled bowl, cover loosely with oiled cling film, and leave to rise in a warm place for 45 minutes or until it has doubled in size.

2 Turn the dough out on to the floured surface and knead lightly. Divide into eight equal portions, then flatten them with your hands. Use a rolling pin to flatten them a little more, then place on a lightly floured baking tray and set aside for 10 minutes.

3 Heat a large frying pan over a medium heat, add one of the circles of dough, and fry for 3 minutes or until brown. Turn it over and fry for 2 minutes. Transfer to a wire rack to cool while you cook the rest.

To give it a lighter texture, this yeast-free bread is made with buttermilk rather than plain milk. For brown soda bread, replace half or all the white flour with wholemeal flour.

soda bread

⊘ **MAKES** 1 LOAF   🕐 **PREP** 10 MINS   **COOK** 30–35 MINS   ❄ **FREEZE** UP TO 6 MONTHS

450g (1lb) strong white bread flour,
   plus extra to dust
2 tsp bicarbonate of soda
2 tsp cream of tartar

1 tsp salt
60g (2oz) butter or lard, diced
300ml (10fl oz) buttermilk

1 Preheat the oven to 220°C (425°F/Gas 7). Sift the flour, bicarbonate of soda, cream of tartar, and salt into a mixing bowl and stir together. Add the butter or lard and rub it in with your fingertips until the mixture forms fine crumbs. Make a well in the centre and pour in the buttermilk, then mix to form a soft dough.

2 Transfer to a floured work surface and knead lightly, then shape into a ball and roll around to smooth the surface. Place the ball on a floured baking tray, flatten slightly, then dust lightly with flour. Use a floured knife to cut it into six sections, but don't cut all the way through to the bottom.

3 Bake for 30–35 minutes or until the bread is well risen, golden brown, and sounds hollow when tapped on the bottom. Transfer to a wire rack and leave to cool completely.

Wholesome and healthy, this chewy bread is made from oats, millet, polenta, quinoa, rice, rye, and bulghur. If you don't have one of these, replace it with one of the others.

seven-grain loaf

MAKES 2 LOAVES **PREP** 20 MINS, PLUS 1½ HRS RISING **FREEZE** UP TO 3 MONTHS
COOK 35–40 MINS

85g (3oz) bulghur
50g (1¾oz) polenta
50g (1¾oz) millet
50g (1¾oz) quinoa
600ml (1 pint) lukewarm water
450g (1lb) strong white flour, plus
  extra to dust
250g (9oz) strong wholemeal flour

75g (2½oz) rolled oats
75g (2½oz) rye flakes
2 x 7g sachets fast-action dried yeast
2 tsp salt
50g (1¾oz) cooked long-grain brown rice
4 tbsp honey
250ml (8fl oz) milk
2 tbsp sunflower oil, plus extra to oil

1 Mix the first four ingredients in a bowl, stir in 400ml (14fl oz) of the water, cover with a tea towel, and set aside for 15 minutes. Meanwhile, mix the next six ingredients in a bowl. Add the bulghur mixture, then stir in the rice.

2 Heat the honey with the milk until it dissolves, then add to the bowl along with the oil. Gradually add the rest of the water or until a sticky dough forms. Knead on a lightly floured work surface for 10 minutes or until elastic. Shape into a ball, place in a lightly oiled bowl, then cover with oiled cling film. Leave to rise in a warm place for 1 hour or until doubled in size. Meanwhile, oil and flour two 900g (2lb) loaf tins.

3 Turn the dough out on to the floured surface and knead for 1 minute. Divide into two equal pieces and, with a floured rolling pin, roll each into a rectangle as wide as the tins and twice as long. Fold both ends to the centre and pinch the edges to seal. Place in the tins, cover with tea towels, and leave to rise for 30 minutes. Preheat the oven to 220°C (425°F/Gas 7).

4 Brush the tops with oil and bake for 10 minutes, then reduce the heat to 190°C (375°F/Gas 5) and bake for a further 25–30 minutes or until the loaves sound hollow when tapped on the base. Leave to cool on a wire rack.

Despite the need for forward planning, this loaf is relatively straightforward to make. The sourdough "starter" gives the bread an agreeably tangy flavour.

rye bread

◉ MAKES 1 LOAF **◕ PREP** 25 MINS, PLUS 1½ HRS RISING **❄ FREEZE** UP TO 3 MONTHS
COOK 40–50 MINS

300g (11oz) rye flour
150g carton live natural yogurt
1 tsp fast-action dried yeast
1 tbsp black treacle
1 tsp caraway seeds, lightly crushed
250ml (8fl oz) lukewarm water

200g (7oz) strong white flour, plus
  extra to dust
2 tsp salt
a little vegetable oil
1 egg, beaten, to glaze
1 tsp caraway seeds, to decorate

1 The day before you want to serve the loaf, make a "starter" by putting half the rye flour in a mixing bowl with the yogurt, yeast, treacle, and caraway seeds. Stir in the water, then cover and leave overnight until bubbling.

2 The next day, combine the remaining rye flour with the white flour and salt, then add to the mixture you made the day before. Mix to form a dough, adding a little water, if necessary. Turn out on to a lightly floured surface and knead for 5–10 minutes or until the dough is smooth and springy. Shape into a ball, place in an oiled bowl, and cover loosely with oiled cling film. Leave to rise in a warm place for 1 hour or until doubled in size. Meanwhile, flour a baking tray.

3 Lightly knead the dough again, then form into a rugby-ball shape and place on the tray. Cover with oiled cling film and leave to rise for 30 minutes. Preheat the oven to 220°C (425°F/Gas 7).

4 Brush the top with the beaten egg, sprinkle with the caraway seeds, then slash the knife along its length with a sharp knife. Bake for 20 minutes, then reduce the heat to 200°C (400°F/Gas 6) and bake for another 20–30 minutes or until dark golden with a hard shiny crust. Transfer to a wire rack to cool completely.

Favourites in the American South, these biscuits are rather like English scones. They are delicious with soup and are best served straight from the oven.

buttermilk biscuits

MAKES 8   **PREP** 25 MINS, PLUS 1 HR 20 MINS RISING   **FREEZE** UP TO 6 MONTHS
COOK 12–15 MINS

500g (1lb 2oz) strong white flour,
  plus extra to dust
1½ tsp fast-action dried yeast
1 tsp caster sugar
1½ tsp salt

45g (1½oz) butter, at room temperature
150ml (5fl oz) full-fat milk
150ml (5fl oz) lukewarm water
a little vegetable oil

1 Mix the flour and yeast together in a large mixing bowl, then stir in the sugar and salt. Rub the butter in with your fingertips until the mixture resembles fine breadcrumbs. Make a well in the centre, pour in the milk and water, and stir with a wooden spoon to form a dough. Transfer to a lightly floured work surface and knead for 5 minutes or until smooth. Place in a bowl, cover with a tea towel, and leave to rise in a warm place for 1 hour or until doubled in size.

2 Dust the work surface lightly with flour and knead the dough briefly again. Divide into eight equal portions, then roll each piece out into a flat round about 10cm (4in) in diameter. Place the rounds on two lightly floured baking trays. Make a small hole in the centre of each one with the handle of a wooden spoon, then prick the rounds lightly with a fork. Cover with oiled cling film and leave in a warm place for 20 minutes or until slightly risen and puffy. Meanwhile, preheat the oven to 220°C (425°F/Gas 7).

3 Bake the biscuits for 12–15 minutes or until risen and lightly golden. Transfer to a wire rack to cool for a few moments before serving hot.

A golden quick bread that is delicious straight from the oven. To ring the changes, add a couple of crushed cloves of garlic, a diced chilli, or some grated Cheddar to the batter.

cornbread

⊘ MAKES 1 LOAF **🕐 PREP** 10 MINS **COOK** 25–30 MINS   **❄ FREEZE** UP TO 6 MONTHS

a little sunflower oil
200g (7oz) cornmeal or
   medium-coarse polenta
75g (2½oz) plain white flour
1 tsp baking powder

1 tsp salt
1½ tbsp caster sugar
300ml (10fl oz) milk
25g (scant 1oz) butter, melted
1 egg

1 Preheat the oven to 190°C (375°F/Gas 5). Grease a 21 x 16cm (8½ x 6½in) ovenproof dish with oil. Place the cornmeal or polenta in a large bowl and sift in the flour, baking powder, salt, and sugar. Stir together, then make a well in the centre. Whisk the milk, butter, and egg together, then pour the mixture into the well and mix thoroughly to form a batter. Transfer to the ovenproof dish and smooth the surface.

2 Bake for 25–30 minutes or until browned at the edges. To test if the cornbread is cooked, insert a skewer in the centre – it should come out clean. Cut into squares and serve warm.

index

acknowledgments

The Soil Association would like to thank:

Darina Allen, Dan Barber, Raymond Blanc, Sarah Canet, Joyce Cellars, Sally Clarke, Jeff Cox, Monty Don, Josephine Fairley, Sophie Grigson, Skye Gyngell, Shaun Hill, Juliet Kindersley, Daphne Lambert, Lorraine Martin, Allegra McEvedy, Clodagh McKenna, Jeanette Orrey, Anna Paszczynska, Arthur Potts Dawson, Thane Prince, Sarah Raven, Eric Schlosser, Charlotte Senn, Rosemary Shrager, Geetie Singh, Rebecca Sullivan, Eric Treuille, and Alice Waters.

Dorling Kindersley would like to thank:

At the Soil Association: Patrick Holden, Roger Mortlock, and Tim Young

Editorial: Susannah Marriot, Diana Vowles, Constance Novis, Lucy Bannell

Recipe testing: Anna Burges-Lumsden, Richard Harris, Lisa Harrison, Rachel Wood

Consultancy: Carolyn Humphries

Prop stylist: Sue Rowlands
Food stylist: Jane Lawrie, Annie Rigg
Art Director for Photoshoot: Nicky Collings

Index: Hilary Bird

Useful websites

Acorn House **www.acornhouserestaurant.com**
Ballymaloe Cookery School **www.cookingisfun.ie**
Blue Hill **www.bluehillfarm.com**
Books for Cooks **www.booksforcooks.com**
Chez Panisse **www.chezpanisse.com**
Judges Bakery **www.judgesbakery.com**
Le Manoir aux Quat'Saisons **www.manoir.com**
Leon **www.leonrestaurants.co.uk**
Penrhos **www.penrhos.co.uk**
Petersham Nurseries Café & Teahouse
www.petershamnurseries.com/cafeandteahouse.asp
Real Food Festival **www.realfoodfestival.co.uk**
Sheepdrove Organic Farm **www.sheepdrove.com**
The Duke of Cambridge **www.dukeorganic.co.uk**
The Walnut Tree **www.thewalnuttreeinn.com**

Picture credits

Text credits

Sally Clarke's Beetroot and tomato soup recipe first appeared in *Sally Clarke's Book: Recipes from a Restaurant, Shop and Bakery* by Sally Clarke, first published by Macmillan and latterly by Grub Street. Jeanette Orrey's Pumpkin and apple soup recipe first appeared as a variation on her Basic cream of vegetable soup in *Second Helpings from The Dinner Lady* by Jeannette Orrey, published by Bantam Press.

british-grown vegetables – what's in season when

	JANUARY	FEBRUARY	MARCH	APRIL	MAY	JUNE
asparagus				●	●	●
aubergines						●
beetroot	●	●	●			●
bell peppers						
broad beans					●	●
broccoli						
brussels sprouts	●	●	●			
carrots	●	●				
cauliflower	●	●	●	●	●	●
celeriac	●	●	●			
celery	●	●				
chicory	●	●	●	●	●	
coriander					●	●
courgettes					●	●
cucumbers						●
fennel						
garlic					●	●
globe artichokes						●
jerusalem artichokes	●	●	●			
kale	●	●	●			
kohlrabi						
leeks	●	●	●	●		
lettuce	●	●	●	●	●	●
lovage					●	●
marsh samphire						●
nettles			●	●	●	●
onions	●	●	●			●
parsnips	●	●	●			
peas						●
potatoes	●	●	●	●	●	●
pumpkins						
rocket	●	●	●	●	●	●
savoy cabbage	●	●				
sorrel			●	●	●	●
spinach	●	●	●	●	●	●
squash						●
swede	●	●	●	●		
sweet potatoes						
sweetcorn						
swiss chard						
tomatoes						
turnips	●	●	●	●	●	●
watercress	●	●	●	●	●	●
wild mushrooms						